BIRTHING
THE WEST

MOTHERS *and* MIDWIVES
in the ROCKIES *and* PLAINS

JENNIFER J. HILL

University of Nebraska Press   Lincoln

Library of Congress Cataloging-in-Publication Data
Names: Hill, Jennifer J., author.
Title: Birthing the West : mothers and midwives
in the Rockies and Plains / Jennifer J. Hill.
Description: Lincoln : University of Nebraska Press,
[2022] | Includes bibliographical references and index.
Identifiers: LCCN 2021037006
ISBN 9781496226853 (paperback)
ISBN 9781496231079 (epub)
ISBN 9781496231086 (pdf)
Subjects: LCSH: Childbirth—West (U.S.)—History. |
Pregnancy—West (U.S.)—History. | Pregnant
women—Health and hygiene—West (U.S.)—History. |
Motherhood—West (U.S.)—History. | Midwives—West
(U.S.)—History. | BISAC: HISTORY / United States /
State & Local / Midwest (IA, IL, IN, KS, MI, MN, MO, ND,
NE, OH, SD, WI) | SOCIAL SCIENCE / Women's Studies
Classification: LCC RG652 .H55 2022 |
DDC 618.2—dc23/eng/20211028
LC record available at https://lccn.loc.gov/2021037006

Set in Minion Pro by Laura Buis.
Designed by L. Auten.

To Ivan and Bob, who mastered the practice of caring

CONTENTS

ILLUSTRATIONS

ACKNOWLEDGMENTS

Research and writing depend on dialogue and engagement, and *Birthing the West* could not have happened without the kind offerings of many. A host of unfailingly generous and intelligent souls enabled this project, making possible everything from the miles of research travel to the unending review of health department statistics.

Stacey Haugland, midwife extraordinaire, introduced me to the contemporary practice of midwifery. She had the audacity to be honest about the horrors that most women experience in delivery, even in our modern era. Her dedication to her profession and to the women she served allowed me to lift the veil of pregnancy and question its impacts on American culture, both past and present. Stacey is no longer catching babies, but her expertise reflected the lineage she so proudly embodied—that of a practicing midwife.

Mary Murphy shepherded this exploration from its very inception. I am enduringly grateful for her exquisite mentorship. Crystal Alegria and Nancy Mahoney persevered through draft after draft, pushing for improved clarity and bolder thinking with each iteration and round of drinks. Ken Robeson offered enthusiasm and support, as did the staff at the Montana Historical Society, the State Historical Society of North Dakota, the South Dakota State Historical Society, the Wyoming State Archives, the Overholser Research Center, and the American Heritage Center at the University of Wyoming. The list of cooperating historical societies from towns and counties across the Dakotas, Wyoming, and Montana runs to more than fifty small institutions, all committed to preserving vital regional history. Humanities Montana, the American Heritage Center, and the Bureau of Land Management provided funding. Clark Whitehorn and the team at the University of Nebraska Press helped make this book a reality; I appreciate their professionalism.

I am touched by the trust that the families of Mary Kassmeier, Catherine Brodhead, and Bertha Emmert placed in me after sharing memories of their grandmothers and great-grandmothers with fondness and attention to detail. The opportunity to tell the stories of mothers and midwives long gone has been a rare honor and an unforgettable adventure.

After delivering each of my children, I swore to myself that I would "never go through that again." There were times in the process of writing this book that I expressed similar sentiments. Those near and dear to me have patiently listened to my laborious explanations of the "progress I made on the book," descriptions of remaining "research I must do for the book," and recountings of "ideas I have about the book." I value their patience and beg their continued indulgence. My oath of abstention absolutely holds true for pregnancy, but I've already conceived another intellectual quest and am itching to start research and writing. Here's to the next one. May there always be another.

BIRTHING THE WEST

Introduction

Across the northern plains the sky stretches out to the far horizon, clouds spread across a great ocean of blue, and the grasses and bugs and birds all commingle in a subtle, yet wildly alive orchestra of sounds and smells. The sweet fragrance of dirt and bruised stems mixes with a slim layer of decomposing matter, teasing the nose with gentle hints of blossoms, seed pods, and fresh cleanness. The wind rushes along in rivers as it folds back the grasses.

Modern travelers through this northern expanse often combat the vast openness by cocooning themselves inside speeding cars on the interstate highways. In fairness, the miles are long—it takes hours and sometimes entire days to get across the spaces we now call Wyoming, North Dakota, South Dakota, and Montana. But for those who step outside, who get away from the double yellow lines and paved roads, who take the time to listen to the land, there is a siren's song of intrigue, of wildness, and the call of something else. This is a special place, special in part because there are still spaces nearly devoid of harmful human impact, spaces where wind and water reign. If you avoid the highly settled valleys of the eastern Dakotas, the tourist streams of the Black Hills, the industrial development of the Bakken oil fields, and the proliferating vacation homes in the approach to the Rocky Mountains, you can still find—or at least imagine—what humans in this unique part of the American West touched and saw and smelled.

Ancient people, making their homes beneath the rotating world of sky, looked up and considered the friendly comfort of Ursa Major, admired the winking beauty of Corona Borealis, and gazed skyward across the angled gaps of Cassiopeia—no doubt speaking their own names for the brilliant constellations but feeling a similar sense of wonder and familiarity. They traveled ancestral lands, harvested buffalo, and dug for camas root. Nations like the Apsáalooke resided year-round in the areas of eastern Montana that I experienced with the aid of forced-air heat and diesel fuel. As the U.S. military confined Native residents to parceled-out reservations, recently arrived Euro-American settlers, my great-grandparents among them, saw opportunity, adventure, and even conquest in this majestic space.

As a child, I explored the landscape of my family ranch. I wandered tepee rings. I picked through old buildings and my grandmother's basement, wondering at the tools of those who came so recently before me and yet lived a life so very different from mine. I took it all in, investigating without prioritization or assessment. As an adult I came to see those spaces and places with new eyes, to ponder the meanings and relics of two cultures so seemingly divided but sandwiched in such a short window of time. I began to ask questions—about ways of living with the land, about how we tell our stories, and about the meanings we give to our pasts.

I went away to college but answered the call of the open spaces and returned to live in Montana. Pregnant with my first child, I had questions about the space of the northern plains that took on a fresh intensity. I had never before considered the experience of giving birth in this openness, looking at the land and the sky and tasting the wind while pregnant, longing to be free of the demanding, rolling, kicking presence that I carried with me, thinking about a future for my impetuous and combustible child in the midst of the grass and the birds and the bugs . . . and the snakes. How did women before

Fig. 1. This Miles City infant, as wonderfully fat as my first child, encountered the world from a relatively privileged position, as is evident from the elaborate christening gown. 945-534, Philip H. Watkins, seven months. Montana Historical Society Research Center.

me navigate these spaces while pregnant, while nursing, with new-born babies and curious toddlers?

As a scholar studying American culture, I had at my disposal tools to analyze and dissect societal norms. Somehow, though, questions of reproduction only rarely appeared in the academic literature. Childbirth, despite being a normal human experience, remained conspicuously absent from intellectual discussion.[1] Was pregnancy a topic somehow unsuitable for scholarly discourse and investigation? Was birth—the very event that brought us all here in the first place—so inherently without value that it did not deserve at least cursory evaluation?

My initial investigations revealed stories about reproduction, reminiscences of hurried deliveries, and the evidence of tilted, settled stones marking short infant lives in abandoned mountain cemeteries. These events had the look of social detritus—bits that fell behind in a great wave of assumed forward progress. In a culture that gave preference to the accomplishments of dominant Euro-American men, a recurring experience like childbirth, traditionally managed and narrated by women, did not merit inclusion in official documentation. The entrance of women into the academy, especially in the 1960s and 1970s, nudged the door of reproductive history open just slightly, but what tenure-seeking female would deign to address such an odoriferously feminine topic? Reproduction did not represent a shrewd career choice.

Little work had been done, at least relative to other fields, to document what I was beginning to perceive as a critical human experience for all participants in American culture, especially in an intriguing geographic milieu.[2] I listened to hours of recorded oral histories and noted that women, often without prompting, mentioned their birthing experiences as salient moments as they looked back over their lives. Men, too, participated in at least their own birth and often that of younger siblings, and most were part of families and kinship networks resulting from birth. How could we not all be impacted by something so common? I became convinced that engaging with the reality of reproduction would bring an understanding of this region that I had so long pondered, with a perspective that might yield some fresh insights.

I followed the trails of existing research, searching for a starting point, yet I struggled to find any beginnings or conclusions. I searched further back in time to explore childbirth practices in human prehistory. I came to see the history of birth not as a single, linear story but instead as a connecting element of human experience.

This book is my attempt to describe just one small node in the rhizomatic monstrosity that is American reproduction: the story of a particular time and a vast space—from the mid-1800s through the 1940s in the Dakotas, Wyoming, and Montana—and the women who miscarried and delivered babies, worried about pregnancy, and celebrated it in a region more famous for the myth of the stoic man on a horse than the nuanced, confusing, and endlessly fascinating realities of childbirth.

Human culture is made tangible in reproduction. When we conceive of an idea, when we give birth to a dream, we mirror the process of creating new human beings. As a family or community welcomes an infant, members narrate identity, tell stories, and enact rituals—even if those practices are as seemingly un-sacred as gender-reveal parties and running strollers. Explaining what it means to be a hardworking Montanan, a loyal Seahawks fan, or the proud member of a particular family is not done for the benefit of the child alone. Verbalizing these identities allows for the re-creation and affirmation of norms, beliefs, and customs. Without new members, a culture withers and its shared meanings waste away. Socializing children reenacts core cultural beliefs and creates a sense of purpose for all who call a particular culture home.[3]

Childbirth is and always has been constructed; birth continues to carry certain meanings for individuals, for communities, and for nations. Those meanings often create "us" and "them"—a sad reality only too true in the northern plains and Rocky Mountains. As cultural historian Patricia Jasen has explained, settlers claimed that Native women existed as wild and uncultured individuals, able to survive childbirth without pain.[4] Constructed assumptions enabled Euro-American settlers to blame infant mortality among tribes on Native women's supposedly incorrect and backward traditions, thus contaminating most early analyses of Native birth.[5] By telling a certain story about the reproductive practices of surrounding Native nations, white settlers constructed a specific cultural identity for themselves. Tales of Native birth often accomplished two interconnected goals: strengthening racist ideas and forming the structure of settler identity.

Childbirth speaks to those who are reproducing, both in relation to their own experience and with reference to other cultural practices. The lived experience of parents, neighbors, and families both contributes to and conflicts with cultural narratives about birth and reproduction. In any exploration of reproduction there are multiple, interrelated parts; an indefinite number of variables form a morphing contraption with bells, whistles, secret compartments, and a host of sensory components. Reproduction is both fiendishly complex and profoundly simple. No matter the era or the people or the place, reproduction creates the physical bodies of new humans and then transforms them from parasitic creatures into seemingly independent and yet culturally embedded sentient individuals.[6]

Across the northern plains and Rocky Mountains, settlers and Native peoples alike addressed birth through the lens of liminality, as "a fluid, transitional stage that must be processed within each culture by various rites of passage."[7] Childbearing, like the processes of death

Figs. 2 and 3. In the northern plains region, women gave birth in a variety of locations, such as in this canvas tent and inside a sheepherder's wagon. Hemry Neg. 32, P70-185, Tent (East of Lost Cabin), 1905; Hemry Neg. 41, Wyoma Hemry in bedroom end of sheep wagon, 1902. Wyoming State Archives.

and dying, occupied an in-between passage in both cultures, and while the marks and measurements of in-between-ness varied, this weightiness dictated a concentration of meaning surrounding the act.

Birth happened—and continues to happen—in all sorts of places and for all sorts of people. The Girls Industrial Institute in Sheridan, Wyoming, hosted births. Started in 1924 to "inculcate habits of industry, order and cleanliness," the institute schooled its charges— underage girls without "suitable relations"—but did not document their experiences of pregnancy and birth.[8] There are no records of whether the girls' pregnancies were the result of violent assault or consensual relationships, but given that 1920s-era standards did not sanction single motherhood, births in that institution were unlikely to have been celebrated events. Pregnancies likely involved shame and blame, leaving women at the institute with a multitude of overtly personal messages about reproduction, all while they struggled to make a future for themselves without any job prospects or the means to care for and keep their children.

Just over 150 miles away from the Girls Industrial Institute, the Heart Mountain Relocation Camp in Wyoming housed U.S. citizens of Asian descent during World War II—single individuals, couples, and entire families—that the U.S. government rounded up as imagined threats to national security. For women who arrived pregnant or who conceived at Heart Mountain, delivery in the confines of the camp became their new reality. Anesthesia and sedation were not used at the camp clinic—although they were becoming quite fashionable for nonincarcerated women at the time—but camp staff did administer a small amount of ether at the final stage of pushing and during episiotomy stitching.[9] Conditions at the camp were rudimentary, and since residents did not have refrigeration, nurses prepared and delivered milk every four hours for those new mothers not breastfeeding.[10] Women at the camp, abruptly removed from homes and communities, transplanted from the verdant greenery of the temperate Pacific Northwest to the comparatively dry and barren plains of Wyoming, likely struggled with issues of privacy, trauma, and separation from all things reassuring and comfortable. Empathy for a woman delivering a baby at the Heart Mountain camp clinic comes naturally; understanding the enormity of her experience is far more difficult.

Women confined to Heart Mountain and those at the Girls Industrial Institute in Wyoming experienced and interpreted their pregnancies and deliveries in profoundly different circumstances but within similar geographic contexts. Topography and weather dictated many of the factors of childbirth in the northern plains regardless of a woman's age or ethnicity.

While the grasslands, buttes, hills, and mountains of Wyoming, North and South Dakota, and Montana offered stunning vistas, they did not host teeming metropolitan centers. Weather and space ranked as critical factors for pregnant women in the area.[11] For Native American women who traversed the region on foot or horseback, concerns included the weather conditions when delivering and the importance of maintaining mobility and returning to full functioning soon after giving birth. For female settlers, distance and travel conditions impacted the assistance they could obtain at delivery. The need to adapt to bone-chilling cold, fierce winds, impassable mud, and desiccating heat before, during, and after childbirth influenced the ways that women residing in the region in 1860 or in 1910 coped with pregnancy and delivery.

Women migrating to the region brought delivery practices ill suited to their new geographic environment. Euro-American women relocated to the northern plains in an era of social childbirth, when the expectations surrounding birth included the care of midwives and the presence of women from the extended family. This system depended on attentive ministrations from numerous individuals: aunts who helped with food preparation, cousins who offered childcare during a mother's recovery, and neighbors who prepared tonics and helped with household and livestock chores.

With the expectation of such a connected and multifaceted healthcare system—one that provided physical, cultural, physiological,

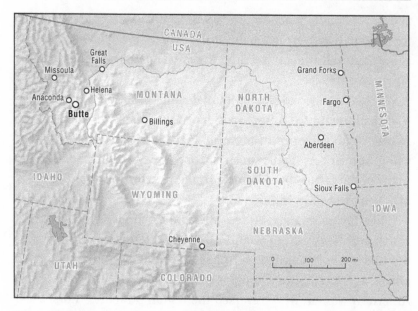

Map 1. Montana, the Dakotas, and Wyoming all saw a flood of immigration in the early 1900s, but with settlers widely dispersed, the area remained largely rural except for the few towns with populations in excess of ten thousand in 1910—Great Falls, Fargo, Aberdeen, and Cheyenne. Butte, Montana, with nearly forty thousand residents, was the largest urban center in the region. Population statistics from the Thirteenth Census of the United States Taken in the Year 1910, Department of Commerce and Labor Bureau of the Census, 568–69. Map courtesy of Erin Greb Cartography.

and personal support—female settlers in the northern plains experienced traumatic delivery in windswept stretches of open prairie. Suddenly isolated and with few close neighbors, reproducing Euro-American women stared into a reality devoid of the most notable quality of the health-care system they had left behind: the consistent companionship of other women. At a time of great vulnerability, women could not access the shared wisdom of their female community. In response, some women framed their minimally supported pregnancies as a challenge, while others experienced anxiety about reproducing in such an environment.

We could look at these women, new to the open landscape of the northern plains, and conclude that they should have anticipated the reproductive challenges of the region. They lived in an era when they had few choices, with little access to capital or even control of their children if they chose to divorce, but they did arrive in the windy grasslands or the foothills of the Rocky Mountains through some measure of their own agency. If these women were not responsible for planning in advance of delivery, who then?

Few of the white women settling the region did so casually; they came because they had little economic hope at home or because they were ambitious for a future for themselves and their families. The responsibility for voluntarily relocating cannot reside solely with the women who traveled the long miles from Wisconsin, Ohio, Missouri, Minnesota, and Iowa. The U.S. government actively promoted western settlement through land grants to railroads, agricultural promotions, and even the specific language of the Homestead Act (1862), which allowed single and widowed women to claim land as individuals.

Seen as essential players in the push to dominate western lands, white women promulgated particular social norms; they were the purveyors of Euro-American culture and served both as evidence and as enforcement of "civilization."[12] According to historian Tonia Compton, "Women as wives, mothers, and civilizers—and therefore a key component to securing the empire in the West—motivated Congress' adoption of legislation that granted women the right to claim the western lands in their own name."[13]

The federal government needed women in the northern plains to accomplish the work of colonization initiated by the military. Academics have identified the U.S. government's explicit aim to have been removing indigenous peoples from the northern plains and Rocky Mountains and securing control of those lands by establishing white settlements and social institutions; scholars have termed this process *settler colonialism*.[14] A settler colonial interpretation includes the initial physical conquest of the geographic space and removal or physical control of the original inhabitants.[15] In the northern plains and Rocky Mountains the U.S. Army accomplished this conquest and its aftermath.[16] With the swift arrival of settlers in the region, the next phase of the enterprise commenced. New residents laid claim to the particular western geography and dominated the landscape through farming, ranching, mining, and other practices that made use of the area's rich natural resources.[17] As Neil Campbell, a scholar who works in the discipline of American studies, has explained, "settling the West has been for so long a key trope of how that land, that space, that political complexity has been discussed. Putting down roots, building communities, taming the land, removing the indigenous populations with their itinerant ways, assimilating the immigrant into the nation, and asserting a national narrative have been intrinsic to western-ness."[18]

I posit a re-visioning of western events in which women's reproductive labor, often disregarded by history, is recognized as an integral component of the deeply racist and simultaneously misogynistic settler colonial enterprise.[19] The U.S. Army confined Native Americans to reservations, but the conquered territory could only be fully Americanized when churches and schools, communities, farms, and growing urban centers dotted the landscape.[20] In short, women were needed to cement the claim of ownership in the northern plains and assuredly wrest it from Native peoples in the region.[21] In this way reproduction in the northern plains region served nationalistic aims and did more than increase the population of sparsely settled western states. Reproduction put the region into service, demonstrated ownership, and began the process of nation-making in a place only recently removed from the control of its original inhabitants.

The white women featured in this study worked to colonize physical space previously controlled by tribal nations. Native and settler women resided in the same geography, albeit with significant cultural remove. Given this geographic cohabitation, ignoring the reproductive practices of Native women entirely is unconscionable. However, providing a full and complete treatment of Native reproduction—

especially since this requires a careful framing of individual tribe and reservation contexts, including land use and ownership, religious practices, and demographic characteristics—necessitates the crafting of separate texts, ideally on a reservation-by-reservation or tribe-by-tribe basis, that are critical stand-alone projects in their own right. This is important work but not the focus of this book. An investigation of Euro-American settlement before, during, and after Native confinement to reservations narrates the formation of social structures and relationships in a newly colonized region and sheds light on procreation, hierarchy, and landscape domination in American culture. That story, at least for this text, is my focus.

Even while the nation relied on western settlement by women, legal statute and social mores of the time denigrated women's value by purporting that husbands owned their wives' labor. Historian Sarah Carter has clarified this seeming contradiction by stating that, "under the doctrine of marital unity, married women had no legal existence. . . . As a commissioner of the U.S. General Land Office explained in 1864, a woman's services and labor were 'due and belonging to her husband.'"[22] As a result, women acting as "heads of household" (due to their being divorced, widowed, single, or abandoned) could homestead as individuals, while the law precluded married women from filing independent homestead claims.

Female settlers chose to relocate to the geographically challenging spaces that would become Montana, the Dakotas, and Wyoming, but they did so within a cultural and legal context that meticulously restricted the rights and opportunities of both single and married women while simultaneously offering a rare opportunity for the upward mobility and independence that often followed.

Regional Specificity

On a bright and humid summer day, with sun streaming through the glass ceiling of the spacious National Archives reading room, I began opening boxes and reading correspondence from western women to the U.S. Children's Bureau staff. Under the watchful eyes of uniformed and attentive archival staff and with fragile one-hundred-year-old letters carefully laid out on my marble viewing desk, I tumbled into the world of Alice Cutting Phelps, a woman who came to be a totem in my process. Phelps lived on a ranch in southwestern Wyoming and penned a letter to Julia Lathrop, head of the Children's Bureau, in 1916. Phelps described her own situation: pregnant, living sixty-five miles from a doctor, caring for not only her own two children but also the baby of a neighbor who had died in childbirth, and begging for any written information that might help her prepare for her impending delivery. In her letter she described the winter journey she had taken to check on her pregnant neighbor. There being few passable roads, Phelps rode horseback cross-country for seven miles to see the family and discovered her neighbor in labor and "nearly dead." After giving birth to a fourteen-pound baby boy, the mother died and Phelps volunteered to take the infant home and care for it. Such large babies often caused injury to mothers, like the extensive perineal tearing that Phelps experienced in her own births.[23] In her poignant letter Phelps requested "all the information for the care of myself before and after and at the time of delivery. I am far from a doctor, and we have no means, only what we get on this rented ranch."[24]

Phelps's letter, meaningful on its own, became far more significant as I read stacks of similar letters telling the same desperate sort of tale. Her story encapsulated the experiences of many western women living in the Dakotas, Wyoming, and Montana—women who cooked on wood or coal stoves, heated water and washed laundry and diapers by hand, and, when they escaped the never-ending cycle of cleaning and food preparation at home, saddled a horse, hitched a team to the wagon, or walked to visit neighbors. As historian Alice Boardman Smuts has commented, correspondence from many "over-burdened, anxious mothers" residing in the region showed "just how difficult and primitive conditions of life were for many American families."[25] Characteristics unique to the northern plains, such as limited rainfall, dispersed settlement patterns, and intense weather, created a

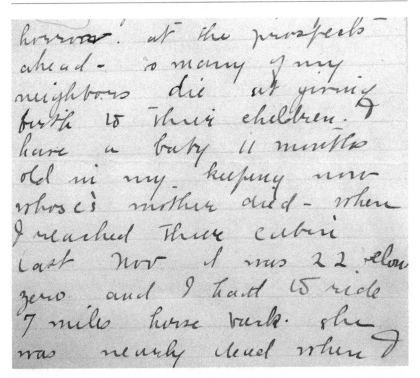

Fig. 4. Alice Phelps's 1916 letter to Julia Lathrop, head of the U.S. Children's Bureau, included a reference to being "badly torn," a birthing injury that created a gaping wound extending from her vagina to her anus. Isolated and without help, she suffered intensely while completing physically demanding tasks with a debilitating injury. File 4-3-0-3, Box 25, RG 102, Central Records of the Children's Bureau, 1914–20, National Archives and Records Administration, College Park, Maryland.

reproductive environment also specific to the region.[26] Forces beyond their control—unpredictable and extreme weather, low population density, and impassable roads—unified the experiences of childbearing women in Wyoming, the Dakotas, and Montana.

A storm of settlement just as intense and dramatic as the regional weather put increasing numbers of isolated reproducing women at the mercy of geographic and weather-related conditions. Homesteaders arrived in an explosive demographic cascade: Wyoming claimed only 9,118 residents in 1870; by 1880 the state's population had reached 20,789.[27] Just across the border from Wyoming, the number of South Dakota residents ballooned from a mere 95,208 in 1880 to 401,570 in 1900.[28] The Montana population more than doubled, from 243,329 in 1900 to 548,889 just twenty years later.[29] The torrent of settlers spread out across the vast spaces of Montana, Wyoming, and the Dakotas, dispersing in ever-diminishing concentrations as they found homes in newly created agricultural communities that lacked rudimentary infrastructure. This great horde of settlers, when tossed about the seemingly endless stretches of open space, fell in isolated groups, like grains of salt in a potluck-sized casserole.

While often separated by distance, settlers nevertheless formed a surprisingly cohesive cultural constituency. The 1920 census recorded members of the racial categories of "Negro," "Indian," "Chinese," and "Japanese" as totaling less than 3 percent of the population for both Montana and South Dakota, leaving both states at 97.3 percent "white." Wyoming was recorded at 97.8 percent "white," with North Dakota an even starker 98.9 percent.[30] Those of Canadian or northern European heritage dominated in many communities, with single men, single women, families, and extended family groups of Norwegian, German, Swedish, English, Danish, and Finnish descent a common presence in towns from Medora, North Dakota, to Miles City, Montana.[31] The overwhelming whiteness of transplanted settlers stood out in a region only recently seized from Native American nations and in states with the highest combined number of reservations as compared to any other part of the country.[32]

While towns and cities did exist, the northern plains region claimed an overwhelmingly rural character, with few metropolitan areas and a decidedly agricultural economy. Residents across the region were all part of this agricultural economy, as the productivity of agricultural lands affected not just those who farmed but entire communities.[33] When drought struck, one scholar writes, "average wheat yields dropped from over 26 bushels in 1915 to less than 3 bushels per acre in 1919," a difference that took many families from surplus to starvation as taxes and bank loans came due and the prospect of bankruptcy loomed.[34]

Early arrivals chose the richer and more fertile cropland, while marginal areas drew those with less capital, especially as land prices rose in consistently watered microclimates. Established areas developed rudimentary social infrastructure, such as churches, schools, community organizations, and local governments that helped to moderate the effects of stressed reproduction. Those with access to capital settled in more established areas; those with fewer resources could only look to more sparsely settled and riskier land.[35] These economic forces conspired to place women of reproductive age in geographic situations that lacked the necessary support systems for childbirth while adding potential physical, emotional, and psychic stressors. Thus, while childbirth was challenging for nearly all women in the region, those with more options, money, and social connections faced fewer obstacles to acquiring care during delivery and postpartum.

Reproducing women needed consistent nutrition, a stable home life, and social and personal connections to moderate the demands of small children and provide rest during pregnancy. In the mobile, reactive, boom-and-bust environment of the northern plains those elements were in short supply, leaving many women chronically depleted, worn, and lacking necessary resources. Men faced many of the same circumstances, as the context of Wyoming, the Dakotas, and Montana proved stressful for all of its new residents, but the unique demands of pregnancy and childbirth meant that delivery and postpartum recovery were increasingly fraught with dangers because of women's poor condition.

The northern plains could not claim a monolithic women's culture; women brought a panoply of languages and birthing traditions with them. But the severity and dominance of regional characteristics such as severe weather and limited access to care created conditions common to most women in the region, from the Red River Valley of North Dakota to the Rocky Mountains of Montana. This context came to characterize the experience of childbearing in the region and also, in an ironic twist, served to maintain women's traditional control of reproduction for decades longer than in some other parts of the country.

Childbirth had long been considered the province of women, in part because it was seen as an act too tiresome and inappropriate for men's involvement. From the late 1700s through the early 1900s male physicians sought to gain access to and experience in delivery. With medicine's push to expand delivery services, male doctors made inroads into this once exclusively female domain. As allopathic physicians organized, sought more clients, and worked to improve their social standing, they targeted midwives in an attempt to reduce competition for birthing services.[36] Support for midwifery remained strong initially but eventually diminished under the onslaught of organized attacks from male physicians. Eventually physicians came to oversee the majority of deliveries, and the "medical model of childbirth emerged unchallenged."[37] This change was most pronounced in the eastern and urban areas of the United States, and because the geographic and weather-related challenges of delivery in the West made it far more difficult to attend and profit from birthing services, demand for midwifery care in the northern plains did not dim as rapidly as in other, more settled and accessible regions.

Western women, including those in Wyoming, Montana, and the Dakotas, retained more control over the birth process than their cosmopolitan counterparts. Doctors defined pregnancy as an illness, so the lengthy transition to medicalized birth in the northern plains region and its sustained direction by midwives meant that beliefs about women's inherent inferiority did not permeate the region in quite the same manner as they did in other parts of the country.[38] Urban centers like New York and Chicago charted the tipping point of physician-dominated birth (when more than half of all births occurred in hospitals or at home with physicians instead of midwives) to the early 1910s, while midwives continued in active practices in the northern plains well into the 1940s.[39]

Fig. 5. This image of an immaculately dressed Wyoming midwife, identified only as Aunt Phillips and photographed around 1890, is a reminder of
the expertise of women—Native American, African American, and Euro-
American alike—who used their professional knowledge in the northern
plains. Sub. Neg. 23506, Aunt Phillips, Midwife. Wyoming State Archives.

This pocket of resistant midwifery impacted both the culture of the northern plains and the availability of evidence about women's experiences there. In the 1970s and 1980s, as social historians recorded oral histories of the region's early white settlers, they documented details that, due to the earlier demise of midwifery in more settled areas, had not been readily available for study.[40]

Historically, public health professionals blamed midwives for high rates of maternal mortality in childbirth. State health departments, in an attempt to explain these high rates in the region, assumed that the scarcity of local physicians created a crisis of care. My findings suggest a different reality, and I claim that the overall conditions of women's existence were far more significant. Poverty and stress hurt men, women, and children, and the existing informal health-care system, moderated by women, did an exemplary job of managing a difficult situation.

Ways and Means

Two of my daughters, Anza and Bethany, then thirteen and nine, accompanied me on a research trip through the Dakotas and Wyoming as I tracked down sources for this book. We arrived at our hotel in Bismarck, North Dakota, late in the afternoon and discovered freshly baked chocolate chip cookies in the lobby. North Dakota was looking good. We toured the North Dakota Heritage Center and State Museum and returned the next morning to investigate the archives.

After repeated research ventures across the region, I was familiar with the refrain—"No, I'm sorry, we don't have any records about childbirth at all"—from well-meaning archivists. To locate sources, I usually scoured oral histories from a repository's collection, and North Dakota, like so many of its sibling states, had a stash of recorded conversations with settlers reflecting on their early years in the state.

Sitting down with a list of oral history interviewees, I went looking for the index of transcriptions, only to discover that the oral histories had never been transcribed and that no survey of topics and no way of searching the hundreds of named oral histories even existed. At around two hours in length each, the recordings (on tape, no less, so they could not be digitally copied) represented at least four hundred hours of listening in place in the oil pump–dotted environs of Bismarck. We were on a tightly scheduled trip with planned stops at a number of research institutions in the coming days. Did this unorganized smattering of old North Dakotans really warrant more time?

One of the girls asked about my frustrated expression, and when I explained the problem, she said, "Well, shouldn't we get started?" Evidently the prospect of multiple long days in Bismarck did not sound appealing to her either. Overcoming my lethargy, I copied out the list of names, and then we both took a handful of tapes into individual listening booths. We agreed on a strategy based on my experience with other similar oral history collections: we systematically pulled all recordings of women (men did talk about their children's births but with far less regularity and specificity than women), listened to the first five minutes or so of the tape to get a sense for the interviewee, and then randomly skipped through the tape, searching for references to reproduction. The list included more women than men, since women usually lived longer and were available when the historians called. I figured we could get through at most a quarter of the relevant tapes in the time we had.

As the voices of North Dakota women from the 1970s, some tremulous with age but many strong and feisty, filled my headphones, my irritation at the perceived inefficiency of my search lessened. I heard about cold winters and failed crops, hardship and sticking it out to survive. I checked in with my daughter. Had she heard anything relevant? Nothing so far, but it was "interesting," she said, to hear the stories. I returned to my tapes and my booth in a decidedly less sour mood.

I sleepily listened on, only to realize that the voice of Amy Nichols was explaining how her mother had emigrated from Norway in 1891 and how she in turn asked Mrs. Braidall, the Norwegian midwife in

Reeder, North Dakota, to help with her own deliveries.[41] Success! I typed notes furiously, stopping and starting the recording to catch all of the details.

At work with her tapes, Anza discovered that a particular interviewer, Larry Sprunk, listened to the interviewees carefully. While he did not ask direct questions about childbirth, his conversations with longtime North Dakota residents often yielded voluntary contributions about delivery and reproduction from the narrators when they sensed he was particularly interested in what mattered to them. We hastily conferred to make sure that we had every interview conducted by the now-beloved Larry Sprunk in the pile.

The discoveries continued. Lulu Larson from Valley City, North Dakota, remembered her midwife with tender affection and admiration, describing her as "so handy, so capable."[42] Karolina Meidinger, also of Valley City, explained that when her mother began having regular labor pains, her father left to get the midwife. The snow was too deep to get a team of horses through, so he walked the two miles. While he and the midwife lunged their way back through the drifts, Meidinger's mother labored on, issuing curt instructions to her older children as she pushed the infant out, cleaned and wrapped it, and then delivered the placenta. A small child at the time, Meidinger viewed the entire process surreptitiously, sure that she would be removed from the scene if discovered but determined to watch the fascinating drama.[43]

My daughter Anza motioned me over to her booth and handed me her headphones. Loretta Thompson, first in hesitant tones, then with growing pride, described how her mother had sent her, at the age of seventeen, to deliver the baby of a neighbor. The more experienced women in the area were already attending births, and Thompson's mother gave her careful instructions. Thompson said, "She told me all the procedures that I was supposed to go through, what I was supposed to keep this way and that way, everything had to be clean, the rags had to be in the oven." Thompson's mother reassured her daughter that everything would be fine if she would be careful to "follow what I tell you." Pausing to consider her long-ago adventure, Thompson said with evident satisfaction, "Kind of rewarding when you do things like that."[44]

As Clara Ramey described giving birth to twins on her own, Larry Sprunk asked her, "Weren't you in pain?" With obvious humor Ramey said, "Of course I was in pain!" and "I had a stick in my mouth" (to help her focus on the task at hand), describing how she pushed one baby out, caught it, scalded scissors to sanitize the blades, and then cut the umbilical cord before wrapping and carefully setting the first baby down and delivering its twin.[45]

Much to my daughters' relief (and mine), we did not spend ten weeks in residence at the North Dakota Heritage Center. We headed to South Dakota on schedule, and I do not know how many details and dramas I left behind, undiscovered. But Lena Vanvig's Norwegian-accented voice tripped along in my head as we hiked through the startling beauty of the Badlands, walked the humid escape of Reptile Gardens, and drove through a dangerous spring snowstorm that closed the road behind us outside of Hot Springs, South Dakota. Vanvig described her training and experience in delivering babies, and when Larry Sprunk asked if "you ladies" worried about childbirth, she shot right back, "What good would it do?" Vanvig's desire to save infants lilted across the miles as we drove into Wyoming. As she told it, "One baby . . . Billy Connell, he was so blue when he was born." The husband said, "Oh, baby's dead," and Vanvig responded, "You take care of Lula [the mother], and I'll see what I can do with the baby." Vanvig kept working with the infant, breathing for him and auscultating his heart. Then, "he start like that, and . . . oh, how happy I was! I never forget it."[46]

Oral histories like Vanvig's formed the basis for my documentation of women's reproductive journeys. In collecting, listening to, and then analyzing the voices of women telling their own stories, I have attempted to piece together a past that has been there all along, noting themes and patterns in the historical record, as well as identifying breaks and incongruities.[47]

My search proceeded to diaries, correspondence, and data from newly formed territorial and state health departments. I evaluated each account in light of my growing body of research, placing it in context as well as recognizing its unique and individual elements. Initially overwhelmed by the unknowns—Why so many twelve- and fourteen-pound babies? Were these women all giants?—I found hints of answers, like lists in diaries of the vast quantities of flour purchased and baking performed, which helped me understand that families subsisted largely on bread-based meals during the long winters, raising the chances of gestational diabetes and large babies. In contrast to settler practices, some Native American women intentionally performed hard physical labor and exercised vigorously during pregnancy to ensure a small fetus and an easy delivery.[48] As I inhabited the lives of 1890s women in Laramie, Wyoming, and Butte, Montana, logical connections appeared, and I assessed potential veracity against the piecemeal public records.

In a process of doubling back, checking, verifying, and listening, I came to understand my expanding collection of observations. These women created culture through reproductive labors, and a specific western ethos emerged as a result of birth practices. The physical exertions of women's everyday responsibilities contributed a sense of place: women's work and women's pay and women's pain and women's productivity came to exemplify the character traits so closely aligned with regional identity.[49] Through their untold efforts, mothers birthed the West.

Their reproductive interactions simultaneously impacted and were shaped by institutions. The state, represented by the governing structures of Wyoming, North and South Dakota, and Montana, as well as the U.S. Children's Bureau, "attempt[ed] to make a society legible" through birth and death registration and the promulgation of laws and policies related to reproductive activity.[50]

Methodically searching records, listening to the voices of the past, considering my own internal ruminations in the present, and assembling what would be, without the blessed benefit of modern technology, a literal mountain of records, brought me to see the emergence of a specific, identifiable system, an ideology of birth practice. This informal health-care network, managed by and for women, operated regionally from the mid-1800s through the 1930s and 1940s. Central to bringing new members into the human community, the woman-centered method contributed to a region of contradictions, a place that trumpeted its individuality while inextricably knitting communities together, a space that promulgated free-for-all extraction while depending for its future on the results of mothers' reproduction.

This text investigates mothers and midwives not because they were saints or otherworldly feminist warriors but because they formed a nurturing, life-affirming practice of passing on knowledge while balancing authority and care. Female-centered reproduction offers insight into women's experiences in another era and also sheds light on ways of being human, of working collaboratively, of giving and receiving respect, of nurturing a creative and productive human culture.

1

Birth in the Big Open

To understand the colonial enterprise of women in the northern plains and Rocky Mountains, we must first pay attention to their quotidian realities. What larger meanings did their daily chores represent? Fertility in all its forms—animal, vegetable, human—marked their lives, and much of women's experience of menstruation, pregnancy, and childbirth remains unchanged even into our contemporary existence. Yet their lives were markedly different from our own. The question "Do I want children?" would have been nonsensical for most of the women whose lives are the focus of this study. Reproduction was a given, assumed as a naturally occurring outcome, especially from a marriage like that of Elizabeth Pope and Edward Maclean.

Pope and Maclean married in South Roundout, New York, on December 29, 1906.[1] Driven and enterprising, Lizzie and Mac, as they called each other, decided to relocate more than two thousand miles from the humid, rolling hills near the Hudson River in New York to the arid grasslands of Montana. They strategized their assault on the homesteading proposition, figuring that to succeed they needed to perform two contradictory tasks: earn enough cash to pay their basic expenses and invest physical energy and effort in the Montana land to which they hoped to receive a deed of ownership.

Success demanded thoughtful planning. Together Lizzie and Mac traveled out to Montana in 1913 to move their household goods and belongings, and then they split their efforts, with Mac returning east to his job building bridges near Pittsburgh while Lizzie established their homestead in Montana. Elizabeth, their young daughter, remained with family in New York. While Mac toiled far away in Pennsylvania as a bridge engineer, Lizzie managed the homestead on her own, fixed the cellar, cut oats, painted the hen house, oversaw plowing and planting and fence building, and tended to neighbors.[2] Glancing up from her labors, Maclean would have looked out on prairie taken from the Blackfeet Nation and cleared of Native inhabitants just forty years earlier.[3]

The Hicks family lived within walking distance of the Maclean homestead, and beginning in June 1915 Lizzie Maclean began staying overnight with a pregnant Mrs. Hicks in anticipation of her delivery. For a full two weeks Maclean completed her own duties and also traveled to check on her neighbor. Finally, Hicks felt the long-awaited signs of labor, and with some relief Maclean first fed her chickens and watered her stock before making a purposeful trip to attend the birth.[4]

In 1916 Alice and Oswald Susag settled near current-day Scobey, Montana, an area originally controlled by Native inhabitants who had since been confined to the Fort Peck Reservation in 1887 and further restricted by an allotment process completed in 1911.[5] Like Maclean, Alice Susag received a message from her neighbor, Mrs. Stenson. Could she come? Susag made a quick survey of her livestock and issued directives to her family about feeding, food, and care. She moved deliberately, without alarm or haste. Birthing an infant required much effort and time; Stenson probably faced hours of labor ahead. With everything in order at home, Susag left for the Stenson place to help deliver the baby.[6]

With the same attention to detail and deliberate care they applied to calculating chicks' hatching dates and rehabilitating injured livestock, Susag and Maclean superintended the process of human birth.

Like other reproductively knowledgeable women of their era, they knew the importance of cleanliness.[7] They used sanitized string to seal off the umbilical cord and clean towels to catch blood and placental fluid.[8] They offered a firm hand and a store of learning grounded in their own experience.

Presentism—the all too common practice of using contemporary perceptions to understand past events—complicates our attempt to interpret reproductive activities like Susag's and Maclean's. Childbirth is a contemporary, deeply personal event, which is translated through the lens of culture. Current perspectives on childbirth wallow in a fear-based atmosphere that describes delivery as an inherently dangerous activity made safe only by trained medical personnel and the reassurance of gently beeping machines. When twenty-first-century women become pregnant, they frequently refer to the medical field to translate their reproductive journey. They note the commencement of gestation with a positive pregnancy test and "meet" the baby through ultrasound images. Pregnancy appears as a far and distant land that can be explored only with the assistance of medical mapping.

My own experience followed this medical routine. After confirming my first pregnancy with the ubiquitously available blue stick, I immediately located a physician in my small Montana town and scheduled a series of prenatal appointments. As I contemplated motherhood, I was suffused with an intense desire to do it right, to discover the one best way to perform this important act. Glad to be pregnant, I also felt entirely unprepared for the challenges and decisions to come. When I was a child and adolescent, pregnant women in my family and social circle simply disappeared to the hospital and then resumed normal life, all without any open discussion or dialogue about their deliveries. I knew far more about cows and calving than human childbirth.

Without any background in the birthing process, I started investigating and began to understand contemporary childbirth as a contrast between two extremes. Those who supported American

techno-birth—the monitor-everything-with-machines approach—
issued dire warnings about the consequences of forgoing a long
battery of medical tests and procedures. They also supplied copious
anecdotes about mothers and infants dying from freak infections
and undiagnosed diseases. The opposing position portrayed mothers as reproductive mavens capable of safe deliveries if left entirely
unmolested to birth in a clump of bushes while chewing on birch
twigs. They promulgated women's ability to achieve nirvana through
female empowerment, deep squats, and primal grunting.

In contrast to these modern caricatures of childbirth, Susag,
Maclean, Stenson, and Hicks looked to each other—not to medical
intervention or to the procreative power of a female deity. Susag and
Maclean claimed a level of proficiency that reassured their neighbors; Stenson and Hicks valued Susag's and Maclean's authority and
expertise. The pregnant mothers guided the delivery from their own
sensations and focused on accomplishing the useful task of delivery—an ordinary duty but also one that held some level of excitement
and import. Each of the participating women turned her attention
both inward and outside of herself: the mothers claimed an active
role in childbirth, while their attendants offered knowledgeable and
supportive assistance.

Honest assessment of historical birth requires a temporary escape
from current assumptions about the necessity of technology, the
preeminence of modern medicine, and the naturalness of childbirth.
Contemporary minds struggle to grasp a reproductive environment
directed and managed by noncredentialed yet eminently capable
women. Embarking on a journey of historical reproductive investigation entails acknowledging this parturient baggage.[9] Discarding
stereotypical notions allows us to observe what we otherwise might
miss: that women birthed without reproductive heroics, they managed delivery within a female sphere, and they were desirous of
consideration and support.

We begin from a reassuring truth: the physiology of pregnancy
remains the same in the twenty-first century as it was for women liv-

ing in the northern plains region in the 1890s. Conception, the gestational progression, and delivery proceeded with a marked consistency into the contemporary era. Knowledge about a mother's pregnancy in the past can be garnered from the current reproductive pattern. We know that pregnancy lasts approximately thirty-eight to forty-two weeks and that, barring complications, the cervix dilates and the mother pushes the baby through the birth canal. We do not need to initiate a nutritional study of historic birth to assess the caloric needs of Stenson and Hicks or inquire about the energy demands of the developing fetus. This reproductively related information is available to us today. Based on the constancy of reproduction, the historical dialogue can flow backward in time, as we interpret past human cultures, and forward, causing us to question our prevailing hubris and learn from the wisdom of our predecessors.

Birth as an Ordinary Occurrence

Women delivered babies across the northern plains—on forced marches to reservations and in mining shacks, army tent camps, and homestead shanties. Birth occurred at all times and in all places, within and simultaneous to more quintessential western scenes. Alongside the Wild West's gold and guns existed the voices, bodies, blood, and babies of women.

Pregnancy and delivery wove their way into the ordinariness of daily life for the reproducing women of the late 1800s and early 1900s. In this era of social birth women usually delivered babies at home and expected to share the experience with female friends, relatives, and neighbors.[10] Girls who lived close to family saw their grandmothers and aunts arrive in advance of a birth and knew that experienced female hands would manage the delivery of a sibling. As young women passed through puberty and reached reproductive age themselves, they could be called upon to help during delivery or at least to care for and entertain younger siblings. Helping with birth became a regular task along with food preparation, livestock management, and household routines.

Fig. 6. Bessie Muth, pictured here with her younger brother around 1890, was probably present at his birth, helping with chores and cleaning up. 944-114, Bessie Muth and baby brother. Montana Historical Society Research Center.

The Constancy of Birth

As the Civil War continued in the eastern United States, Lucy Nave left Missouri with her family and made the long trip to Montana, arriving in 1864. Along with her sister and niece, she opened a dressmaking shop in Virginia City. Their storefront stood just across the rutted street from the Wells Fargo stage office, where William Tinsley worked. The couple met and subsequently married in 1867. As a young adult, Lucy Tinsley no doubt attended births, but upon marriage she quickly transitioned into her own phase of active reproduction. She navigated her first pregnancy through the end of 1867 and beginning of 1868, giving birth to her son Floyd in the spring. By 1869 she was pregnant again. The year 1870 concluded with the birth of Quiteria. Tinsley, now with a two-year-old and an infant to care for, became pregnant for the third time in 1871. With Lillian's birth, Tinsley had three children all under the age of four as she became pregnant for a fourth time in 1872. Tinsley delivered Ida in 1873 and quickly became pregnant for the fifth time, giving birth to William in 1874. Perhaps desiring a brief respite from constant childbearing or worn out from the quick succession of pregnancies, Tinsley nursed William through 1875 and conceived again in 1876. She delivered Enoch in 1877 and soon discovered herself in the midst of her seventh pregnancy, which resulted in Edwin's birth in 1878. Floyd and Quiteria, then ten and eight, were old enough to help with household chores when in 1880 Tinsley became pregnant for the eighth time and gave birth to Lucy Mary in 1881.[11]

Tinsley began her marathon of childbearing at the age of twenty-four and concluded thirteen years later as the thirty-seven-year-old mother of eight children.[12] During that period she may have gone for as long as one year without being pregnant, and she breastfed for more than a decade. She also raised a garden, looked after livestock, prepared food, did laundry, sewed the family's clothes, managed the homestead, and helped neighbors. She raised all eight children to adulthood, losing none of them to illness or infectious disease, a noteworthy accomplishment in a time of high mortality rates.

Tinsley's reproductive success likely stemmed from several sources, including her own planning and hard work. Martha, Tinsley's sister-in-law, lived close by, and the two women stepped in for each other as needed.[13] During each of Tinsley's deliveries, Martha likely cared for the children, prepared meals, and assisted during labor. Most women bleed for a number of weeks after delivery of the placenta, and while the quantity of blood tapers off quickly, the need to contain the flow and launder additional menstrual rags for a period of time would have substantially increased the quantity of laundry in the household. In Tinsley's case, Martha's help with such

Fig. 7. The Tinsley children, along with their parents, Lucy and William: Floyd, born in 1868; Quiteria, in 1870; Lillian, 1871; Ida, 1873; William E., 1874; Enoch, 1877; Edwin, 1878; and Lucy Mary, who ended the procession with her birth in 1881. 83.73.10, William Bailey and Lucy Ann Nave Tinsley and Family. Museum of the Rockies.

physically demanding tasks would have been particularly helpful by allowing Tinsley to rest and also be at ease in the knowledge that her skilled replacement could ably manage any problems.

Birth loomed as a constant for females of reproductive age and also for the men, postmenopausal women, and children with whom they shared their lives.[14] Accounts of delivery reveal birthing as a time of celebration and some distress. Regardless of the emotions that accompanied the event, reproduction remained an integral part of daily existence and presented concrete issues that women grappled with on a regular basis.

Reproduction ran a continuous thread through both daily routine and the upheaval of relocation. A mother contemplated moving to a western territory while exhausted from early pregnancy weariness; she worried over the difficulty of planting the garden with the growing bulk of later pregnancy and allowed time for the demands of a nursing infant while baking bread and butchering chickens for ongoing meal preparation. In addition to her own reproductive status, her thoughts rested on pregnant sisters, nieces, neighbors, and even her mother; she commiserated with their discomfort and shared in their excitement. At any community gathering, females in all stages of reproduction would be present, from menopausal women to nursing mothers, from pubescent girls to women pregnant for the eighth time.

As settler women constructed rudimentary systems of care, they called men into service as assistants when women were not available. Historian Nanci Langford has explained that "childbirth was a family affair, and every available adult, including hired men, had a role in the delivery of each child."[15] Given the regularity of animal reproduction, including the all-night work of calving and lambing and foaling, birth in the northern plains region moves from the periphery to a place of preeminence. Everyday reproductive encounters—from taking a message to a neighbor, helping at a delivery, or watching over a cow during calving—saturated the ordinary experiences of regional residents.

Fig. 8. Over time the Tinsley clan expanded to a sizable crowd, pictured here circa 1900. 85.64.8, Group Portrait of the Tinsley Family Gathering. Museum of the Rockies.

Conception

Before the availability of the pregnancy test, women relied on physical clues and personal observation of their menstrual cycles to determine fertility.[16] Women today can look to tests like ultrasound to measure fetal development and predict due dates, but settler women in the late 1800s and early 1900s had no such aids. Estimates of conception depended on remembered dates of sexual activity and menses. Tracking cycles proved difficult for women migrating to the northern plains and Rocky Mountains, since the physical demands of their new lifestyle often left them depleted enough that they ceased to menstruate. Eighteen months into her homesteading experiment, Lizzie Maclean noted that she "weigh[ed] 123 pounds," and while there is no available point of comparison for her weight prior to her arrival in Montana, 123 pounds on any frame does not allow for abundant fat reserves.[17]

Mothers guessed in the early stages of pregnancy about whether or not they were expecting and wondered at the end of pregnancy about when they might actually deliver. With scarce and ineffective methods of contraception, they could not reliably prevent pregnancy. Some of the signs, like the absence of menstruation, were inaccurate indicators. As a result, Euro-American women of the late 1800s and early 1900s existed in an undefined state of potential pregnancy for great stretches of their actively reproductive years.

In contrast to Euro-American settlers' relative ignorance about contraception, Native Americans in the region employed multiple contraceptive methods, as well as particular plant-based treatments during delivery. Historian Jane Lawrence has explained that "Native American women . . . us[ed] various natural methods to prevent conception," including red cedar, deer's tongue, and juniper.[18] Since many Native women could identify when they were fertile, they adjusted their sexual activity accordingly and exercised some measure of control over the timing of their pregnancies.[19]

For recent Euro-American settlers without such efficacious knowledge, stepping into a zone of possibly continuous pregnancy required a sometimes unwelcome shift in perspective. Laurentza Koch married her husband, Peter, in 1874. She left her family behind in Mississippi and moved to Bozeman, Montana, where Peter worked as an attorney and banker. As was typical, Koch became pregnant within the first year of marriage, and she struggled to accept her reproductive future. While it is probable that she put on a brave face with casual acquaintances, she wrote her mother that she felt "rebellious and ugly" when she realized that she was pregnant.[20] At a time when childbearing was the epitome of the female role, Koch had few options, a realization that no doubt contributed to her claustrophobia and frustration.

Most midwives of the 1700s and 1800s grew, harvested, preserved, and dispensed herbs that induced abortion, prevented conception, and increased milk supply. These plants thrived in specific climates and areas of the country, and as settlers headed west to the Dakotas, Montana, and Wyoming not knowing what plants might be available, they relied more heavily on transportable contraceptive devices like diaphragms or condoms.[21] The Comstock Act, signed by President Ulysses Grant on March 3, 1873, prohibited these manufactured contraceptives from being imported to the United States and forbade their manufacture, advertisement, or sale. The law allowed for the seizure and destruction of any materials related to birth control and deemed such items obscene. These prohibitions on contraceptive availability remained in effect well into the 1950s and were not officially repealed until 1971.[22]

While Comstock-era rhetoric drew a firm line between socially acceptable women and sex workers, contraceptive and abortifacient use occupied a gray zone in the lives of ordinary Americans. Personal letters, advertisements, and trial transcripts showed that the Comstock Act dampened the availability of contraceptives and reproductive knowledge (by stifling open conversation about the topic) but in no way eradicated it.[23]

Many turn-of-the-twentieth-century women actively searched for ways to prevent conception, even going so far as to contact professional staff at the Children's Bureau, the first government agency devoted to serving women and their infants.[24] A North Dakota mother wrote the bureau begging for information and explaining that she

Figs. 9 and 10. Laurentza Koch, pictured here first as a young woman and later with her two sons, had her first child in Bozeman, Montana, in 1875. She endured at least four more pregnancies, carrying five infants to term. It is possible that Koch, like so many other women, miscarried during her years of active reproduction, potentially increasing her total number of pregnancies. Collection 2476, Edward D. Nelson Papers, Merrill G. Burlingame Special Collections, Montana State University, Bozeman.

was twenty-two years old and already had seven children. According to her letter, she "did not want any more after [she] had two."[25] Birth control activist Margaret Sanger published an entire volume of letters she received in the early 1900s from women pleading for ways to prevent pregnancy. Given the social shame associated with the use of contraceptives, the boldness of women in openly seeking such knowledge spoke to the depth of their reproductive distress.[26] Even while motherhood defined the core of female identity, some women of the era openly resisted and even more voiced their worry and consternation about the potential for repeated conception.

Edna Cox McCann dealt with the confinement of consistent childbearing in the early 1900s by escaping into the nearby foothills to "prospect." She hired a neighbor to stay with her children and would "take the saddlehorse and go." McCann credited her exploratory forays with offering benefit "more than anything" when she had a young family and faced repeated pregnancies.[27]

Like Koch, women at the start of their first pregnancy acknowledged the physical demands of reproduction, as well as the cultural burden of motherhood. Becoming pregnant involved far more than the arrival of a child forty weeks in the future. Mothers considered their childbearing role in marriage; the involvement, concern, or pride of extended family and relatives in the pregnancy; and the changes that pregnancy might bring to their social standing within communities. Conception raised all of these issues and represented the point at which women took on the mantle of motherhood, an often overwhelming burden.

Pregnancy

Most turn-of-the-twentieth-century mothers monitored the details of their pregnancies individually. Pearl Johnson gave birth to her children in 1916, 1918, and 1928, without having received any prenatal care.[28] Faye Hoven, born in 1894, said she "never went to a doctor all the time I was pregnant or when [the baby] was born because we were thirty-five miles [from town] and no cars. We just . . . had a team and a wagon at that time."[29] Like Hoven, Katie Adams rarely traveled away from her homestead near Joplin, Montana. Born in 1888, Adams recalled going to town only twice in ten years.[30]

Nine months of pregnancy without any outside consultation stands as a marked difference from current standards of prenatal care, but it was routine for pregnant women in the early 1900s. Faye Hoven "just didn't think anything of it" because her neighbors, family, and friends followed the same policy.[31] Finding assistance for the birth presented enough of a challenge; receiving medical care prior to delivery ran against the cultural norm. Women considered pregnancy a part of the typical female experience, and the idea that they might benefit from medical attention prior to delivery only gained regional acceptance in the 1920s and 1930s with the expansion of hospital care.[32]

Women did seek medical attention for miscarriage. Idora and Herbert Guthrie married in 1904, and one year later Guthrie commemorated their anniversary by noting in her diary the anticipated arrival of "one more."[33] Regular missives traveled from Guthrie to her mother over the course of the pregnancy. "A letter from mother tonight" or "wrote to mother this p.m." occurred more than once a week in Guthrie's accounting.[34]

Like most western women, Guthrie rode horseback of necessity. Trains were used for long-distance travel, while horses provided daily transport. On September 17, 1905, one horse bucked her off, and when she mounted another, it lay down with her still on it. She was "not hurt either time" and called the doctor for an apparently unrelated stomach complaint two days later. But September 20 she "dragged all day" and noted her discomfort again the next day. Guthrie felt poorly enough to call the doctor again, and he indicated that no diagnosable illness existed aside from the chance of "mountain fever," a bacterial infection carried by ticks. Guthrie shook off her symptoms until October 10, when she worried that some intermittent vaginal bleeding might "mean trouble." Spotty bleeding could indicate nothing other than slight overexertion. It could also be a portent of more significant problems, and Guthrie's concern proved legitimate. Two days later she experienced "a good deal of pain all day," and the next evening she felt "such pain [she] could scarcely work."[35]

Despite her misery, she prepared dinner. When her friend Belle stopped in, Guthrie told Belle how poorly she felt. Then, as Guthrie phrased it, she "had a flood." The sudden rush of blood signaled the end of her pregnancy. The doctor arrived within an hour and a half, and Belle applied cold cloths. Despite their efforts, however, "the foetus came about half past eight." Belle left soon after, and Guthrie wrote nothing in her diary for the next fifteen days.[36]

Women rarely recorded details of miscarriage, and no state or federal agency existed to investigate or tabulate its occurrence in Montana, the Dakotas, and Wyoming during the late 1800s and early 1900s.[37] Catherine Brodhead, a midwife and lay physician who worked in North Dakota and Montana in the 1920s, 1930s, and 1940s, made note of the women she treated for miscarriage.[38] About 4 percent of her maternity cases involved miscarriage, an unfortunate but common event for turn-of-the-twentieth-century women like Guthrie in the northern plains.[39]

In calling a local physician on several occasions, Guthrie represented an anomaly. Because of lack of funds and the scarcity of doctors, many women in the region took a piecemeal approach to reproductive care, both leading up to delivery and for the birth itself. A mother might find a neighbor to attend the birth but be left without any postpartum help, or she might make arrangements for a physician to be present at the birth but deliver with the help of a close neighbor if an emergency case took the doctor miles away.

In situations where the family had ample financial resources and access to help, multiple providers could be hired. Once she resigned herself to her pregnant state, Koch arranged for delivery and postpartum care from Mrs. Rich, a local midwife, and consulted with Dr. Whitefoot, the local military post physician. Whitefoot prescribed calomel, a common but poisonous mercury-based purgative used to treat nausea.[40] As an urban and well-to-do resident of the northern plains, Koch sought a certain kind of treatment from one provider and arranged additional services from another. She approached her impending delivery focused on remediating her physical symptoms, assured that, if an emergency called Dr. Whitefoot away from her delivery, she could fall back on the assistance of Mrs. Rich. Koch's wealth and location made sufficient care available, especially in contrast to women like Faye Hoven, Pearl Johnson, and Katie Adams, who endured multiple pregnancies with a minimum of assistance.

In a context of inconsistent health care, women mined their own physical and emotional resources to meet their reproductive demands. When no one else could be called on, mothers ate less, slept less, and performed more physically demanding tasks while pregnant. Pushing, and often exceeding, the limits of their reserves, women experienced complications and pregnancy-related death at high rates.

Despite the fact that women in the northern plains and Rocky Mountains were largely removed from the impacts of urban squalor and isolated from the disease epidemics that city dwellers experienced, early state health records show that mortality rates in the region reached startling proportions.[41] Western states followed the lead of their eastern counterparts and, witnessing an influx of settlers, began collecting public health information. State governments across the region faced challenges in justifying this governmental function, in obtaining the necessary funding, and most particularly in convincing residents to share birth and mortality information with data collectors. Nevertheless, when health officials gathered even patchy and insufficient evidence, the numbers told a grim story. Women could not draw on personal resources unendingly. When unsupported, women struggled with pregnancy-related complications; when under stress, their babies died more frequently.

Delivery

Women worried about the dangers of childbirth, but their fear of being entirely alone during delivery overshadowed these concerns. Mothers expressed a profound desire for female companionship and a vital need for other women to be present. When Nannie Alderson miscarried, the doctor was one hundred miles away. When a hired hand offered to make the journey to fetch the doctor, Alderson said, "I don't want a doctor. I want a woman."[42] Pregnancy and childbirth, perceived as important life events and not medical emergencies, demanded commonality and connection with other females who also experienced the intrusive regularity of reproduction.

If they could not find a suitable attendant and had the necessary funds, women often chose to leave the region and make the arduous journey to be with family during the delivery and postpartum period. Months later, recovered from childbirth and strong enough to make the trip, mothers returned to the northern plains with their infants. The uncertainty of due dates made for lengthy absences. A woman might be gone for as long as six months to allow for travel well before anticipated labor, with additional time for subsequent postpartum recuperation. Only those families with significant financial reserves could make use of this strategy, as costs involved included train fare and also replacing the value of the mother's lost work, a monetary outlay far in excess of many families' resources.[43]

A survey of births occurring from 1911 to 1919 in a sparsely populated Montana county hinted at the kinds of care available to rural women across the region. The Children's Bureau—formed in 1912 as the first federal agency to focus on the needs of the nation's children—performed analytical surveys throughout the United States and selected a rural Montana homesteading county as the site of one such study. The report, published in 1919, detailed the living conditions, birth environment, and mortality statistics in the entire county. Bureau personnel interviewed mothers of all children born during a five-year period, amassing information from a total of 463 visits. From 1911 to 1919, one in four women in the county left the state to deliver closer to family and medical care. Trepidation—and recognition of their statistical danger—prompted 25 percent of the county's rural pregnant women to leave the state, actions that were expensive both in time and money.[44]

Women who remained in the northern plains for delivery faced potentially serious complications.[45] Faye Hoven remembered a neighbor, Mrs. Anderson, who had a "terrible time." Mrs. Anderson labored for several days, but the doctor could not get to her because the "coulees were overflowing" from a spring thaw. Mrs. Anderson lived; her baby did not.[46]

Some women survived childbirth yet succumbed soon afterward to delivery-related problems. Peggy Czyzeski's mother, pregnant herself, went to attend her son's wife in 1909. As Czyzeski described it, "the baby couldn't come . . . the doctor had to break her pelvic bones down so . . . the baby could be born." Surprisingly, both mother and infant survived this brutal birth. However, nearly two weeks after the delivery, the new mother who had appeared to be recuperating died suddenly, likely from a blood clot in the heart or lungs.[47] When she was still an infant, Beatrice Kaasch lost two older siblings, one in 1910 and the other in 1911, and when Kaasch's mother delivered twins prematurely in 1916, "the little boy died on the day of birth" and the infant girl, Marie, "lived for a week."[48]

Just as women grudgingly resigned themselves to continual pregnancy, northern plains residents accepted the risk of delivery-related death—with certain caveats. If an infant died during delivery or a mother perished from illness weeks after childbirth, filing legal charges did not immediately come to mind. Birth attendants offered services but no guarantee of results, and when a doctor, neighbor, or midwife provided poor service, women removed the attendant from the birthing space and refused to render payment. In contrast to women's later role in the 1950s and 1960s as passive consumers of health care, mothers actively participated in delivery and controlled the physical context of labor.

Sophie Guthrie married in 1899 at the age of seventeen. She and her husband raised sheep at their ranch twenty-five miles from Big Timber, Montana. Guthrie's mother, who birthed twelve of her own children, came to help with Guthrie's first birth, passing along a lifetime of accumulated birthing expertise. Guthrie successfully delivered her next five babies at home. Pregnant with her seventh child, Guthrie hired a newly arrived local doctor but discovered that she did not like his methods. With the wisdom of six trouble-free births, she knew "well and good that he shouldn't be doing what he was—trying to lift the child when nature was taking care of it slowly and gradually." Guthrie told her husband to evict the doctor and then, after laboring through the night, delivered the baby by herself, "just all right."[49] Doctors, neighbors, and midwives worked in homes as invited guests. Mothers engaged these trusted friends and providers to perform a certain service. Assistants could easily be removed from the home without the need for deliberation or outside involvement.

Turn-of-the-twentieth-century settler mothers sought out the companionship and help of other women during delivery. Because they controlled the confines of the home and the birthing environment, mothers could invite or remove visitors and caregivers. This was a boon for urban women, but the scarcity of female friends, relatives, and skilled attendants in rural areas meant that women potentially excused less than optimal care out of concern for being left entirely without assistance.

Prioritization of Postpartum Care

Turn-of-the-twentieth-century women in the northern plains paid little attention to prenatal care; pregnant women considered themselves capable of managing a relatively heavy workload prior to delivery. Still, they diligently arranged for help in the postpartum period, as mothers generally acknowledged that full recuperation from childbirth necessitated additional help.

Midwives offered postpartum care in both rural and urban locations, helping out with delivery and then staying on in the home or making regular visits to cook meals, watch children, and manage the running of the household.[50] In the absence of longer-term midwifery care after delivery, women made alternate arrangements with neighbors. One young mother asked Vina Stirling, living with her family in Montana, to hire out. At the age of fourteen, Stirling had never before worked for wages. She was "really scared" but agreed to stay with the family and tend the baby.[51] Stirling, while not able to perform at the level of a highly trained midwife, still played a role in the infrastructure of birth by competently performing important tasks in the absence of someone more skilled.

In contrast to more settled areas, where women allowed themselves about a month to recover from birth, those residing in the northern plains shortened the recuperation period.[52] It was commonly believed that the uterus returned to its pre-pregnancy location and size a little more than a week after delivery, so women in the region often reduced their recuperation time to less than a fortnight, sometimes even to a quick ten days of bed rest.[53] McCann, the prospector of Trout Creek, Montana, echoed this routine, hiring a neighbor for at least ten days of postpregnancy help.[54] Doctors did not offer postpartum care, so women who called a physician for delivery still sought birthing-related assistance from other women during the recuperation period. According to historian Sylvia Hoffert, "Women on the frontier were more likely to bemoan the lack of domestic help during the recovery period than the absence of doctors during delivery."[55]

Similarly, Native American women placed special importance on the postpartum period. Childbirth and reproduction occupied significant and sacred spaces in the lives of Native American women, both precontact and continuing through the reservation period. The birthing experience and traditions of Native peoples resided primarily in oral tradition and tribal memory—a contextualized repository of culturally impactful wisdom frequently inaccessible to academic study—but some details shared through oral tradition made the transition to the written record and shed light on the indigenous culture of birth.

Infants slept with their mothers, received skin-to-skin contact, and breastfed on demand for an approximate twenty-four-month period. Native women used herbs to increase their milk supply when necessary, and the extended period of breastfeeding provided Native infants with an ample supply of vitamin D and resulted in lower occurrences of rickets as compared to settler infants and children. Native practices for pregnancy, delivery, the postpartum period, and early childhood included "highly developed systems for health care and maintenance" that evolved through generations of observation, testing, and careful implementation.[56] Settler women did not widely adopt the herbal pharmacopeia and full armory of Native reproductive practices, because they sought to distinguish themselves from, not follow the lead of, Native women.

Birth as a Space of Female Intimacy and Expertise

As participants in this century-spanning conversation, we can recognize women's need of other women, but coming from a cultural context where we make sense of pregnancy by reading a text like *What to Expect When You're Expecting*, can we understand it? Why were women so focused on having other women present during delivery and after the birth? Informed interpretation requires familiarity with the routines of childbirth, as well as the beliefs and assumptions surrounding reproduction in the late 1800s and early 1900s.

Parturient women needed specific assistance during pregnancy and delivery: help with and respite from the constancy of physical demands, trained care during the birth, and emotional and physical support to recuperate and return to a full workload. The tasks commonly relegated to women—like cooking over a wood or coal stove, skinning and preparing wild game or domestic livestock, and milking farm animals and processing dairy products—required a specific skill set. Women who took in laundry or worked as cooks and dressmakers performed these tasks at a high rate of speed for long hours each day. For those who managed a household and raised poultry, their daily round included essential activities such as feeding children, tending livestock, and ensuring basic cleanliness, all of which had to be accomplished in the midst of the melee of seasonal harvest, hailstorms, blizzards, and childbirth. Given the gendered nature of labor, these were not tasks that men could accomplish with the alacrity that other women could. Even single men parted with their scarce cash to obtain freshly baked bread and churned butter. For a new mother contemplating the unending tasks of daily feeding, cleaning, food preparation, laundry, and sewing, any time spent recuperating came at a steep cost in catching up later. It is no surprise that women felt overwhelmed when anticipating a delivery without the presence of another woman and desperately sought out skilled help in anticipation of imminent birth. Parturient women needed other women not only to help with the demands of physical labor but also as empathic companions in the shame-charged cultural context surrounding female reproduction, including birth control.

Contraceptives existed but required additional effort to obtain, and women exercised great care in discussing or revealing the products or methods that they employed.[57] The social stigma surrounding contraception meant that many settler women in the northern plains at the turn of the twentieth century hesitated to openly discuss matters related to contraception and often relied on breastfeeding as their primary means of controlling the frequency of pregnancies. As Mary Zanto remembered of her early days in Montana, "They nursed all the kids, there wasn't no baby bottles or nothing [in] them days." She explained that the caloric commitment of breastfeeding impacted fertility for some women, allowing them to reduce, if only slightly, their odds of conceiving while nursing an infant.[58] Whether they intervened more actively in controlling pregnancy or relied on breastfeeding to decrease fertility, women thought carefully about with whom they could discuss their reproductive choices.

In a cultural environment where broad statements and swift judgments about women's moral standing abounded in the public sphere, the presence of another woman at delivery brought both the opportunity for empathy and an opening for castigation. Inviting another woman not only to see but possibly touch the almost always covered genitalia invited a deep sense of intimacy, not simply because of the close physical contact but also because of the trust placed in a birthing companion who would make no judgments and show a willingness to help in ways that might expose vulnerability. Signs of abuse or venereal disease might be visible and need to be addressed in the process of delivery.[59]

This tender intimacy carried a balance with it: women invited their chosen birthing companions into their vulnerable spaces, but the inviting women could also remove their potential caregivers. Both women—the laboring mother and her attendant—carried a certain value, as well as certain constraints. The laboring mother needed and wanted help. The attending woman offered expertise and a willingness to work, but she entered the mother's space only by that mother's request and could be easily removed. While not without its pitfalls—there were undoubtedly overbearing neighbors who would not leave or mothers who harangued their daughters throughout labor and delivery—the opportunity for a balance of power offered a space for sharing and vulnerability, a place of deep understanding and concern.

This reciprocity-based system of reproductive care embodied some remarkably consistent themes. Mothers and their attendants held to a policy of negotiated authority. The caregiver offered expertise and claimed authority over its use, while the mother retained control of her body and home, the locus of care. A midwife or neighbor, sensing an uncooperative or willfully disagreeable mother, did not have to participate or offer birthing instruction. A mother who disliked a provider's manner, practices, or comments could limit physical contact or remove the midwife from the home. Both parties—mother and caregiver—could alter and adjust the terms of their service and conditions pertaining to body and space without recourse to legal maneuvering, instead negotiating through conversation and dialogue. Both held power in the relationship, and both claimed overlapping yet delineated areas of authority. Just as Sophie Guthrie of Big Timber, Montana, refused to follow the questionable direction of a young doctor and removed him from her home during delivery, so too could mothers swiftly eject objectionable attendants.[60]

A woman helping a mother during birth could stand in for her in every way, both physically and emotionally. The laboring mother could depend on her female attendant to care about what she would care about, to tend to tasks both life threatening (like keeping a small child from getting too near the wood stove) and merely important, to care for animals that needed to be watered, or to prepare the next meal. The shared experience and sense of trust, the reliance on contextualized judgment and decision-making ability, and the personal and revealing experience of birth made female-supervised delivery a potentially intimate and desired exchange.

Native women in the region also depended on female wisdom and intimacy, but the long-term effects of oppressive control, war, violence, and cultural instability meant that many pregnant women in Native American communities did not have regular contact with female elders and did not receive instruction in the traditional practices of birth. With extended families devastated by infectious disease epidemics and forced relocation, the transmission of cultural practices through oral traditions faced a serious challenge.[61]

Typically, trained birth attendants, called "wise ones," assisted Native women in labor. Pretty-Shield, an Assiniboine elder, explained how her attendant drove two stakes into the ground inside the lodge and arranged robes to support Pretty-Shield's arms while she knelt. In the final stages of labor Pretty-Shield grasped the stakes while pushing. Once she delivered the baby, she wrapped it in a skin with buffalo hair to serve as cushioning and a piece of firm rawhide to support the head. Like other women of her tribe, she carried her infant in her arms until the child was about six months old, when she transferred it to a back cradle. Native birth attendants did use herbs and roots, particularly in prolonged or difficult labors, and their community prized their knowledge and compensated them, often handsomely, with gifts of horses, blankets, or other valuables.[62]

In contrast to Native cultures' highly systematized and culturally integrated birthing structure, settler women arriving in the region brought with them delivery practices that were a poor fit for their new geographic environment, where women were separated by long distances and thus unable to provide close and attentive care for frequent births.

Fear

Within this context, how do we understand the supposed terror that women felt when facing labor and delivery? Existing literature on turn-of-the-twentieth-century childbirth focuses on women's likely anxiety about childbirth, and given what they faced, a certain amount of fear was warranted. Judith Walzer Leavitt in her classic *Brought to Bed* suggested that women in the early 1900s delivered about five infants on average, and "one of every thirty mothers . . . could expect to die in childbirth during her fertile years."[63] According to Nanci Langford, these fears were "realistic," as the dangers of complications and the few treatments available made childbirth a relatively dangerous endeavor.[64]

It is important to remember, though, that everyday life in the northern plains and Rocky Mountains included dangers that seem stark and frightening to modern realities. The commonality of infectious diseases, the frequency of physical injury from blunt-force trauma such as having a horse lie down on you or getting kicked at close range by a cow, the brutal disfigurements from mining or even just an ax swung a little off target that severed a set of toes—all of these offered legitimate reasons for northern plains residents to cultivate a healthy sense of fear.

Childbirth fell into the "fear and prepare" category but did not warrant the overwhelming or irrational panic that is often applied to women's emotional landscapes. Delivering without an on-call emergency room staff might elevate a twenty-first-century mother's heart rate, but a woman of the early 1900s would have felt no need of full-scale medical intervention. Despite centuries of rhetoric about the delicate condition of the female anatomy, mothers making their way in the northern plains in the late 1800s and early 1900s did so with a physicality that would challenge many contemporary women and men. For women drawn to the adventure-and-accomplishment ethos of the region, childbirth stood as the ultimate challenge—and women, some willingly and some from a seasoned pragmatism—often understood the event as one in which they could succeed or at least perform admirably.

This "resourcefulness and fortitude"—a phrase applied to area women by regional expert Nanci Langford—did not require ignoring the dangers and fears associated with delivery. Instead, the risk of death and women's proactive responses coexisted in a logical pairing.[65] In hours of oral history research, in pages of diaries, in reams of correspondence, I came across not a single mention of in-the-moment terror and fear. This in no way indicates that women did not feel apprehension—quite the contrary, in fact, when we acknowledge the odds they faced—but rather that they framed their worries within a particular context. As Jodi Vandenberg-Daves explains it, "the female body came to represent a complex set of conditions: it was driven by reproductive organs while possessing both dangerous fragility and disturbing power."[66] In full recognition of the dangers they faced, women embraced a sense of their own power, their ability to produce a living, breathing human being. The capability to reproduce offered a point of pride, a legitimate and lasting creation in the midst of meals hurriedly consumed and clean clothes quickly dirtied.[67]

Childbirth in this northern plains environment induced a medley of emotions. Women felt "rebellious and ugly" about childbirth; they also savored their accomplishments and experienced justifiable pride when they delivered their babies "just all right."[68] Whether birth occurred in a newly settled western town or in a lonely mountain cabin, if a woman looked to multiple attendants or delivered her infant entirely on her own, when a mother miscarried or succumbed to a pregnancy-related death, Euro-American inhabitants of the northern plains counted conception, gestation, and delivery as recurring and important events guided and directed by females in their newly acquired western realities. Women like Lizzie Maclean, establishing a homestead on her own in northern Montana, or Alice Susag, tending her milk cows in eastern Montana, participated in the everyday events of reproduction.

In this nuanced regional context, Alice Susag and Lizzie Maclean served the reproductive needs of their neighbors. Leaving the dairy operation to the capable management of her children and husband, Susag stayed through the night at the Stenson place, superintending labor and delivery, and she remained there the next day to stand in for Stenson. Susag eventually returned home, tired but satisfied, and announced the birth of a "little baby girl."[69] Maclean celebrated Laila Olive, Mrs. Hicks's newly arrived nine-pound infant, by sewing a "baby skirt."[70] Hicks paid Maclean for her help during birth and offered a gift of embroidery; she thus placed a monetary value on services rendered and also recognized the generous offer of hours and expertise that could not be monetized.

The services of women like Maclean and Susag, rarely mentioned and infrequently recorded, tied residents of the northern plains and Rocky Mountains to each other and their adopted home. Settler women in the northern plains created humans to populate the collaborative communities they lived in. Women like Susag, Maclean, Stenson, and Hicks established an unrecognized infrastructure of health and human connection and performed the labor of production—in gestation, delivery, infancy, and childhood—by supplying bodies and families to live in the region and work its farms, mines, and forests.

2

The Expertise of Women

The settlement narrative recites the deeds of pioneers—the "heroic" men who rode the range and their "supportive" wives, who tended to domestic chores. This token inclusion of women treats them like a condiment, akin to the ever-present cruet of vinegar on my grandmother's lengthy dining table. As the story goes, female settlers supplied a dash of housekeeping and a side of laundry. But when we attempt to quantify women's labors, we discover that their contributions to the meal of western advancement comprised the meat and potatoes of the national repast.

Because male efforts had numerical handles—measurable quantities of bushels produced, wages paid, and track laid—historians could assess and weigh their production. In contrast, women supplied expertise and time, typically ignored in the absence of credentialed female professions and the assumption that women could give unendingly of each twenty-four-hour span allotted to them. The formation of the U.S. Children's Bureau, as well as Julia Lathrop's appointment to lead the agency, paired the work of women with the novel idea of data collection.

Lathrop grew up in a progressive Illinois household; her mother ardently supported women's suffrage and her father served in the state legislature. After graduating from Vassar College in 1880, she studied law in her father's practice. No demure intellectual, Lathrop crafted her education and training to address poverty, the exploitation of immigrants, women's equality, and care of the disabled and mentally ill. Determined to find solutions to pressing social ills, she passionately advocated for the use of science and statistics in combination with compassion and care. Lathrop sought to move beyond "the era of rule by thumb and a kind heart" to a new and "more effective" practice where "kindness of heart" paired with training and knowledge to bring about measurable and significant social progress.[1]

After completing her legal training, Lathrop went on to work in Chicago with other social reformers, such as Jane Addams at Hull House. In 1912 the U.S. Congress created a federal department to focus on the needs of the nation's children, and President William Taft named Lathrop as its director. She became the first woman to serve as head of a bureau in the history of the U.S. government.[2]

In an era that lampooned women as hysterical and irrational, Lathrop exercised logic, reasoning that effective solutions relied on clear-headed and data-based identification of problems. Determined to wield the power of statistical evidence, Lathrop directed the Children's Bureau to assess existing conditions of women and children. Under her supervision, bureau staff implemented what might be termed a revolutionary method: they took the time to ask women about their living conditions, they documented the details of children's days, and they compiled the evidence-based results. Babies at risk—infants without maternal caregiving, bottle-fed babies, and infants whose mothers lacked the income necessary for a reasonable standard of living—were the ones who died. In short, the bureau determined that poverty caused infant mortality regardless of the race or social standing of the parents. Despite public opposition, Lathrop tenaciously publicized her conclusions.[3]

In an ambitious effort to expand the bureau's sphere of influence, Lathrop trumpeted the correlation between mothers' well-being and that of children. When mothers did well, children thrived. When mothers suffered, so did their children. Lathrop determined that the cause of supporting children equated to furthering the interests of women and reasoned that issues surrounding the welfare of women justifiably resided within the jurisdiction of the Children's Bureau. In a move that no doubt unhinged her overwrought critics (*Is she going to listen to even more women? And believe them?!*) Lathrop initiated an assertive plan to gather maternal and infant data from an even wider selection of communities across the United States.

Beginning with its creation in 1912, the bureau served as a clearinghouse for mothers' concerns. Women across the country who could look to no other governmental or institutional advocate wrote letters to Lathrop seeking advice and assistance. Some of these missives, like the note from a pregnant Alice Cutting Phelps that I encountered in the sun-filled reading room of the National Archives, came from women in Wyoming, the Dakotas, and Montana, and highlighted conditions unique to the rural West. In an effort to address birthing conditions in this northern plains region, bureau staff members Dr. Grace Meigs, Viola Paradise, May Lane, Stella Packard, Helen Dart, Dorothy Williams, Janet Geister, and Letitia Fyffe prepared to conduct fieldwork in Montana in the summer of 1917.[4] These intrepid bureaucrats set out to collect data from residents of Chouteau County, a rural expanse of prairie in northern Montana. Meigs, Paradise, Lane, Packard, Dart, Williams, Geister, and Fyffe started by identifying the names and locations of all women in the study region who had given birth from 1912 to 1917. Given the rudimentary nature of birth registration at the time, the task of compiling just under five hundred names represented hours of sleuthing, poring over incomplete county records, and questioning area residents.

With their list of mothers in hand, bureau staff traveled dusty, rutted roads—or, in the case of rainy weather, they navigated slippery, impassable stretches of clinging mud—to locate all the mothers residing in the approximately fifty-five-hundred-square-mile study area. Bureau staff arrived at solitary shacks, dugouts, and cabins, introduced themselves, explained the project, and performed an evaluation of the family's living conditions. They queried each mother about the care she received before, during, and after giving birth, as well as her housing, daily tasks, sanitation, and access to water. Bureau staff reported widespread community support for their work and gratefully paid tribute to the "intelligent cooperation" they received from mothers.[5]

The bureau's eventual report arrived at what must have seemed obvious conclusions to residents of the northern plains. Bureau analysis acknowledged "difficulties" for women in the region, especially in the way that "isolation intensifie[d] both the need and the difficulties of safeguarding life."[6] Study details chronicled the appalling challenges of childbirth, discussed the difficulty of locating delivery assistance, and documented the absence of prenatal care. Bureau staff took photographs to document impassable roads and untenable living conditions in houses that failed to provide shelter from winter storms and summer heat. They noted invading hordes of flies from open privies and lamented the numbers of easily preventable maternal and infant deaths.[7]

With an unremitting list of tasks, chronically fatigued mothers living in isolation faced greater physical and emotional burdens than urban women. Dovie Zehtner and Hazel Dorr, both pregnant in turn-of-the-twentieth-century Montana, kept up with their usual workload all through pregnancy: chopping wood, hauling water, milking cows, and performing the heavy labor of stockkeeping, laundry, and household management.[8] A Montana physician bemoaned the condition of local women in the early 1900s, stating that hard physical labor, "excessive child bearing," and "loneliness" wore them out, and by the time mothers asked for his help, "there [was] nothing [he could] do."[9] The constancy of both pregnancy and work, especially in the absence of reliable birth control, left those without abundant resources in a state of moderate to severe exhaustion over a period of many years. Unsurprisingly, this continued depletion resulted in gestational problems and trouble during delivery.

Fig. II. Seemingly intrigued by the condition of Montana roads, Children's Bureau staff included a number of pictures of "winding" and "furrowed" wagon roads in its landmark report. Viola Isabel Paradise, *Maternity Care and the Welfare of Young Children in a Homesteading County in Montana* (Washington DC: Government Printing Office, 1919), 16.

The data collected by Meigs, Paradise, Lane, Packard, Dart, Williams, Geister, and Fyffe provided official documentary evidence of the problems that women in the region experienced. Women of reproductive age ventured into potentially dangerous territory when they migrated to northern plains spaces in the late 1800s and early 1900s. They faced an assemblage of risks altogether different than those looming on male horizons. Women left essential health care—the skilled hands and collective wisdom of other women—behind, while men traveling with women brought their health-care providers along. Men could count on their wives, mothers, or sisters to tend them in sickness. Women could not be certain of finding other women when they needed them.

As they considered leaving family and friends and heading west, women's hesitation rested on more than separation from loved ones. The reality of sparse settlement and long distances meant that family visits would be rare and that women might at times face a total absence of the kinds of care they had come to expect, with no one to help during illness or to call in case of emergency. For those who depended on family and friends for health care, the thought of leaving behind the infrastructure that dealt with illness, convalescence, and childbirth must have been sobering. Heading into the sparsely settled northern plains and Rocky Mountains meant abandoning resources that could not be easily replaced.[10]

Early Euro-American regional settlement followed a gendered pattern, with an influx of men, either single or without their wives, outnumbering the arrival of families or single women. The 1890 census revealed nearly two men for every woman in Montana, an imbalance that directly impacted health care. As historian Dawn Nickel has explained, "women were expected to provide care, yet there were so few of them."[11] In a situation of such lack, women, by serving as midwives, nurses, or knowledgeable female family members, provided the essential services necessary to bring the next generation into the world. They also cared for those who faced traumatic injury, infectious disease, or death.

Those who migrated with extended relations were perhaps in the most enviable position, because they could look to female family members for care. Isabella Mogstad, born in 1886 and married in 1906, moved to the Fort Benton, Montana, area in 1912. She tended chickens—four hundred of them in one year—cultivated a garden, milked cows, and raised pigs. For each of Mogstad's five deliveries, her sister stayed with her, providing birthing assistance and also helping with daily work, giving Mogstad the time to recover from childbirth.[12]

Some migrants settled in areas with practicing midwives. Susie Clarke Huston came to Montana in 1914 and relied on the help of a midwife for the births of her two children.[13] Faye Hoven gathered information about her neighbor, Mrs. Rutledge, who served as midwife for "a lot of the women around there." Satisfied with Rutledge's competency, Hoven paid a call to see if Rutledge could help with her delivery. After comparing dates, Rutledge "said she would come," committing to assist with birth and in all likelihood an extended period of postpartum care.[14]

According to the Children's Bureau study, midwives performed the bulk of maternity care.[15] As the most common type of delivery assistant at the time, midwives provided invaluable help, sometimes in surprising moments. Mary Zanto hired a doctor to assist at her delivery, but impenetrable snowdrifts blocked his progress. Assuming that no help could reach their dwelling, Zanto and her husband planned to manage the delivery on their own. Fortunately, a local woman, a "kind of a midwife," arrived. Zanto expressed gratitude for the unexpected assistance, especially since the couple did not "know whether we would've tied the cord or not."[16] We might wonder how the midwife found a way through the otherwise impassable drifts. Perhaps midwifery training, later derided by doctors and health department officials as lacking intellectual sophistication, included a lesson missing from the more cultured medical school curriculum: how to push onward through driving snow to reach laboring mothers.[17]

In the absence of family or midwives, neighbors stood in and served in a supportive role for each other. As Ethel Eide of Spartan, North Dakota, explained, in cases of illness or childbirth, community women stepped in to clean, cook, and perform all the tasks necessary to "take care of them."[18] Mary Zanto remembered being sent to fetch a neighbor, Mrs. Fleming, to help out when Zanto's mother gave birth. Fleming arrived and sent the children up the ladder to their beds in the loft for the night. The next morning, when Zanto woke up and climbed back down the ladder, her mother "had somebody wrapped up in the blanket." Zanto joyfully discovered her sister Rose, "the cutest doll."[19] For Rose's birth, Fleming performed the tasks traditionally assigned to multiple family members: helping with and cleaning up from delivery, tending to the mother and infant, and remaining in the home to feed the family and oversee management of the household while the mother recuperated.

Women like Fleming, Mogstad's sister, Eide's neighbors, and Zanto's blizzard-braving midwife, when viewed in the aggregate, formed a functioning infrastructure of care. Without compiling a business plan or outlining a crisis-management action strategy, community women nevertheless identified those in need, made adjustments to their own schedules and workloads, spent nights, bathed children, cooked meals, tended livestock, helped deliver babies, and disposed of blood and human waste. As interviewee Lydia Keating explained it, in Utica, Montana, at the turn of the twentieth century, there were "no doctors, no hospitals," but she did find a woman to come when she was delivering.[20] Just as Idora Guthrie looked to her friend Belle for support during a miscarriage, settler women across the region stepped in to help each other deal with the realities of reproduction, taking on tasks from meal preparation and laundry to assistance at births and treatment of complications during pregnancy.[21]

Without a central organizing structure, a triage-like process emerged: women in a community delegated responsibilities to ensure the provision of necessary care. The details of solo homesteader Lizzie Maclean's efforts on behalf of the Hicks family exemplified the workings of this adaptive caregiving system. On May 13, 1915, Maclean "went over to Mrs. Hicks a little while."[22] Hicks, nearing the end of a pregnancy in May 1915, could most certainly sense the loosening of her pelvis and the preliminary contractions of late pregnancy. With a number of pregnancies and births to her credit, Hicks had her own delivery experiences to reflect on and knew that birth was near.[23]

For the next six nights Maclean slept at the Hicks home, walking back to her own place during the day to tend to chores and livestock. In the midst of this daily migration, Maclean's mare, named Snip, delivered a foal and then injured a hoof. Maclean confined the mare to the stable, "doctored Snip's foot," then "pulled grass for her," and checked on the "10 little chicks" that hatched while Maclean was away at the Hicks home.[24] A neighbor, Mrs. Berger, relieved Maclean of her nighttime duties at the Hicks homestead for one night, and then

Maclean completed another six-night sojourn away from home. After nearly two weeks under Maclean's supervision, Hicks gave birth to a nine-pound baby girl, Laila Olive, on June 1, 1915.

The day after the birth Maclean remained with the new mother, only briefly stepping away to return "home to do chores." For the next three days Maclean stayed at the Hicks homestead, going "home twice" daily to catch up on animal care and a bit of housework. The fifth day after the birth Maclean "lost 2 little chicks drowned."[25] The effort of caring for another homestead had a cost beyond lost sleep, as Maclean's chicks needed hands-on attention to thrive.

Three weeks into an intense effort at the Hicks home, Maclean arranged for a Mr. Elliott to plow fields on her land, and she "came from Hicks to get a lunch" for him. She returned to her midwifing duties, and Elliott "got supper" for himself after completing his work at the Maclean homestead. Lizzie cut her next two days at the Hicks homestead short, catching up on work at home but returning to the Hicks place for the night. On June 11 she "made [a] baby skirt for Mrs. Hicks in pm" and then on the twelfth "came home early to catch Snip." After once again getting things in order at home, Maclean "went back to Mrs. Hicks to do up work" and then "washed at home in pm." For the next five days Maclean traveled to the Hicks home to help manage the household as the new mother tended the baby and resumed her normal workload. By June 23, a little more than three weeks since the birth of the Hicks baby, Maclean turned her full attention to tasks at her own homestead.[26] Maclean's terse diary entries revealed the structure of women's active support of childbirth. As caregivers who gained their reproductive knowledge by working with and observing other women, individuals like Maclean called on a hefty dose of Lathrop's "kindness of heart" and also leveraged a store of accumulated knowledge built on the radical practice of "asking women." A young woman in labor with her first child could remember scores of birth experiences, presentations, and outcomes, as well as recall the circumstances and details of a multitude of delivery dramas. From early Euro-American settlement in the 1600s to that of the northern plains of the early 1900s, women knew firsthand the hazards of childbirth, as well as its normal and reasonable outcomes.[27] Attentive observation of women's reproductive processes, whether to understand the routine of normal birth patterns or the causes of infant mortality, offered essential and usable data. Women focused their attention on each other. They observed, they learned, they remembered, and they put their arsenal of skills to use. Performed by women in the routine of everyday life, these seemingly mundane actions embodied current practices with grandiloquent titles like "evidence-based medicine" and "participant-observer data collection"—terms that represent the gold standard of contemporary academic practice. By making the female body and the birth process the subject of their attention and study, some northern plains women succeeded in accessing a trove of experience-based knowledge that contemporary birthing practitioners have yet to integrate into hospital-based birthing routines. As participants in an informal and unrecognized health-care system, female providers served as the kinds of "trained individuals" that Lathrop advocated. These midwives, nurses, and neighbors, regardless of title, operated effectively because they were "governed by intelligence."[28]

In addition to providing birthing services, this kind of care also allowed for information gathering and data sharing under the cover of women's sociability. Simultaneous with Hicks's delivery, Maclean's neighbor, Mrs. Latreau, also neared the conclusion of pregnancy. With Maclean committed to helping at the Hicks homestead, Mrs. Berger (neighbor to the Hicks family) traveled to the Latreau residence, where she assisted in the birth of Juanita Evelyn, weighing ten pounds, on July 2. Just six days later Maclean and Hicks convened with Latreau and most likely Berger, still in residence at the Latreau homestead, to celebrate the babies, recognize the effort that went into their safe deliveries, and most certainly augment their already copious reservoir of birthing knowledge by reflecting on the details of the two most recent births.[29]

Four homesteads—those of the Macleans, Bergers, Latreaus, and Hickses—spent June and July 1915 consumed with the labor of childbirth. Two mothers delivered babies, but the entirety of the local adult female population turned their energies to supporting the demands of reproduction, spending hours performing the tasks necessary for successful childbirth and recovery. Individual homesteads made do as the female members of the community helped the postpartum mothers and infants back into the ongoing routine of intense work. Hicks compensated Maclean, at least in part, by paying her ten dollars, and Maclean evidently saw such compensation as justified. At a time when a horse cost twenty-five dollars and the sale of a calf brought fifteen dollars, Hicks's payment accorded at least some level of value to Maclean's efforts.[30] However, the investment of time by the female members of the immediate community far exceeded the value of the cash exchanged. The birth of one infant demanded the full attention of both Maclean and Hicks for at least six weeks.

The delivery of one child required a minimum of twelve weeks of "woman-work." Oral histories suggest that the Hicks delivery followed a normal progression, and using it as a pattern helps us understand the significance of reproduction for turn-of-the-twentieth-century women. When women followed the typical reproductive cycle and delivered one child every two years, the cost in time per healthy, uncomplicated pregnancy was three months out of every twenty-four. Giving birth with just one delivery attendant who also took on the responsibility of postpartum care represented the absolute minimum of necessary assistance. For those women able to enlist the help of a neighbor, a midwife, and a female relative—a far more realistic expectation given the time-consuming nature of the work involved—the investment in reproductive labor increased to six months out of every two years. Based on these estimates of reproductive care, it is possible that northern plains women allocated from 10 to 25 percent of their total labor to activities associated with childbirth and reproduction.[31]

Just three years after the birth of Laila Olive, Hicks delivered another baby girl, Bertha, who weighed eight pounds. This time another neighbor came to assist, freeing Maclean from on-call reproductive duty. Maclean remained attentive, though, visiting immediately after the birth and completing Hicks's washing and ironing for the next two weeks.[32] Records do not exist to determine how many births Maclean assisted at during her lifelong tenure in the community, but eight years after Laila Olive's birth Maclean was still at work, "walk[ing] 2½ miles" to help another woman deliver.[33] During the remainder of her life in the community, Maclean served as the "neighborhood doctor," assisting with childbirth, sickness, and even death.[34] Over the years, she continued to travel to neighboring homesteads to help women through labor and recovery. Maclean's skilled assistance brought support and confidence to mothers, both during the delivery and in the weeks that followed, even though such efforts never entered the ledger or record book of any county courthouse or business enterprise.

Since there was constant demand for reproductive assistance, providing the necessary care required trade-offs. When a community lacked a highly trained practitioner, a woman in the community often stepped forward to offer what knowledge and caregiving capabilities she had. Annie Knipfer, before moving to Baker, Montana, in 1919, worked with physicians in Massachusetts and served as a nurse. After settling in the northern plains, Knipfer could not stay silent when neighbors in barren and sparsely settled eastern Montana found themselves without any assistance at all. She volunteered to help, offering her skills and watching over four separate births. Because of this type of voluntarism, few areas faced a total dearth of services.[35]

In emergency situations when pre-arranged help did not arrive, mothers called upon men to assist in deliveries. Entering into a female realm, men participated in an inversion of gender expectations by deferring to the expertise of their wives.[36] Men acted as assistants, bringing water, catching the baby, and cleaning up the placenta, all under the trained eyes of delivering mothers.

Any system, fully documented or unofficially structured, can be assessed by both its successes and its failures. The unrecognized system of health-care delivery in the northern plains undoubtedly consumed copious amounts of women's time and energy across the region. Notwithstanding good intentions and kindness, did the process function? How often did this de facto arrangement fail to provide services or deliver adequate care? Women feared delivering entirely alone, yet limited evidence hints that the reality of truly solitary childbirth rarely materialized. The 1919 Children's Bureau study *Maternity Care and the Welfare of Young Children in a Homesteading County in Montana* documented that only about 1 percent of the women studied had experienced an entirely solo birth, a remarkable finding given the overwhelming challenges of delivering services to a small, scattered, and often transient northern plains population. Children's Bureau staff chose the study area precisely because of its isolation and limited services, so it is unlikely that conditions in other locales were significantly worse. Additionally, my chronicling of births recorded in oral histories and correspondence revealed the details of just one solitary birth in the multitude of stories relating delivery experiences recorded in the Dakotas, Wyoming, and Montana.[37] These scarce sources hint at solo deliveries as anomalies, as noteworthy occasional happenings to be wondered at and retold as part of local lore evidencing the grit of pioneers and the conditions they endured.

Women like Maclean, Mogstad, Huston, Rutledge, Fleming, Berger, and Knipfer, all of whom devoted much time and skill to the structure of female health care, did not belong to a professional organization or document the details of the care they provided. In fact, they may have diminished their own knowledge and expertise, believing their efforts to be part of the necessary work of women, work that went unrecognized.[38] Identifying their contributions remains difficult, especially with few bureaucrats like Lathrop taking the time to observe, record, and thereby legitimize the experiences of women.

Fig. 12. This photograph, included in the Children's Bureau study, offers some sense for the badlands terrain that residents faced when traveling to town, to see neighbors, or to fetch help when a woman was in labor. Viola Isabel Paradise, *Maternity Care and the Welfare of Young Children in a Homesteading County in Montana* (Washington DC: Government Printing Office, 1919), 23.

Historian Anne Butler, noteworthy for her recognition of women's work, documented the physical labor done by Euro-American residents of the northern plains and concluded that women were "substantial, if undercompensated, contributors to western economies."[39] These rare sorts of calculations, which take into account the butter and egg production women managed, often miss the integral role of reproduction. Just as income from dairy and chicken operations formed the backbone of a family's financial well-being, the exchanges of reproduction—intellectual, experiential, monetary, and relational—established the structure of community.[40]

Native American women also occupied a central role in serving the reproductive needs of their communities. Native birthing practices included the "presence of supportive and experienced women" and the full use of an extensive pharmacopeia of medicinal plants to reduce pain, hasten prolonged or difficult labors, expel the placenta, and increase milk flow.[41] Native American attendants received com-

Fig. 13. Children's Bureau researchers' notes stated that this dugout (an earth-sheltered dwelling) claimed the added improvement of a "fenced roof" to keep wandering cattle from walking over the top, breaking the timber supports, and falling down on the people inside. Viola Isabel Paradise, *Maternity Care and the Welfare of Young Children in a Homesteading County in Montana* (Washington DC: Government Printing Office, 1919), 65.

pensation—as, for example, when Assiniboine elder Pretty-Shield's attendant received a horse and robes in payment for her assistance—and held positions of respect in their communities.[42]

While it is not possible to tabulate the economic impact of female-provided health care in the region, we can employ time as a stand-in for money to quantify the significance of this very open—from the perspective of lived experience—and yet numerically hidden enterprise. Reproductive exchanges, just like sales of butter and eggs, were not motivated solely by maximizing profit but instead focused on fair transfers and the goal of maintaining relationships. One winter day Susag drove her team and sled through deep snow and crusted, windblown drifts to deliver butter, fifty pounds of which she planned on selling to her regular customers for thirty-five cents a pound. The train, unable to get through the drifts, had been delayed for a week, and the owner of the restaurant in town offered Susag one dollar per pound for all of her butter, an additional profit of nearly thirty-three dollars. She refused, citing her relationship with her customers "who had depended on her for so long." This level of human connection, even in the face of a potential and most likely urgently needed windfall profit, characterized the basis of her business model. With the local population being vulnerable to economic downturn, food scarcity, and weather-related emergencies, the existence and maintenance of such a reliable structure of support made living in the area tolerable and even a source of pride for area residents.[43]

Mischaracterizing or even just missing this important element fails to capture the meaning of exchanges. When *work* is defined as a profit-driven activity done outside the home by men, the operational framework creates an affected reality in which relational efforts are not counted as valuable. When labor is understood to be that which provides narrowly defined monetary value to an unrelated person or entity, much of the work of women who mentored and cared for their own or neighboring children, or the efforts of women like Susag to support her community, are not recognized or tabulated. These critical, value-laden activities, the sorts of behaviors that sustain communities and families, disappear from view before they are even seen.[44]

Our typical economic renderings of historical transactions ignore the fact that in a system of informed transactions, appropriate adjustments could be made. Neighbors knew who faced particular family, relational, and financial challenges. Some exchanges warranted monetary transfer—Maclean earned $2.50 a day cooking for a neighbor's threshing crew—while other identical services, like Maclean's cooking dinner for harvesters at the Berger place, were offered without demand for payment and as a means of developing connections of caring. Redirecting the lens of history from its typical focus on large-scale enterprise to ongoing and regular relational exchanges allows a host of critical nurturing activities to appear.[45] If reproductive labor required up to one-quarter of women's work, then childbirth, delivery, and postpartum care constituted a core, essential, and enduring western activity. Women's reproductive relationships—generous, reciprocal, and often monetized—helped to create a unique culture where relationships and profitability coexisted.[46]

Mere recognition of these investments misses the nuance, depth, and significance of women's reproductive contributions. Birthing events should not be seen as addendums to cattle drives and military campaigns but rather as a pattern of exchange and sociability that questions the raw capitalism of the frontier ethos. When neighbors called for Susag's help delivering a baby, she went; Pretty-Shield's attendant arrived to help prepare the birthing lodge; Maclean received payment for her work before, during, and after Hicks's delivery.[47] Back-and-forth transfers for eggs, butter, or care during childbirth fit the nature of their northern plains relationships.

The behaviors surrounding reproduction established reciprocal connections and a community ethos. In addition to buying, selling, and trading, Maclean also gifted, distributing at no charge bread, laundry services, and help during childbirth. Her diary entries kept careful count of money earned but also recorded a notation for acts of neighborliness, generosity, and concern. Maclean charged at times, and at others she determined that forgoing monetary profit and investing in relational connections served personal and community interests. When Maclean worked at an adjacent homestead, she created a sense of common cause and made her small community a place where neighbors received and gave support. When she walked to the Hickses' place to do the weekly washing, she acted in response to a need. When she taught her bachelor neighbor how to bake bread, she transferred an essential skill. The practice of gifting supplied a regional identity, imbued a harsh lifestyle with meaning and purpose, provided job training, and served as a social safety net. When the efforts of women like Maclean all across turn-of-the-twentieth-century Montana, Wyoming, and the Dakotas are considered en masse, a personalized, on-the-ground, adaptable, and highly mobilized structure for cultural caregiving emerges as an animating principle for those residing in the region. Reproductive care, horses, eggs, butter, and land were sold, purchased, traded, and gifted within a constellation of exchanges that included visiting and shared life experiences, as well as advantageous economic arrangements.[48]

In the northern plains of the early 1900s, women provided unrecognized birthing and reproductive labor. They created communities by simultaneously earning appropriate profits and investing in relationships—an essential and often overlooked element in the chronology of the American West that flies in the face of tropes of the inherent independence of settlers and the harshness of the frontier. The inclusion of human reproduction changes the heart of the western narrative. Instead of a series of lone actors, we see women engaged in exchanges—both social and monetary—that provided family sustenance and community viability. The shared labors of childbirth and postpartum recovery emerge as central organizing activities that utilized female expertise in the provision of necessary health care. Some women, whether due to personal interest or necessity, specialized in the details of delivery and postpartum recovery. In a landscape of reproductive challenges, these female professionals possessed the bulk of available reproductive expertise and made it available to their neighbors in the settler communities they called home.

3

Midwives among Us

Women's reproductive activities drew communities together in relationships and exchanges, and midwives participated as one of the primary parties in these social, economic, and nation-making transactions. The profession of midwifery followed specific, identifiable practices that contributed a particular flavor to reproductive care in the northern plains and Rocky Mountains. Midwifery claimed an enduring history that began long before Euro-American settlement of the region, predating the formation of the United States itself. While midwifery stands as one of the longest-lasting professions, we can look to 1500s France and the writings of Louise Bourgeois for documentary evidence of midwifery's core tenets.

As official midwife to Marie de Médicis and trusted birthing practitioner to noblewoman, French midwife Louise Bourgeois held the position of national expert on childbirth. At the height of her career, she publicly reprimanded a physician for his willingness to surgically intervene in a birth in order to charge a higher fee. She authored three midwifery texts, trained midwives and physicians, and altered the trajectory of reproductive care across Europe.

Born in France in 1563 to a well-placed family, Bourgeois initially had no interest in pursuing a profession; her status allowed her to care for her children and enjoy a relatively stable position in sixteenth-century French society. But her husband went to serve in the military in 1589, leaving her without regular financial support. Bourgeois took up midwifery as a steady source of income and received her midwifery license from the city of Paris in 1598. Her reputation as a savvy, likable, and skilled birth attendant caught the attention of the royal court and Marie de Médicis, wife of King Henry IV, in particular. Providing reproductive care for rulers brought stress and worry but also financial reward. Bourgeois oversaw six deliveries for Marie de Médicis and received a pension for her service, as well as a cash payment for each birth.[1] Bourgeois was literate, unlike most French citizens during the early 1600s.[2] Her ability to record the details of midwifery practice, even more than her renowned skill in dealing with complicated deliveries, made Bourgeois instrumental in spreading midwifery knowledge and techniques.[3]

A typical sixteenth-century midwife expanded her knowledge base with each pregnancy, whether it was her own delivery or that of a friend, relative, or client. A skilled practitioner often transmitted this accumulated expertise by training apprentices or describing methods or herbal treatments in conversation with other midwives. The one-on-one structure enabled midwives to communicate contextual information and ensure hands-on experience, but it also constrained the sharing of innovations and techniques. Geography and time limited the process of acquiring and honing midwifery skills. In order to improve her delivery acumen, a woman depended on serendipitous contact with more learned providers. This mirrored the practice of Native American women, as aspiring Native midwives received intentional tutelage from more knowledgeable women and accumulated skills and insight over the course of many births.[4]

In contrast to this deeply personal method of instruction, Bourgeois's ability to spread her midwifery knowledge via the written word allowed her to impact the practice of birth hundreds of years later and thousands of miles away. By documenting her expertise in reference texts, she promulgated the importance of caring for the mother's comfort and identified numerous "malpresentations." Her texts offered detailed instructions on remedying these unusual but treatable conditions.[5]

Bourgeois's work positioned France as a regional leader in the professionalization and practice of midwifery. With the oral and practical experience of midwives made available in text format, a growing number of practitioners—nearly 30 percent of French residents were literate by the 1650s—shared a baseline body of knowledge to which they added over subsequent decades.[6] Midwives were training medical students in France by the 1800s, and over the next century the Netherlands, Russia, Sweden, Norway, England, and Denmark followed France's lead and instituted state-sponsored midwifery, licensing protocols, and formal training.[7]

Women took advantage of these rigorous training and apprenticeship programs in their home countries. Apprentice midwives mastered a delineated skill set and adopted a specific professional title. They learned to guide the labor of childbirth, began to accumulate knowledge about the female body and reproductive processes, and dispensed that information for the benefit of individual women. After completing their training, they practiced as midwives, and their diplomas, textbooks, and governments testified to that identity. More than half of all settlers in Montana, the Dakotas, and Wyoming came from places with strong midwifery traditions, such as Canada, Germany, Norway, England, Sweden, Ireland, Denmark, Scotland, Austria, and France.[8] Newly settled American communities thus looked back to traditions of midwifery in their countries of origin and had clear ideas about childbirth practices, as well as a belief in the competence of female birthing attendants. European midwives relocating to the distant plains and mountains of Montana, the Dakotas, and Wyoming brought their specialized birthing skills and put them to immediate use.[9]

Desiree Frichot Madeliane, born in France more than 250 years after Bourgeois, came to the United States with her family in 1864 and married Julius Villian in 1885. The couple settled in Anaconda,

Montana, where Julius worked as a smelter watchman and Desiree Villian opened her practice. Leveraging the reputation of French midwifery, Villian advertised herself as "The French Nurse and Midwife" and had a room for client visits at the Palace Hotel in Anaconda.[10] Anna Karstedt, also an immigrant, trained in Prague, where she received a midwifery diploma. She worked in the Montana cities of Butte, Anaconda, and Helena from 1891 through the early 1900s.[11] Amelia Topliss emigrated from Wales in 1854 and listed her occupation as midwife in the 1900 census. After she was widowed, she supported herself and her family of nine children with her midwifery work in Anaconda.[12] Anna Valleen emigrated from Switzerland and advertised her midwifery services in Butte, a mining city with slightly more than thirty thousand residents in 1900. Valleen eventually moved to Seattle, where she continued her work as a midwife.[13] Anna Hamalainen completed her midwifery education in Helsinki, Finland, in 1906 and proudly brought her diploma and midwifery equipment with her when she established a practice in Butte.[14] In addition to Hamalainen, Karstedt, and Valleen, the Butte midwifery community in the early twentieth century included Bertha Wallace, Martha Noble, Julie Moe, Ellen Thomas, Rose Brown, and Bertha Watmer.[15] All advertised their services in the city directory or listed their profession as midwife in the 1900 census.[16] Women like Villian, Karstedt, Topliss, Valleen, and Hamalainen served urban and ethnically diverse communities. Because they came from cultural contexts that identified midwifery as a specific, skilled profession, they willingly claimed a professional title and charged a standard fee for services.

Women who practiced midwifery also resided and worked in scattered rural enclaves. When asked about doctors in her area, Hilda Peterson, born in Fort Ransom, North Dakota, in 1892, said with a gentle dismissal that physicians were not involved because mothers "had their children with the midwives."[17] Midwives like Stella Jane Bauer, who served the hamlet of Noxon, Montana, in the early 1900s, offered care to those residing in and around their small towns.[18]

Edna McCann of Trout Creek, Montana, never went to a hospital for delivery "because back then they had midwives" or the help of skilled neighbors who, while they might not label themselves as professional midwives, "knew all about it."[19] Liiza Honkala, Hilma Ylenni, and Agnes Rahkola assisted Finnish women in the southwestern Montana mining town of Red Lodge.[20] Anna Kjas worked in Circle Diamond, Mary Jenkins helped women in and around Toston, and Gertrude White maintained a practice in Bozeman.[21] In the far more rural expanse of eastern Montana, Verona Barnes assisted with deliveries in Gold Butte; Percy Clauton, Viola Ebaugh, and Mary Robertory worked in Malta; Inga Johnson practiced in Havre; Nancy Lease helped women in Glendive; and Borghild Ronning served the women of Plentywood.[22] Cornelia Mowatt worked in and around Lewistown, a central Montana enclave that claimed an impressive one thousand residents in 1900.[23]

These rural midwives modeled the same theory of practice as their urban sisters. They saw childbirth as a natural event, not a disease to be cured. They offered care and support to the birthing mother. They used herbs, ointments, salves, and tinctures and eschewed surgical interventions, ether, and chloroform. They knew that birth followed a general pattern and that each birth involved its own variations and peculiarities. These methods of practice remained consistent with those of urban midwives even though, unlike their more educated colleagues, the rural midwives gained their experience from practice, observation, and shared information acquired without the aid of lectures and textbooks. While most urban immigrant women willingly took the professional appellation of "midwife," many of their rural compatriots embraced the work but not always the title.[24]

As Euro-American settlement occupied increasingly wide swaths of western lands and midwives trained in Europe practiced their trade across the northern plains, Native midwifery and birthing traditions suffered. Contact with Euro-American immigrants and armies of the U.S. government brought threats to long-held, efficacious traditional practices. The policy of the federal government, beginning in 1788 with the ratification of the Constitution, identified Native Americans as "savages" and alternately made alliances with and war on tribal groups. From the 1820s to the 1850s the U.S. government followed a clear policy of removal, encouraging and forcibly moving Native Americans from their ancestral lands. During this time the Cherokee, Creek, Seminole, and Potawatomi peoples were all "removed"—a deceptively passive term used by a series of commissioners of the federal agency that dealt with Indian affairs. Native women pregnant during removal faced an entirely new and danger-filled reproductive landscape. Leaving traditional food supplies behind, traveling unfamiliar terrain, enduring violence and coercion at the hands of soldiers, seeing support systems and family networks disrupted—all these events assailed the reproductive patterns that had been in place for generations. While the U.S. Army did offer vaccines for infectious diseases to Native Americans during this time—the first mention of the smallpox vaccine occurs in an 1832 report by Commissioner of Indian Affairs Elbert Herring—it appears that the motivation for provision of rudimentary health care was to curb the spread of these infections to non-Indian populations at or near military posts. Beginning in the 1830s, some treaty language (like that of the Fort Laramie Treaty) between the federal and tribal governments stipulated the provision of medical supplies and the services of a physician. In these situations the U.S. government took on the responsibility for providing health care not out of compassion or duty but as a negotiated service in exchange for ownership and control of large tracts of land. The treaties were numerous and contained varied language detailing the agreement between the parties.

From the 1850s to the 1870s policies toward Native American nations with treaties focused on reducing their land base and forcing tribal groups to adopt more sedentary lifestyles on reservations. The military used force to keep Native Americans confined to reservations and to restrict their movement to any areas seen as off limits or out of bounds. For women who survived the instability and chaos of relocation, war, or the loss of traditional foods and social practices, pregnancy and delivery only became more dangerous. In addition to the impacts of stress, mothers and their infants faced threats to their personal safety from insufficient shelter, lack of food, and unregulated and unsupervised soldiers who faced no penalties for assaulting Native women.

Native women like Pretty-Shield, Alma Snell, and Agnes Yellowtail Deernose documented their recollections of traditional childbirth practices in the northern plains. For these women and their people, childbirth represented a source of strength and a locus of knowledge and expertise. Their communities valued birth and marked it with ceremony and ritual, even as the physical attacks by the U.S. Army on encampments of women and children clearly challenged even the opportunity for peaceful deliveries.[25]

Once they had been confined to reservations, Native women with experience as midwives could no longer travel to gather the herbs, plants, and roots that they used for medicinal preparations. With substandard housing, pregnant mothers could no longer plan for safety from the elements during delivery, and with the upheaval of relocating, they often did not have access to or the freedom to collect the absorbent plant materials typically used to keep both mother and baby clean after birth.

In addition to all the seemingly small restrictions that made traditional practices difficult or impossible, the federal government actively restricted Native health care, banning and outlawing certain Native American practices, even going so far as to "aggressively sanction" some traditional practitioners.[26] The U.S. government directed the structure of reservation life and instituted regulations. Policies like the Allotment Act, or Dawes Act—instituted in 1887 by the U.S. government to deed communal Native lands to individuals, thus freeing up vast tracts for sale to nontribal buyers—prioritized the nuclear family over the larger and more supportive clan and extended familial relationships that brought stability and care to so many Native American men, women, and children.[27] By the time that reservation confinement was complete, "nearly every aspect of Indian life was subject to the almost uncontrolled discretion of Indian Service officials."[28] The northern plains and Rocky Mountains, once home to knowledgeable and experienced Native American midwives, became the site of an array of settler birth practitioners, some describing themselves as midwives while others worked without a title or occupational definition.

Some Euro-American women working as midwives identified as such and saw themselves as active members of a valued profession. Others who performed seemingly identical work perceived their labor as part of reciprocal neighborliness or even denigrated their own service and skills. Individual states and municipalities codified the licensing of midwifery in the United States, in contrast to some national programs in Europe. The treatment of American midwives varied from outright support, like the colonial settlement that hired an official midwife to serve its residents, to New York's 1907 requirement that all midwives register annually. Enforcement of licensing requirements varied, especially since many women practiced without licensure even when statutes delineated licensing requirements. Montana, North Dakota, and South Dakota did not offer a licensing protocol for midwives in the early 1900s, while Wyoming did. Interestingly, Wyoming allowed license applicants to take the exam in languages other than English.[29]

The murkiness of midwifery history in the northern plains and Rocky Mountains, especially in contrast to the institutional support for the profession in some European countries, intrigued me.[30] Why were midwives in France credited with advancing national aims while women performing the same services in their new American homes not only received no recognition from their government but sometimes even encountered outright hostility? How could these women, all providing essential and life-saving reproductive care, range from openly claiming delivery successes to maintaining near-complete silence about their skills, even with family members and close friends?

Curious about this ambiguity, I began hunting down the stories of individual midwives whenever possible. I expected to find a few renegades who had stumbled into the profession and offered birthing services in conjunction with running boardinghouses, managing family farms and ranches, or teaching school. I collected anecdotes about these women, including names and locations, when I encountered them during other researching forays. As I talked about my quest in public lectures, discoveries came to me. One woman stopped me after I presented on the topic at a local museum, pulled a stack of labeled file folders from her quilted bag, and laid out the details of her grandmother's likely death from childbed fever. She also showed me an impressive selection of archival evidence and family pictures. Families from the hinterlands of eastern Montana tracked down my contact information and sent me accounts of their grandmothers' work in local communities, with accompanying photographs and documentation. Archivists and museum staff, initially stumped by my questions regarding records of childbirth, forwarded snippets they later discovered in uncategorized collection boxes, with details that included records of births, mentions in diaries, and even unpublished manuscripts. As I pored over these multiplying stories of reproductive expertise, my impression of a haphazard collection of scattered anecdotes evaporated into a sense of wonder at the torrential evidence of women's reproductive labor and childbirth practices.

Upon hearing of my expanding investigation into regional midwives, Ken Robison, the director of the Overholser Historical Research Center in Fort Benton, Montana, generously shared the details of a treasure donated by a local family—a photo album documenting more than one hundred babies that Mary Kassmeier, a Fort Benton resident and local midwife in the early 1900s, helped to deliver. Hoping to add to my expanding midwifery stash, I arranged to visit the picturesque river town and investigate for myself.

Like many women, Kassmeier valued the work she did and saw her service to Fort Benton families as important. She wanted evidence of her accomplishments, and she took the audacious step of

Fig. 14. This photo of the Kassmeier family was taken in Chouteau County, Montana. Leonard, the youngest child (pictured here as a toddler), was born in 1920. Courtesy of the Kassmeier family.

recording her work and life in tangible form. Kassmeier requested a baby picture from each family that she helped, and she assembled these photographs into an album, taking the time to carefully affix each image and, in many cases, record the babies' names. Kassmeier did not display the album at social events or discuss her work with friends, but she did make sure that at least one family member, her daughter-in-law, knew about the pictures and their meaning. It seems that Kassmeier kept the album as a personal history; her midwifery experience was an important part of her identity, and she wanted a way to preserve evidence of the births she attended and the families she cared for.[31]

Basing my research on this photographic evidence, I hoped to identify the nature of Kassmeier's practice. Did she work with fam-

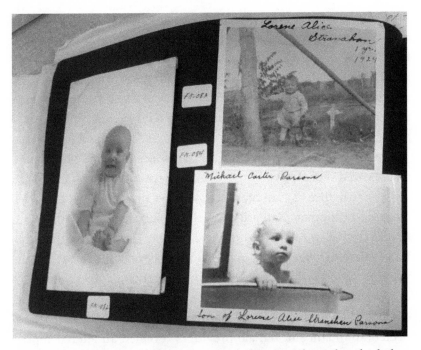

Fig. 15. Mary Kassmeier's photo album includes more than a hundred photographs of infants and children. Some are formal portraits, and others are more casual images in home settings. Mary Kassmeier Album, Overholser Historical Research Center, Fort Benton, Montana. Photograph by the author.

ilies all across Chouteau County or limit her assistance to close-by neighbors? How many babies did she actually deliver? The high-ceilinged vault that housed the records of the Chouteau County clerk and recorder promised some potential clues along with refreshing air-conditioning on a blisteringly hot July day.

The historic space held floor-to-ceiling records, including bound ledgers with documentary details on area residents extending back more than a hundred years. It appeared that residents of Fort Benton and the surrounding farmland mostly looked to a handful of male doctors who faithfully served the region's residents from the 1860s through the 1930s. Standing over the slanted surface of a metal desk amid the orderly stacks of records in Fort Benton, I began scanning the list of area birth attendants.[32] With the pleasure of familiarity, I carefully turned the fragile, musty-smelling pages and recognized the names of attending physicians: multiple entries for Murphy and Bassow, along with an occasional listing for Anderson.[33] After a couple of minutes I realized that although these known doctors showed up with a pleasing regularity, a host of other individuals also delivered babies in the Fort Benton area. Bernina Park, Carrie Rucker, Josephine Harant, Dora Bell VanDoren, and Thora Phalen all appeared repeatedly in the ledger. In between these prolific providers, the names of even more reproductive practitioners came into focus: Ella Chipman, Katherine Coruthers, Elizabeth Reynolds, Ruth Blanchard, Ellen Steven, Janie Boyd, Evalyn Hamann, Wilhemina Lohse, Sarah Dolan, Nellie Vos, and Magdalene Kolnitschar. These women signed birth certificates as birth attendants; they were out-and-proud midwives. Even with the preponderance of named male doctors, the number of listed women left me stunned. This unexpected abundance of female providers revealed an altered reproductive context, one in which a great many women offered delivery assistance.

Still struggling to comprehend a potentially transfigured reproductive landscape, I made note of the expanding array of practitioner names and pressed on. The register listings, arranged by the last name of the delivered infant, ran from the earliest—with some even in the mid- and late 1800s—through the 1930s. Now into the alphabet, past *F* and *G* and even *H*, Mary Kassmeier had not appeared; through the *S*, the *T*, the *U*, and the *V* listings, her name still remained noticeably absent. How could an established practitioner whose family and community knew of her expertise remain entirely absent from the official state-sponsored historical record? Kassmeier ran a busy practice, which was at its peak from 1915 to 1925, and claimed verifiable skills with herbal remedies and difficult births.

After finishing the *Z* names and still without a Kassmeier sighting, I emerged from the cool darkness of the clerk and recorder's office into the blazing sunlight of the July afternoon, determined to parse the conundrum of Kassmeier's story. Conversations with local historians and community elders, another round of oral histories with Kassmeier's family, extended genealogical record searches, and a review of local newspapers revealed that Kassmeier operated a routine practice in collaboration with one or more local physicians. She delivered babies in private homes and at St. Clare's, the local Catholic hospital. Her regular presence at the hospital for deliveries indicated that she maintained at least tacit cooperation with area doctors, especially James Murphy, who signed the majority of certificates for the births Kassmeier supervised.

Kassmeier's situation embodied a collaborative structure in which women delivered babies in independent practices and also worked with doctors in areas of specialty.[34] Male physicians undoubtedly maintained some awareness of these female providers and even openly cooperated with them. For example, Elizabeth Rae, who opened a maternity home in Livingston, Montana, in the 1890s, had honed her skills as a nurse and midwife in Scotland. Montana neighbors greeted her as "Aunty Rae" and fondly remembered her warming premature infants on the open door of her stove.[35] While Rae delivered infants on her own, she also took referrals from area physicians who requested her services for preterm babies.[36]

These types of arrangements, in which female providers performed the bulk of the hands-on reproductive care with the involvement of male physicians as occasional consultants, fit the practice needs of women like Kassmeier and Rae. Many others like them performed a similar and essential community service across the region but neither dealt with the state nor signed forms. As a result, they were often passed over in official historical accounts.

Still, fragmentary evidence of women who delivered babies across the region in the early 1900s could be found in local newspapers, oral histories, and family lore. Given how frequent these mentions were and how the size of my collection expanded over just a few years, the quotidian prevalence of women like Kassmeier took me aback.

My mental picture shifted as I added those incomplete yet multi-tudinous records to those of the women in early state and county sources bold enough to list themselves as providers. These were not scattered malcontents searching for reproductive risk but rather the norm, the routine, the ordinary. In searching for Mary Kassmeier, I discovered a landscape full of women: women exerting themselves in the effort of birthing babies, women assisting at births, women cleaning up from deliveries, women talking about their pregnancies, women teaching and learning from each other, women being present when a child died, and women visiting each other's homes before, during, and after birth. Instead of anecdotes about a few maverick midwives, my research documented the uncounted details of a story written, acted, directed, and produced by women.

As I began to comprehend the size and significance of the scattered records pointing to the widespread existence of off-record midwives like Kassmeier, I thought back to the Children's Bureau study published in 1919. The bureau's work, based on data assembled from women's actual delivery experiences, calculated midwifery deliveries at about half of all births.[37] A midwifery delivery rate of about 50 percent, within the bounds of reason and appropriately conservative, tracked with my knowledge of rural and urban communities across the region. Yet I wanted a more concrete estimate.

Although college calculus left me with lingering trauma, I adore numbers. Data are illustrative. Numbers give us a way of assessing the commonness or rarity of particular human experiences; they establish context and relationships; they let us know how general-izable our conclusions are. Reflecting on the forgotten history of reproductive care in the northern plains and Rocky Mountains, I focused on counting births in the hope of achieving some statistical conclusions with percentages, charts, and diagrams. I was concerned to avoid either over- or understating the volume of midwifery pro-viders. For women who had already been dismissed as irrelevant, both by their own era and subsequent generations, the inclusion of statistical information became particularly relevant. I worried that the absence of quantifiable percentages would allow these reproductive caregivers to again be ignored.

For the midwives who completed birth certificates for the babies they delivered, the signature affixed to the bottom of the page might be the only evidentiary proof of their hours of work heating water for cleaning, massaging the cramping muscles of mothers in labor, carefully supporting infants as they took their first breaths of air, encouraging exhausted mothers to deliver placentas, and washing mounds of stained linens and clothing. But birth certificates preserved by county governments remain private information in North Dakota, Montana, South Dakota, and Wyoming, available only to the named individual and immediate family members. Even if, by some legislative dispensation, I obtained all turn-of-the-twentieth-century birth certificates from a particular county, the Kassmeier conundrum demonstrated how misleading that information could be. How many women in the rural landscape of the Upper Missouri country and across the expanse of Montana, Wyoming, and the Dakotas shared a story like Kassmeier's? How many women learned their trade but did not claim the title? How many saw birth as female and private while viewing the government as public and belonging to men? If even one-quarter of births—a grotesquely conservative estimate—were deliveries supervised by midwives but recorded by male doctors, the data would be useless. Evidence indicated that across the northern plains in the early 1900s, female midwives often performed the work of delivery and male physicians received the credit. Unfortunately, accessible resources did not exist to tabulate how many midwives served in the region.

The majority of these women were forgotten by history and remain so, in a reality that seems irreversible. For those women who delivered babies, even in the twentieth century, their legacy of knowledge, compassion, service, and struggle disappeared with their deaths. There is no way to recapture their lives or the value ascribed to them by the mothers they helped, the communities they supported, or the infants they caught.

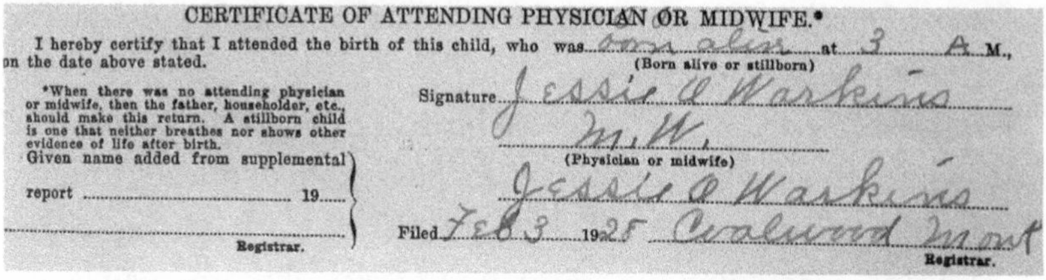

CERTIFICATE OF ATTENDING PHYSICIAN OR MIDWIFE.*

I hereby certify that I attended the birth of this child, who was born alive at 3 A. M., on the date above stated.
(Born alive or stillborn)

*When there was no attending physician or midwife, then the father, householder, etc., should make this return. A stillborn child is one that neither breathes nor shows other evidence of life after birth.

Given name added from supplemental report .... 19....

.... Registrar.

Signature Jessie O Warkins
M.W.
(Physician or midwife)

Jessie O Warkins
Filed Feb 3 1925 Coalwood Mont
Registrar.

Fig. 16. Jessie Warkins worked in sparsely populated Powder River County, Montana, and, unlike many midwives, regularly signed as the attending midwife for deliveries. Significantly, she also held the position of county registrar and was responsible for recording all of the births and deaths across the county. Birth certificate held by the Powder River Historical Society, Broadus, Montana. Photograph by the author.

Where does that leave us as we gaze into the reproductive past? We know that women working as midwives delivered babies all across Wyoming, the Dakotas, and Montana. Some of them signed birth certificates and some did not. It is likely that every turn-of-the-twentieth-century regional community, rural and urban, relied on the services of at least one female reproductive provider. Even without the statistical detail that I was hunting, it is clear that the infrastructure of health and caregiving in the northern plains and Rocky Mountains rested firmly on the shoulders of midwives and those who acted as midwives.

The inability to firmly and conclusively tabulate representative numbers does not diminish the important work that individuals like Villian, Hamalainen, Ylenni, and Ebaugh performed. Instead, it serves as a reminder that access to institutions matters, that history is most often written by those who control the recordkeeping, and that our understanding of our human past is at many points desperately limited. Exploring these lesser-known and less complete histories allows us to understand the intimate details of past experience and forces us to craft strategies for exploring these critical yet neglected human stories. Assigning a reliable “percentage of deliveries” figure to midwives and midwife-like providers remains out of reach, but sufficient evidence does exist to enable an examination of the nature of the work they performed, the kind of care they offered, and the impact their profession had on the experience of birth.

The Theory and Practice of Midwifery

A multitude of lay midwives spread out across the northern plains and Rocky Mountains, delivering babies and caring for parturient women in a highly effective mass of health-care professionals. These women called on a wide array of training and varied backgrounds to provide health-care services. Their diversity accompanied a common characteristic: they shared an attentiveness to the needs of pregnant women. They came to the task of childbirth with a sense of necessity; it was important work and someone needed to do it. Some of them served as midwives in a professional capacity, advertising in the newspaper and charging for their services. Others labored as resident lay physicians in small communities, delivered babies, tended sick children, and managed infectious disease epidemics. These individuals typically defined their work as part of their feminine role, sometimes claiming the title of midwife but often serving without recognition or acclaim.

The absence of a unifying or identifying title played a role in their historical dismissal. Many of these women struggled to define and value their contributions: they acknowledged the important work they did but nonetheless felt constrained about claiming a professional title. Ethel Eide served her North Dakota community in the early 1900s and oversaw the delivery of six infants. When asked if she was a midwife, she replied, "No, I wasn't anything," a telling assessment of the indefinable role these female caregivers filled. Even though she did not claim a title or skilled profession, Eide took pains to educate herself. She searched for information about childbearing and "read up" on delivery problems. After talking with and learning from other women, she tested her knowledge, explaining that she "just had to go ahead" and offer care to improve her skills. In addition to delivering babies, Eide helped when children had colic or convulsions, and she concocted and applied remedies for sick and injured neighbors. Eide, in describing the nature of her duties, initially said she "[wasn't] anything"; she then grudgingly acknowledged, "I was kind of a doctor."[38] Her equivocation demonstrated the deep ambivalence she carried about the definition of her work.

Anna Hamalainen, immigrant midwife from Finland, exemplified the essence of competent and care-based midwifery practice. Arriving in the United States with her midwifery diploma in hand and her skills at the ready, she worked in New York–area hospitals before moving to Montana. After setting up an initial practice in Butte, she relocated to Red Lodge in 1916, presumably gravitating toward the Finnish population working the coal mines amid the stunning panorama of the Beartooth Mountains. Hamalainen married in 1919 and operated her Red Lodge midwifery practice through the Depression and on into her later years.[39] She helped women establish approximate due dates and encouraged them to eat well and get enough rest during pregnancy. When notified of an impending delivery, she arrived with her sanitized tools and delivery supplies. Her straw bag included a wooden fetoscope, towels, linen cord, forceps, scalpel, and thermometers. Hamalainen stayed with the mother through the delivery and for about ten days afterward, providing the necessary support to put both mother and infant on the way to full strength.[40]

Like Hamalainen, Charley Hanson's grandmother studied midwifery in the "old country" and received instruments from the Swedish government. She brought her training, expertise, and tools with her when she immigrated to America and thereupon delivered babies all over McLain County, North Dakota, charging a two-dollar fee for delivery.[41] Most midwives like Maclean, Hanson, and Hamalainen charged a delivery fee but also took payment in trade, like foodstuffs or chopped wood, or, like Maclean, in embroidered fancywork.[42]

Midwives like Villian, Topliss, and Karstedt worked in urban areas and could draw on a population large enough to provide full-time employment, but rural midwives often supplemented their income with poultry and dairy operations. As demographer Irvine Loudon pointed out, rural midwives "who were fully employed and delivering a hundred or more women a year were rare for the obvious reason that most rural populations were small and scattered."[43]

Midwives fit no distinct or definable profile but did share a certain level of life experience. Mrs. Braidall, the midwife in Reeder, North Dakota, could refer to at least eight pregnancies of her own, in addition to the births that she supervised.[44] Ordinarily, midwives claimed personal experience of delivery through the births of their own children. It would have been unusual to find a young woman without children working as a skilled midwife, unless, like Hamalainen, the midwife had formal institutional training. Lulu Larson of Valley City, North Dakota, remembered her midwife as "so handy, so capable."[45] Age and experience brought expertise and skill, and mothers appreciated the competence and mastery that midwives employed during childbirth.

Midwifery Practices

While midwives of the northern plains challenged simplistic categorization, three distinct types of practice can be identified. Some midwives, like Valleen and Hamalainen, set up solo professional practices and advertised their services in local publications. They worked alone (not in partnership with doctors or other midwives) and typically preferred cash payment, although they did sometimes receive their fees in trade goods. They often had formal training or extensive practical experience with delivery and usually came from countries that recognized delivery care as a remunerated service.

In contrast to these solo providers, other midwives operated blended practices, in which they delivered babies independently and also collaborated closely with physicians. Childbirth was (and remains) a lengthy and laborious process, and physicians frustrated with the tediousness of waiting on mothers or overloaded with patients suffering from traumatic injuries could avoid spending days tending to the needs of a woman in labor by establishing an association with a midwife. In these cases midwives like Kassmeier and Rae cooperated with physicians to deliver routine births while keeping the local doctor apprised of possible delivery complications.

Finally, some women began assisting with birth out of necessity when no other support was available, and they developed a certain amount of knowledge. Over time some of these "occasional" midwives gained confidence in their abilities after assisting with a number of deliveries. Lena Vanvig, born in Norway and an immigrant to North Dakota, "took care of quite a few babies when they were born," and she had particular success in saving nonresponsive infants. During one birth the husband lamented that the "baby's dead," but Vanvig cleared its mouth and nose and rubbed the baby repeatedly with hot water. Eventually the infant boy "start[ed] like that," to Vanvig's and undoubtedly also the parents' intense pleasure.[46] Ethel Eide, the midwife and lay physician who explained that her work "wasn't anything," served in this category, accumulating knowledge and generously offering care out of necessity but without any assumption of professional status or title.[47]

Midwifery and Nursing

The fact that some women practiced as both nurses and midwives complicates an understanding of these vocations. But despite assumed similarity, examination of the structures and core elements of the two professions offers a clear distinction. With an expanding northern plains population and a growing demand for nurses, nursing schools sprouted across the region. In the state of Montana nurses organized in 1912 and met in Missoula for their first state convention.[48] Augusta Ariss, an early Montana nurse and historian of the Montana Nurses Association, explained that nurses desired a distinction between trained nurses and "untrained women who were caring for the sick as means of livelihood."[49] This reliance on a credentialed hierarchy cut to the core of the nursing profession, which embraced a careful ranking and apportionment of power and authority. As a result of this mind-set, the state's Nurse Practice Act of

1913 differentiated between registered nurses and licensed practical nurses. Women with hands-on nursing experience but lacking the academic requirements to be licensed as registered nurses in 1913 continued to perform nursing duties and received the designation of practical nurses. Practical nurses did not gain access to professional licensing until 1953.[50]

The emerging field of nursing adapted a mixture of male-dominated and female-led internal structures. In the northern plains and Rocky Mountains various religious orders often oversaw the professionalization and training of nurses and organized, staffed, and maintained medical institutions. For example, Catholic orders operated throughout the state of Montana, and Methodist and Episcopalian organizations also started hospitals. Religious sisters and deaconesses hired doctors, raised funds, trained nurses, set rates, and established formal business procedures.[51] Nursing leadership and female administrators guarded their power base but did so with carefully chosen gender-appropriate behaviors. Couching their concerns in the language of request, spirituality, and assistance, they avoided using directly forceful or confrontational terms whenever possible.[52] Louise Bourgeois's forthright challenge of a male physician's methods would have been startlingly out of place in the deferential practice of nursing.

The nursing profession emphasized the cultivation of character appropriate to a nurse; such character included compliance with existing social structures. Nurses disciplined each other, even over the objections of male doctors, and refused to certify individual nurses of questionable morality. Desperately concerned about the image of nursing, the profession's self-policing ensured that nurses demonstrated the ability to perform particular nursing procedures and also met specific character and gender norms.[53]

The day-to-day work of midwives and nurses appeared similar, but the rationale and underlying structure of the two practices could not have been more divergent. As the profession of nursing established governing bodies and rules, it developed a practice of rank-based deference, from novice nurses to their teachers and from nursing supervisors to physicians. While it retained its desire to offer care and reduce pain, nursing did so within an institutional and hierarchical bureaucratic system of hospitals. The religious emphasis of many nurses' training only intensified the moralistic tone of the profession.

In contrast, women acting as midwives, even if they had nursing training, did so outside of any bureaucratic structure, negotiating rates and establishing services directly with their clients. Midwives answered only to the women they served; they claimed no governing body or ranking structure. For the women who gained expertise in the process of childbirth, theirs was the knowledge of normalcy. They were not treating the sick. Midwives saw the range of individual differences in female reproduction and could identify and describe illness, but their focus was on the normal function of the female form and methods of support for parturient women in all stages of reproduction.

Despite the philosophical differences between nursing and midwifery, many women who trained as nurses also practiced as midwives, delivering babies and helping pregnant women. Erminia Josephine Maggini graduated from nursing school in 1917, entered the military, and served during World War I. Upon discharge, she married Chester Eide and moved to Froid, Montana, in 1920. Chester and Erminia Eide homesteaded near Dagmar, and she worked as a midwife throughout Sheridan County. She undoubtedly experienced overlap between midwifery and nursing but identified her professional skills, according to her family, as "nursing" and "midwife for Sheridan County."[54] Eide's background allowed her to work in two distinct professions with different structures. As a military nurse, Eide reported up a rigid chain of command, while as a midwife she answered only to her own standards and those of the women who employed her.

Coming from a contemporary reproductive culture of sterile and regimented hospital birth, readers today might find it difficult to comprehend the degree of intimacy a midwife like Eide shared with

Fig. 17. After homesteading in Dagmar, Montana, Erminia Eide's family relocated to Fort Peck to work on the construction of the dam there. Courtesy of
Elizabeth Douglass.

birthing mothers. The necessary woman-to-woman sharing between mother and midwife would have revealed potentially shameful and most definitely private matters, like overall health, financial condition, sexually transmitted diseases, and physical or emotional abuse. Even in situations where Eide might have arrived for the birth without any prior knowledge of or conversation with the mother, the physical closeness of birth—holding or supporting a mother during contractions, bathing the thighs and genitals after delivery, or even performing nipple stimulation to hasten stalled contractions—would have brought her into an intensely intimate physical space with her clients. Midwives guarded secrets that could bring shame and judgment on mothers but also knew that the sharing of personal matters would effectively bar them from practicing. Across the profession of midwifery, practitioners structured a relatively balanced give-and-take with mothers while engaging in close and guarded reciprocal intimacy.

The Power of Midwifery

Whether it meant resuscitating an infant or guiding a first-time mother through the delivery process, midwives all across the northern plains bore witness to the important reproductive work of women. Their involvement in delivery helped to shape the reality of life in the northern plains, and despite the dangers of childbirth in the region, it is safe to say that without the assistance of midwives the death toll would have been far more significant.

The midwifery model of care, going all the way back to Louise Bourgeois, offered clear advantages to mothers. The stated belief that women's bodies were normal, not aberrant, diseased copies of the "superior" male form, and that childbirth was a healthy human process offered a sense of ease for pregnant women. Mothers received comfort from a birthing ally who brought confidence to childbirth and a firm conviction that delivery could be competently managed. The respect mothers and midwives tendered to and received from each other reduced the risks of abuse and domination, especially in the vulnerable atmosphere of childbirth. Midwives, with their historical emphasis on practical experience and contextual knowledge, preserved the essential components of professional practice.

If someone saw Erminia Maggini Eide "on her horse with one of her three boys behind her, there was a baby on the way." As her family remembered, "she was gone sometimes for days."[55] When she rode out on horseback to tend the women of Sheridan County, she followed a path worn by her predecessors, from Louise Bourgeois to unrecorded and illiterate practicing midwives of earlier centuries. Their skills and methods went with her, as she treated and cared for the pregnant women in her rural community.

As mothers and midwives constructed the American West by creating families, farmsteads, and communities, their intimate knowledge of reproduction and their operational system of shared power and negotiated authority stood in stark contrast to the ambitions of the medical profession.

4

The Practice of Birth

The work of midwives and mothers in informal birthing networks helped to create settler communities in the northern plains and Rocky Mountains. At the same time, however, the far more structured apparatus of organized medicine dabbled in childbirth, promulgating negative ideas about midwives and actively disseminating falsehoods about reproduction that carried into contemporary thinking.

In the fall of 2017 I attended a lecture, advertised as an analysis of midwifery care in the United States. The presenter intended to show that licensing protocols, ostensibly aimed at improving the quality of midwifery care in the early 1900s, successfully reduced maternal mortality. His was a well-funded study, employing student assistants and reams of data, that concluded in favor of licensing—a not-very-contentious position—and asserted that the process of credentialing midwives, enacted by municipalities and state governments, resulted in a public health benefit. He claimed that governmental control over midwives brought about a public good—a significant and quantifiable reduction in rates of maternal death—not measurably achieved by the licensing of other professions.[1]

On the surface his conclusions sounded ordinary enough to fit the "dismal science" reputation of economics. But the underlying assumptions made about midwifery—and, by extension, women and race—left me seething. The author asserted that turn-of-the-twentieth-century American midwives, "many of whom were black or foreign-born," needed training in cleanliness from physicians and health department workers.[2] The clear implication was that midwives were dirty and that their ignorance and incompetence caused the deaths of American mothers and infants. The lecture concluded with a statement suggesting that countries in the developing world could follow the lead of the United States and implement policies like the ones that proved so successful in controlling African American and migrant midwives in turn-of-the-twentieth-century America. After all, the speaker concluded, many contemporary birth attendants are, like midwives of a century ago, lacking any "formal education or training."[3]

The majority of audience members in the room were students, and few noticed the racial and gender bias revealed by the study's assumption that female birth attendants in Africa and Asia are ignorant and dirty. Most attendees willingly believed that American midwives of a century ago did not understand the importance of cleanliness, that perhaps they wandered the countryside with rusty knives, grimacing at passersby and muttering incantations.[4] The audience had no background in the history of childbirth. They did not know that American physicians created and subsequently fostered the deadly epidemic of puerperal fever in the early 1900s through their complete disregard for basic sanitary measures. And like the general public, attendees assumed that physicians occupied the moral high ground when it came to cleanliness and common-sense medical knowledge.[5]

As a scholar of American culture and women's history, I felt no surprise at this view. There are some myths about women—and midwives in particular—that are tied so tightly to cultural tropes that they remain with us, despite copious historical evidence to the contrary. Fevered tales of midwifery incompetence, typically vague and histrionic, remain standard fare.[6] Understanding the history of the birthing space, inhabited first by midwives and then by physicians, helps to explain this continuing disconnect between fact and fiction in our knowledge of childbirth practices.

A Brief History of Medicine

In the late 1800s patients seeking medical assistance chose from a plethora of practitioners, including herbalists, homeopaths, and phrenologists.[7] With such an array of methods of medical practice, the title "Doctor" required explanation. Medical certificates could be ordered through the mail, and physicians earned their reputations based on the quality of care they provided, not the type of degree they held or school they attended.[8] Allopathic practitioners—the branch of medicine that dominates medical services today—lacked systematized education, licensing, and procedures and delivered inconsistent results.[9] As medical historian Todd Savitt notes in his description of the situation in Montana, "anybody could claim to be a healer and charge money to care for patients."[10]

In an era when multiple titled practitioners offered their services, patients had little expectation of a standard of medical care from physicians. Medical historian Richard Shryock has explained that "many general practitioners, prior to 1900, had received a mediocre education at best. Yet patients were either unaware of this fact or considered it irrelevant."[11] For many in the northern plains and Rocky Mountains, health care represented a luxury good, accessed only in cases of extreme emergency. Home remedies filled the gap between expensive and often ineffective medical care and living with chronic pain, infection, or illness.[12]

By the late 1800s allopathic physicians had seen the need for a professional rebranding. They recognized the benefits to be gained by ensuring that practitioners delivered a consistent product and understood certain baseline biological systems. But how were they to achieve some level of medical consistency? Prior to the 1830s, medical schools, state boards, and medical societies all vied for control of standards to be set for the profession. This cacophony of bureaucratic institutions caused confusion, so over time and with the backing of the American Medical Association, licensing schemes were eventually passed and had been implemented in individual states by the 1920s.[13]

In the midst of this professional turmoil, obstetrics emerged as a specialized area of study. Following the formation of the American Medical Association in 1847, the *American Journal of Obstetrics and Diseases of Women and Children* began publication in 1868. The American Gynecological Association appeared in 1876, and the American Association of Obstetrics and Gynecologists established itself in 1888.[14]

Cognizant of their profession's poor image, doctors organized and mobilized to reform their practice in the early twentieth century. At their request Abraham Flexner, an educational consultant, conducted a full examination of the medical educational system and came to some dramatic conclusions in his 1910 report. Flexner recommended that the number of practicing physicians be reduced and that medical schools simultaneously implement rigorous educational standards. His report reserved particularly harsh words for obstetric programs, noting that doctors lacked training, with many physicians attending their first births only *after* receiving their licenses. Few were skilled in directing labor and ensuring a safe delivery.[15]

Following Flexner's report, the medical profession worked to improve the reputation of obstetrics. By standardizing procedures and utilizing teaching hospitals, the profession ensured that licensed doctors observed births and gained familiarity with the use of instruments. Poor urban women, unable to afford any attendant, exchanged their privacy for medical assistance and became hospital training tools, delivering in operating theaters ringed with audiences of male medical students.[16] Little if any obstetrical training provided information on the normal course of labor and delivery, focusing instead on the specific tools of medicine—instruments like forceps and drugs such as ether.[17]

After numerous attempts at reform, medicine could claim significant improvement in training and licensure by the mid-1900s: state medical boards oversaw far more consistent licensing processes, and medical students across the country, from Milwaukee to Montana, thus shared at least a general body of knowledge.[18] However, commonly held obstetric theories and beliefs, like the practice of viewing pregnancy as a disease, informed physician interactions with and treatments for female patients across the northern plains and Rocky Mountains and around the country.[19]

The Assumptions of Medicine

From the colonial era to the rush of Euro-American settlement in the northern plains and Rocky Mountains, physicians often saw birth as unworthy of their attention. This historical disregard for women and their reproductive labor made the process of birth off limits to men, reserving it as a solely female activity. But as physicians began experimenting with tools and technologies like anesthesia, cervical dilators, and uterine sounds—all in common usage by the mid-1800s—they argued for the expansion of birth boundaries to include a formal role for men in the delivery process.[20]

Birthing change came slowly—and in many communities not at all. Doctors found little demand for their services at deliveries, and midwives generally filled the role of birth attendant to the satisfaction of eighteenth- and nineteenth-century mothers.[21] On the occasions when male doctors were invited into the women's world of birth, they faced challenges of Victorian-era propriety. Based on standards of appropriate male-to-female contact, doctors performed physical examinations under full or partial cover, and their resultant blind groping did little to elicit useful medical information or put mothers at ease.[22]

Without a history of maternity care treatments, physicians in the early to mid-1800s worked to develop and expand a battery of procedures. Medical doctors, most especially those involved in the institutional arm of the profession, gravitated toward an interventionist approach to childbirth, preferring action over observation and advocating the use of new technologies even when significant harm to mothers resulted.[23] The emptying of bladder and bowels via catheter and enema, seen as unnecessary and invasive by midwifery, became routine medical practice. Doctors bled laboring women and administered ergot to strengthen contractions. Mothers were subjected to blistering and purging, common remedies in the nineteenth century, especially during lengthy labors when other treatments failed to deliver results.[24] Despite the known dangers associated with the use of anesthesia in labor—hemorrhage, lengthening of labor, and reduction of the strength of contractions, as well as newborn breathing difficulties—many physicians felt that its calming benefits (to avoid mothers' unladylike outbursts during labor) outweighed the risks.[25] Forceps, another questionable technological advancement, provided assistance in difficult deliveries, despite the potential for great damage to the mother and infant if misused.

In direct contrast to the focus of midwifery, which ensured a healthy infant and safe delivery by providing care based on a mother's needs, medical treatment as advocated by the American Medical Association and leading obstetricians evolved according to the needs and interests of doctors. It is no surprise that many male physicians, socialized in a system that recognized their needs as paramount, failed to act empathetically on behalf of laboring women or to render assistance based on mothers' requests. Instead, medical teaching— and by default a growing number of trained physicians—followed the standard cultural course of action and sought ways of reducing their own discomfort.[26]

After working to gain entry into the birthing room, organized medicine moved to alter the circumstances of childbirth in ways that eased doctors' own experience of delivery. Doctors did not kneel in front of squatting mothers to examine them—instead women lay in bed. No more moaning, cantankerous mothers: physicians administered ether and cleared the room to ensure silence and calm.[27] Forcibly emptying bladder and bowels with a catheter and enema increased mothers' pain but ensured that physicians need not encounter bodily excreta during delivery.[28]

Unfortunately, this desire for a controlled birth managed by the physician brought an increase in discomfort and danger for mothers. Lying prone in bed during labor immobilized the muscles necessary for pushing; sitting up in bed created a right-angle bend in the birth canal that made delivery more difficult. Neither bed-based position worked for women; for thousands of years women had naturally assumed a squatting or all-fours position during birth.[29] The physician-advocated position slowed labor and intensified pain, which in turn led to women's willingness to accept drug treatments. Ether and other anesthetics such as chloroform decreased the efficiency of women's labor and sometimes resulted in extensive blood loss.[30] Enemas caused anal contractions that, experienced simultaneously with the intense contractions of labor, only increased mothers' pain and worry.[31]

In fact, medical procedures brought a unique violence into the birthing room. Tools such as forceps crushed tender tissues and ripped at the structure of the female genitalia.[32] Anesthesia rendered mothers unconscious while their bodies were subject to the pulling, twisting, and prying of physicians. Ideas about women—the need to keep them quiet, to render them passive, to disregard their comfort—found their way into the specific practices of medicine, often at the hands of otherwise kind and gentlemanly purveyors of medical care.[33] The reality of reproductive violence remains a part of contemporary health care, with mammograms in which breasts are forcibly compressed, annual exams that include cold speculums inserted into vaginas, and the overall sense that one must be friendly, pleasant, and a good sport about painful and invasive procedures.

As doctors experimented with obstetric technologies, scientific thinking about the female body adapted to justify evolving treatments. Londa Schiebinger, a specialist in the history of science, explains that physicians from the 1600s through the turn of the twentieth century used anatomical studies to classify women as "incommensurate" to men, with the physical and emotional capabilities of females ranked as inferior.[34] Medical science shifted from a mystical interpretation of childbirth focused on its unknowability and instead shifted to emphasizing labor as a mechanistic process.[35] This change in theory meant that birth could be separated from the woman, understood as an event independent of the mother, and managed by the physician. Science thus freed the uterus from the female body and made physicians, formerly handicapped by their sex and limited knowledge, authorities in women's reproductive processes.[36]

As part of this theoretical evolution, the late 1800s heralded the oft-voiced physician belief that childbirth was an inordinately dangerous undertaking.[37] Women tended to describe childbirth as a painful, sometimes worrying, but ultimately routine event.[38] In contrast, the profession of medicine often perceived birth as critically unpredictable, as it certainly appeared to men who had never experienced the process.[39] Childbirth, a lengthy series of physiological events involving unobservable internal activity, put doctors in the position of waiting. Male physicians were understandably fearful, and having had little if any practice in observing or collaborating with women in the birthing room, they responded by attempting to take charge of delivery externally, by means of surgical intervention. In the event of birthing complications, evolving standards of obstetric practice favored a course of action that allowed the highest level of physician control, diminishing communication with and cooperation on behalf of the laboring woman.[40] For example, a physician might attempt to hasten delivery by rupturing the amniotic sac with an unsterilized tool, an intervention common in medical practice in the 1800s and one that could introduce foreign bacteria into the uterus and cause life-threatening infection.[41]

According to their training, doctors saw their goal as bringing about a standard progression of delivery with as little deviation as possible.[42] Many processes, however, with childbirth chief among them, are hindered and even harmed when made to follow a pre-established routine. As anthropologist James Scott has explained, situations that are "broadly similar but never precisely identical" demand "a quick and practiced adaptation that becomes almost second nature to the practitioner."[43] Childbirth stands as the quintessential embodiment of both *broadly similar* and *never precisely identical*.

Delivery remains remarkably consistent from mother to mother, across generations, continents, and centuries: dilation of the cervix precedes the work of pushing the baby out; the infant emerges from the vagina and remains connected to the mother via the umbilical cord; the laboring woman delivers the placenta.

Even with these general similarities, each delivery, as Louise Bourgeois eloquently noted in 1617, is uniquely individual.[44] The position of the baby when entering and leaving the birth canal, the strength of contractions, the length of labor, the size of the infant, and even the mother's strength and stamina all differ from delivery to delivery. In these situations attendants must adapt their care based on experience. When contextual knowledge is called for, training by rote, according to Scott, "resists simplification into deductive principles." Competent adaptability required a certain kind of training: extended exposure alongside someone with the experience to differentiate normal birthing diversity from troubling complications.[45]

That very learning was extirpated by the efforts at controlling the birth setting. In removing the company of women from a social birth setting, organized medicine also removed the intrinsic tending and caring that is now understood to be central to normal, physiologic birth. When physicians evicted female attendants, it often meant that the mother could no longer receive physical support from friends and family while laboring in an upright or squatting position. Unable to gain extra birth canal clearance from a spreading pelvis meant that women labored much longer in the prone position with a wedged baby. Some of those babies eventually died, and physicians tried to prove their worth by breaking the woman's pelvis to extract the dead baby, an intervention that midwives certainly did not attempt but also one that they assiduously avoided by advocating for intelligent birthing positions.[46]

Optimally, practitioners combined intellectual acumen with hands-on training under the supervision of an expert practitioner, much like Lena Vanvig, a North Dakota migrant midwife from Norway, who attained just such a combination by working for a doctor, thereby gaining familiarity with the technicalities of birth interventions, as well as receiving the mentoring care of an experienced midwife, who expanded Vanvig's understanding of the range of normal birth.[47]

So it was that medical training ran contrary to the more effective midwifery mentoring model.[48] By advocating for physician intervention without knowledge transmission that could differentiate normal variations from potential complications, the medical model attempted to bypass traditional ways of knowing and acquisition of skill sets. Superintending safe deliveries required a practitioner to listen and adapt. Unilaterally acting according to a preordained plan and regimenting the birth process created its own birthing complications.

Birth interventions began to gain public acceptance, and delivery migrated from communal to medical space. In the early twentieth century fewer than five in one hundred babies were born in the hospital, but by the 1920s hospital birth was the choice of 30 to 50 percent of women in urban America. The trend accelerated into the 1950s, when hospital birth became the widespread norm, replacing the home as the default delivery venue.[49] The attendance of male physicians and their desire for quiet and controlled birthing environments reduced the number of friends and relatives in attendance and changed the delivery from a social event to a medical and procedural one.[50] As the number of attendants decreased, the authority of the physician increased, and the birth space, formerly viewed as unworthy of the attention of the doctor, became inhabited by male physicians directing the course of action.[51]

From the mid-1800s through the turn of the century, notable leading physicians worked to legitimize medical care for delivery and supported their case by making lofty claims about the role of their profession. Charles Meigs, a prominent American obstetrician, exemplified this rhetoric when he declaimed in his introductory lecture at the Jefferson Medical College on October 9, 1854, that "there can be none more ennobling, none more elevating to the soul than the sciences we pursue in order to obtain the knowledge of those principles, out of which we deduce our power to act as physicians and surgeons among mankind."[52] Obstetrics worked to elevate the status of the physician; the specialty wore the mantle of a virtuous pursuit, noble in its sacrifice to help humanity escape the unpredictability of the female body. Medicine's growing cultural cachet helped to make restructuring the act of birth acceptable to mothers and the general public in the United States.[53]

Making the Case for Medicine

After making the male doctor the central player in the act of birth, organized medicine turned its attention to the competition. Even as the profession made great efforts to enhance the training and licensing of general practice physicians and obstetricians, doctors faced lingering resistance. Midwives provided lower-cost care with comparable (and often better) results, and many women remained loyal to their midwives, hiring them to supervise subsequent births. The practice of general physicians in the late 1800s and early 1900s consisted of treating recurrent ailments like digestive troubles and joint pain, as well as providing crisis care for traumatic injury. In the northern plains military doctors were commonly called upon to treat gunshot wounds and infections, while their general practice counterparts dealt with the burns and maimed limbs resulting from mining explosions and cave-ins. Doctors stitched up the soft tissue tears and performed the amputations related to railroad and agricultural work. Physicians also attempted to contain infectious disease and treated victims of epidemics, from influenza to tuberculosis.[54]

In the late 1800s physicians searched for ways to broaden and cement a business model that suffered from inconsistent demand. As the medical industry "actively look[ed] for arenas of expansion," health-care services typically provided by women, such as delivering babies, became prime targets for professional annexation.[55] Doctors across the country realized that adding routine services to their business mix would diversify their income and perhaps smooth out the vagaries of medical practice.[56] Birth provided just such an opportunity, and physicians struggled to gain access to a recurring source of non-disaster-related calls. The birth rate in 1905 stood at 3.8, meaning that on average a woman of reproductive age would experience about four pregnancies, or more with miscarriages—meaning there would be enough work to conveniently supplement the income from more traditional types of medical care.[57]

The Midwife Problem

With an eye to gaining birthing business, the profession of medicine encountered a challenge, which was referred to as the "midwife problem."[58] Many doctors were unable to match the quality of care provided by midwives and equally unwilling to reduce their fees to the level of midwives' more affordable rates. Instead of encouraging an organizational shift to adapt the practice of medicine to compete with midwives on the basis of substance, some members of the profession strategized about how to reduce competition by abolishing the practice of midwifery entirely.[59] Obstetrician Joseph DeLee framed the issue as one of keeping medicine as the private domain of physicians instead of allowing it to become a public service. He explained that if American midwives received the kinds of public support many of their European counterparts took for granted, they would "come under public supervision, often as a salaried employee in a public clinic" and the "survival" of midwifery would "necessarily strengthen the public sector of medicine." Governmental support for midwifery would, DeLee continued, invalidate medicine's claim that reproductive care required the specialized skills and higher fees of physicians. The ability of "an uneducated woman of the lowest classes" to competently manage deliveries would thus discount the marketing of organized medicine.[60]

Midwifery thus stood in the way of medicine's potential expansion and profitability, so the American Medical Association instigated organized and widespread attacks on midwifery. Social historian and demographer Irvine Loudon has described the "savagery" of organized medicine's assault and noted the stunning contrast between American attempts to abolish midwifery and the "European plan of educating [midwives] and regulating [their] practice." He noted that medical malevolence toward American midwives resulted from "crude self-interest in the competitive world of American medical practice" and explained that obstetrics required an elite classification for specialty status. Thus, the destruction of midwifery formed "an essential part" of medical tactics.[61]

Acting on this strategy, the medical profession orchestrated a public relations battle and drew a clear line between doctors and midwives. Doctors attacked midwives for their lack of knowledge and their adherence to out-of-date, old-country traditions.[62] In 1917 Philadelphia physician William Nicholson gave voice to common antimidwife themes, describing immigrants as "ignorant in every sense of the word . . . do not speak English . . . have but little money . . . are prolific breeders, and . . . come here with definite and fixed ideas in favor of the midwife rather than the doctor."[63] Medical journals regularly included statements like the 1926 pronouncement by a Mississippi bureaucrat characterizing midwives as "filthy," "ignorant," and "not far removed from the jungles of Africa."[64] While common in publications across the United States, these sorts of broadsides also showed up in the northern plains press. As early as 1911 the Harlem, Montana, newspaper offered details about the "meeting of the American Association for the Prevention of Infant Mortality," which "ended in an attack on midwifery" and a "resolution that midwives should be abolished."[65]

As migrants working within their own particular ethnic working-class communities—like Anna Hamalainen's Finnish clientele in Red Lodge, Montana—midwives were vulnerable to these racist and classist tirades.[66] Organized medicine painted midwifery as the choice of crude illiterates in contrast to educated physicians, who were portrayed as cultured and cosmopolitan birth practitioners.

Those who wished to assimilate into American culture saw that, in the United States, American physicians delivered American babies in American hospitals. Thus, the choice to employ a physician became a badge of civic pride.

The combination of racial, gendered, and classist themes provided a powerful propaganda tool in a country with residents anxious to belong, and the option to choose a conclusively American birth proved irresistible. Even as immigrant midwives assimilated and a generation of American-born women entered the ranks of midwifery, the familiar tropes continued to prove powerful. They were so powerful, in fact, that those same ideas were proudly on display—and virtually unchanged a century later—as new and innovative findings in the lecture I attended on the campus of an acclaimed research university.

Obstetrics in the Northern Plains

For mothers delivering in the context of the Rocky Mountains and northern plains, the assumptions of medical doctors probably felt far removed from their experience. However, the historical and theoretical underpinnings of both midwifery and medicine created a particular experience for mothers, even if they had no knowledge of medicine's attacks on midwives.

Settlers in Wyoming, the Dakotas, and Montana certainly encountered licensed physicians who began practicing without ever having overseen a delivery. Given that mothers preferred midwifery care through the turn of the twentieth century, many doctors had little experience with childbirth, and they lacked the time to become highly informed about it while so many other critical cases demanded their attention. Lucy Russell, in labor with her first child in 1905, was able to find a doctor—"a very poor one," she recalled, who "let his beard grow to make him[self] look older." Russell concluded that her birth "was his first delivery."[67] It would have been a relatively common occurrence for the delivering woman to have had far more exposure to birth, through her own previous deliveries and by watching and helping with the deliveries of friends and family, than the doctor called to supervise her labor. Even experienced physicians new to the area lacked familiarity with regional conditions and the particular stressors on pregnant women in the northern plains and Rocky Mountains.

Because childbirth could be most effectively managed by a combination of fact-based learning and abundant hands-on experience, trained midwives like Red Lodge's Hamalainen, especially later in life after she had experienced her own pregnancy, were best prepared to attend women in delivery. Midwives who lacked formal training but still had practical experience were able to provide care that, while somewhat less than optimal, still allowed for safe and supported births. Physicians, with enough book learning to be dangerous but little experiential sense for the process, could easily do more harm than good. By imposing a mechanistic practice, northern plains doctors reduced the potential for a reciprocal relationship and made it difficult for the mother and physician to work together toward a common goal—the element that formed the core of healthy childbirth.[68]

Physicians' lack of respect for women and their reproductive processes extended even into ideas about cleanliness. Delivery was a physiologically intense process accompanied by sweat, blood, mucus, and even urine and feces. The typical untidy-ness of childbirth seems unnatural to us now only because we vacated the birthing room and lost touch with the sounds, smells, and general disarray of reproduction. Childbirth is not and has never been sterile. Humans, and other mammals as well, enter the world accompanied by a great deal of effluence and noise. Some laboring mothers yell, swear, and even call down pestilence and painful castration on every penis-bearing human within a five-mile radius. Midwives did not fear the mess common to birth, which, based on our current knowledge of the shared mother-infant immunity, did not pose a high risk to the newborn.[69] However, midwives saw outside contamination—germs foreign to the mother's system, particularly those from outside the home—as dangerous and requiring that protective measures be taken.[70]

The midwifery perspective of evaluating bacterial dangers from an empathetic perspective meant that women offering reproductive care prioritized sanitation. Children's Bureau staff recorded that "nearly all the women [who assisted with births in the northern plains] realized the need, if not of complete asepsis, at least of cleanliness in caring for their patients. Antiseptics such as boric acid, carbolic acid, Lysol, and mercury bichloride were reported. One woman had persuaded a small country store to stock bichloride tablets. Nearly all used scorched linen and boric acid on the umbilical cord and a boric acid solution to wash the baby's eyes."[71]

Loretta Thompson, sent to assist in a delivery at the age of seventeen, received clear training in cleanliness from her mother. Prior to her hasty departure to the birth, Thompson listened attentively while her mother "told [her] all the procedures" and explained exactly how to superintend the process. Thompson's mother mandated sanitation, saying that "everything had to be clean" and the rags had to be sterilized "in the oven."[72] The wealth of experience evidenced by midwives, especially the care taken in being rigorously clean, allowed laboring women and their children to recover from childbirth without the additional challenges of bacterial infection.

Puerperal Fever

In the mid-1800s two doctors, Ignaz Semmelweis in Europe and Oliver Wendell Holmes Sr. in the United States, independently came to the same conclusion: examining physicians in hospitals were transmitting childbed fever via their hands from the birth canal of one woman to the next. Physicians did not routinely sanitize their tools or wash their hands before a delivery, and as a result they exposed laboring women to bacteria from other women by going from patient to patient (and sometimes deceased patient to laboring mother) without properly cleaning their hands in between examinations.[73]

Puerperal fever afflicted women in the maternity wards of hospitals in unprecedented fashion, causing as many as 75 percent of maternal deaths. Obstetric patients would often seem to be recovering from delivery, only to take a sudden turn and die from infection. When studies showed that aseptic procedures prevented puerperal fever, the profession of medicine resisted the idea that the unwashed hands of doctors could spread death. The mind-set of the medical profession denied physician culpability, refusing to acknowledge that doctors infected their patients.[74] The efforts at cleanliness that doctors did employ, like emptying the bladder and bowels, focused on the comfort of the doctor rather than the mother and dismissed the physician's role as potential disease carrier.[75]

For women attended by a midwife at home, the odds of contracting puerperal infection were significantly reduced. Midwives, according to early nineteenth-century health workers, "realize[d] their limitations, and [did] not attempt to interfere with the natural course of delivery."[76] With their predisposition to nonintervention, midwives generally did not probe the uterus to break the amniotic sac or insert forceps into the vagina, thereby minimizing the chances of transmitting any infectious agents their hands or tools might be carrying. Additionally, midwives performed a variety of tasks, including food preparation and laundry, both of which involved contact with water and hand washing. Because midwives spent time with one client at a time, they were more likely to wash their hands, change their clothes, and bathe in between caring for pregnant or newly delivered mothers.

By the 1910s and 1920s regional health departments had begun highlighting epidemic numbers of maternal deaths. A 1925 Montana State Board of Health report dedicated a section to the problem of puerperal fever and its dramatic increase, especially as women in the state responded to medicine's mandate to deliver in the hospital at the hands of doctors. Such conditions made an already common health tragedy all the more widespread, as the Montana Health Department's data revealed. In 1921 ninety-two women in Montana died of causes related to delivery. Fifty of those mothers, more than half, perished from infection contracted immediately after childbirth.[77]

Puerperal fever, common into the 1930s and 1940s, continued to kill needlessly until the widespread use of penicillin and other antibiotics finally reduced its effects.[78] Despite the efforts of many health professionals to encourage simple hand washing to prevent infection, only the availability of pharmacological treatments like antibiotics lessened the impact of childbed fever. Over a period of nearly a century organized medicine disregarded the loss of life that resulted from puerperal infection.[79] This vanity led to widespread death of new mothers across America, including Montana, the Dakotas, and Wyoming. For the forty-eight Montana women who died of puerperal septicemia in 1925, their physicians' choice to forgo the basic cleanliness that Loretta Thompson, at the age of seventeen, managed to achieve, remains an outrageous act of collective negligence.

Childbirth and Social Class

The great irony of medicine's intrusion into the birthing room and the subsequent move of childbirth to the hospital ward was that upper-class women willing and able to pay physician fees found themselves more susceptible to the dangers associated with physician-directed birth and the specialty of obstetrics.[80] Judith Walzer Leavitt, historian of women's health, has documented how, through the 1910s and 1920s, women with the financial means to hire a physician increasingly chose to do so, while "poorer and migrant" mothers turned to midwives, who "seldom administered drugs" and followed a less interventionist approach.[81]

Social commentators of the era noted these differences. Physician Henry Smith Williams, writing in 1914, argued for the virtues of reducing or eliminating the pain of childbirth. He claimed that pain in birth for "civilized" women represented an evolutionary error because it caused white upper-class women to avoid numerous pregnancies and thus reduced the birth rate of the "optimal" citizens who should be reproducing. He promoted the use of an experimental cocktail of drugs administered during labor to alter the pain of delivery. Williams posited that women might willingly endure repeated pregnancies if they could escape the sensations of delivery. The use of drugs would result, according to his thinking, in an increased birth rate among white women of means. He explained that an upperclass woman "not unnaturally shrinks from the dangers and pains incident to child-bearing; yet such cultured women are precisely the individuals who should propagate the species and thus promote the interests of the race."[82] Turn-of-the-twentieth-century birth practices were inextricably connected by a web of racial and gender concerns, which both physicians and mothers reacted to in advocating for or requesting particular birth interventions.

The use of anesthetics presented complex issues for women in the Dakotas, Wyoming, and Montana in the early 1900s. One of the new technologies offered by physicians and requested by upper-class women was called "twilight sleep." To perform the procedure, which was usually done in the hospital, a physician dosed the mother with scopolamine, a drug that induced amnesia, before the pushing stage of labor. Under the influence of scopolamine, women thrashed about and screamed, so nurses secured them to the delivery tables with tethers. During delivery, women felt the pain of childbirth, but after metabolizing the drug from their systems they could not recall the experience.[83] Even with its likely regional scarcity, the procedure did represent the extensive reach of medicine's foray into birth by allowing for a consummately male delivery and triumph over the frustrations of the female form, along with a subsequent erasure of any memory of the mother's participation in childbirth.

For novice physicians attending medical school in turn-of-the-twentieth-century America, official instruction portrayed female reproduction as an illness to be treated, with pregnancy, childbirth, and menstruation receiving the attention given to diseases. Individual doctors practicing across the northern plains undoubtedly desired to provide pregnant women with the best care possible, but the overall tone of the profession framed these doctor-mother inter-actions. From the perspective of male medicine, childbirth was an anomaly, a strange and fearful happening that required treatment and intervention.[84]

In contrast, midwives' and mothers' shared femaleness brought, if not celebration of the female body and reproduction, at least accep-tance of it. Midwives treated pregnancy and childbirth as normal, routine events. Having a baby was not something to be ashamed of but to be accepted as part of the experience of womanhood. Since midwives almost always had children of their own, they came to the task of treating childbirth as the mother's comrade, as someone who had navigated the routines of pregnancy, labor pains, and breast-feeding herself. Midwives shared the cultural weight of femaleness with the women they cared for, and their presence as women helping other women through a typically female experience offered some element of normalcy to childbirth and the postpartum period.

A More Accurate History

Before I began my deep dive into the history of midwifery, I assumed that physicians provided verifiably superior service, with results supported by scientific research. Data for all turn-of-the-twentieth-century maternal births and deaths by type of provider do not exist, thus preventing a full assessment of the relative success of mid-wifery delivery versus physician-assisted birth, but indicators point to comparable if not better birthing safety at the hands of midwives.[85]

According to historian Joan Jensen, "Midwifery in rural areas did not seem to be a cause [of high maternal and infant mortality]. In fact, some of the lowest infant mortality rates existed in counties with the highest numbers of midwives."[86] Reproductive historian Mary Melcher, after a thorough review of contraception and child-birth in the American West, concludes that, "despite their paucity of professional education, American midwives had lower [maternal and infant] mortality rates in the early twentieth century than general practitioners because they had more practical experience and did not use interventionist methods which often caused problems for physicians."[87] Turn-of-the-twentieth-century midwives regularly delivered breech babies vaginally, as well as twins and triplets—conditions that present-day physicians treat with far more invasive and expensive procedures, such as caesarean sections. Comparisons of midwives' and physicians' maternal death rates indicate that midwifery delivery was just as safe, if not safer, than birth at the hands of a physician. Additionally, the long-term and collaborative working relationships physicians established with midwives—like Mary Kassmeier in Fort Benton—would suggest that birth attended by a midwife met and possibly surpassed the results that physicians thought they could achieve. Finally, women's preference for midwifery care, often over the course of multiple pregnancies, attests to the quality of care they experienced at the hands of their local attendant.[88]

It would be naïve to think that all midwives in the region spent their lives delivering premium service of the highest order. There were undoubtedly women who offered better, cleaner, and more informed birthing assistance than others. But there exists no evidence to support the claim made by the medical profession and advanced during the drive to increase the status of medicine in the 1910s that midwives harmed their clients or caused infant death. Quite to the contrary, midwives furnished a relatively high level of care to the pregnant women they served.

Attempts to pit midwifery care against hospital-based physician-provided assistance, both in the past and present, have exacerbated issues of essentialism. Women were told and certainly participated in spreading the idea that there was *one* right way for a mother to deliver. This reduced women to their reproductive capability and prescribed one simple treatment for all humans with uteri. Medicine gave women a choice: give up control over the birthing space and the female body in exchange for a medical seal of approval and social status or deliver at home with midwives, who, if the medical rhetoric of the time was to be believed, endangered mothers and their infants. This bifurcation, the disallowance of mothers as active

Fig. 18. Fort Benton, Montana, midwife Mary Kassmeier delivered these twin babies, Elsie and Ellis Chaney, in 1921. 2011-FK-044, Mary Kassmeier Album, Overholser Historical Research Center, Fort Benton, Montana.

participants and acknowledged experts in the birthing process, had longer-lasting implications than the medical move to gain market share at the expense of client safety. In attempting to remove midwives from delivery, organized medicine succeeded in removing mothers from the birth process, a result that still impacts legions of women in America.[89]

Outcomes of the Birth Battle

As we look at turn-of-the-twentieth-century northern plains reproductive providers, a schematic emerges, with a range of qualities beneficial to birthing mothers, such as birthing expertise and intimacy, as specific categories. Midwives collectively claimed the highest level of experience and knowledge of the birth process, followed by nurses and then doctors. The negotiated authority of midwifery practices made high levels of intimacy possible. Delivery with a male doctor offered few opportunities for establishing a reciprocal relationship of care and compassion. Some individual doctors undoubtedly considered the needs of delivering mothers, but they would have been behaving in an intentionally contrarian manner relative to the precepts of their profession.

Midwives were not nurses and not doctors. They were women who acted on the assumption that delivering mothers needed other women to offer specific guidance during labor, as well as to prepare a meal, do laundry, and hold the baby. For reproducing women, these services were essential. In the history of American culture they were often ignored and rarely recorded, but the unseen process of midwifery had real, tangible components that constructed the social fabric of the northern plains and Rocky Mountains. The routine of pregnant women in the region often included tending to the demands of life, from crying young children to dirty dishes to a legion of hungry farm animals. Midwives allowed the delivering mother to do just that—deliver—by taking on her responsibilities. For a woman whose family and livestock depended on her for constant tending, for provision of food and water, and for the emotional sustenance of caring, knowing that those needs were being met allowed her to devote her attention to moving an infant from the internal uterine world to an external reality. Midwives served as interlocutors and allowed mothers to tend to the internal mechanics of birth. As women themselves, midwives could be trusted to empathically understand and respond to the process, emotions, and demands of delivery.[90]

Unfortunately, the very qualities that made the services of midwives so desirable—their practice of sharing authority, establishing intimacy, and working within a relational context—also rendered them particularly vulnerable to the attacks of organized medicine. If reproductive care in the northern plains had followed a logical progression, midwives would have been called upon to train nurses and physicians in the processes of normal birth and the protection of mothers' authority and control, leading to dramatically improved success rates and quality of care. Instead, the stakeholders least incentivized to concern themselves with women's well-being— government entities and the profession of medicine—collaborated to bar the most experienced providers from the field. Ironically, as the practices surrounding childbirth developed, the doctor, the least beneficial childbirth attendant, was enshrined within the bureaucratic public health system as the provider of choice.

5

Death in the West

The female-centric reproductive networks of the northern plains and Rocky Mountains relied on transformative methods—like sharing authority, establishing collaborative intimacy, and respecting relational context—that shaped the American West. Sadly, the very same settler West in which women had so heavily invested in establishing subsequently disregarded their expertise. As public health efforts expanded in the region, the critical cultural elements of care and connection so essential for the health of families, communities, and nations were undermined by institutional structures that valued male physicians over female reproductive professionals. This loss impacted both longer-term residents and those more recently arrived, including new immigrants like the Kummer family.

Elisabeth Kummer gave birth to Bertha Lina Kummer in Limpach, Switzerland, on November 11, 1879. Bertha joined an older sibling, Elise, and over the next eleven years their mother delivered ten more babies, including one set of twins. With a reproductive pattern similar to that of Lucy Tinsley (chapter 1), Elisabeth spent more than a decade engaged in continual childbearing. Tragically—and unlike Tinsley—four of her children died in infancy: one daughter lived only nineteen days, another son survived just sixteen days, and twins born in mid-December 1888 had both perished by the end of January 1889.[1]

In 1902 daughter Bertha and her sister Elise, both in their twenties, left Switzerland and immigrated to the United States. In 1903 the remaining eight members of the Kummer family, from twelve-year-old Johanna to twenty-two-year-old Ernest, including mother Elisabeth and father Albert, traveled by ship to Boston. They eventually settled in Logan, Utah, where they adapted to their new American home.[2]

At the age of twenty-eight Bertha married John George Emmert, who went by his middle name. Also an immigrant, George came from Bavaria and worked as a brewer. After their marriage Bertha became pregnant with Margaret, and Erma, a second daughter, soon followed. In search of suitable work for George, they moved first to Washington and then to Montana, where George took a position as a brewer at the Dixon Brewery near Townsend. The job offered on-site housing for the family, a welcome benefit, as Bertha was pregnant with the couple's third child.[3]

Young Margaret, then three, often visited her father at his workplace. One December day when she was at the brewery, George climbed into a large cask to perform some routine maintenance. Suddenly, the alcohol lamp he carried ignited inside the barrel, engulfing George in flames. Fortunately, a coworker pulled George to safety, but all three—George, Margaret, and the coworker—suffered burns.[4]

Bertha, nearing the end of her third pregnancy and deeply concerned for both her husband and daughter, tended to George's and Margaret's immediate needs. Inconceivably, an unrelated fire broke out within the hour at the Emmert home. In the midst of the chaos of the brewery blaze, all available hands worked to put both fires out. They salvaged most of the furniture and contents from the house, but the fire demolished the structure.[5]

After the two fires, the four members of the Emmert family, all alive but understandably traumatized, moved to the nearby community of Townsend. Bertha, dealing with the loss of belongings in the

Fig. 19. Bertha Lina Kummer and John George Emmert married on July 3, 1907. Courtesy of the Kummer/Melton family.

fire, the stress of her husband's and oldest daughter's injuries, and the demands of her youngest child (about eighteen months old at the time), also faced the arrival of a newborn. Just about ten days after the fire, Bertha felt the unmistakable pain of contractions. Willing herself to persevere through labor, she delivered her infant, a baby girl, alive and breathing.[6] The birth of this third daughter offered a hopeful moment in the midst of a difficult time, and Margaret and Erma were no doubt excited about their new sister.

After giving birth to two previous children, caring for her daughter and husband after the fire, moving the family belongings to another house, and settling everyone, Bertha's reproductive system still functioned as intended. Her intense effort resulted in a new baby and a moment of happiness for this young family. Tragically, just a few days after the delivery, Bertha contracted a bacterial infection—puerperal septicemia, the all too common childbed fever—and died on December 11, 1911. Her newborn daughter passed away just two weeks later.[7]

George Emmert, now the sole caregiver for two young children, needed to make funeral arrangements for his deceased wife. He decided to return Bertha's body to her family in Utah for burial but had no support system or local extended family to care for Margaret, aged three, and Erma, still a toddler. Making what must have been a wrenching decision, he took both girls to Helena, about thirty-five miles away, and admitted them to the St. Joseph's Home for Orphans on December 21, 1911.[8] In the span of just a few weeks, the girls saw their home go up in flames, lost their mother and newborn sister, and said what likely seemed a permanent good-bye to their father.

It is hard to imagine what overwhelming grief and terror the girls must have felt that first night at the orphanage, especially since the staff separated Margaret and Erma from each other, a typical policy for institutions that operated according to a rigid age-based system.[9] The girls, stripped of siblings, parents, and home and only able to glimpse each other across the grounds during outdoor play times, lived in the same building but could not see each other or share their grief. The experience undoubtedly left a permanent mark on their childhoods and their lives.

Happily, three months later, in March 1912, George Emmert returned to claim the girls, and the orphanage staff noted in their records that Margaret and Erma were "released to father." The girls' aunt and Bertha's older sister, Elise, came to stay with the family and care for the children. She and George married, and Elise's presence no doubt comforted Margaret and Erma during the intense upheaval and loss their mother's death brought to their young lives.[10]

Bertha Emmert's death impacted many: her siblings lost a caring sister, her parents mourned a daughter, her husband floundered without her presence, and her young children undoubtedly felt lost and bereft. Bertha's death also impacted the larger community, from the sadness of George's coworkers at the brewery to Dr. Gilham, who signed her death certificate. Those who knew Margaret and Erma grieved for the young children. As friends, neighbors, family, and community mourned Bertha's death, her loss became far more than a personal event. She died as Bertha Lina Emmert, mother to Margaret and Erma and wife to George, but also as one death among many young mothers who perished in an area promoted as the embodiment of the American dream.

With far-reaching ripple effects, the deaths of mothers like Bertha created a seismic public health event and left husbands without partners and children without loving care. The absence of state-sponsored services—like access to contraception and basic health care—and women's essential role in providing the infrastructure of care in newly formed communities meant that the death of each mother left a critical gap that no one else could fill. While most mothers of Bertha's era delivered without mishap, far too many women, as well as their newborn infants, died of preventable conditions in the northern plains and Rocky Mountains in the early 1900s.[11]

Euro-American migrants entered a space in which they were ill suited to successfully reproduce but failed to understand or respect the value and wisdom of traditional Native practices.[12] Emmert or

Fig. 20. Given what the two young Emmert girls experienced, it is heartwarming to see in this image the visible signs of affection between Elise (Bertha Emmert's older sister [seated], who took over the role of mother) and Erma Emmert, who was about eighteen months old when Bertha died. Courtesy of the Kummer/Melton family.

those around her could have sought help and instruction from knowledgeable Native midwives confined to a reservation not far from Townsend. Instead, settlers often characterized Native labor and delivery practices as simplistic, painless "non-event[s]."[13] These dismissive assumptions meant that valuable reproductive information, mastered by Native attendants and specific to the region, was not shared or passed down to new settlers.

The Dakotas, Wyoming, and Montana claimed a surprisingly high number of maternal deaths as compared to their eastern counterparts.[14] In addition to revealing higher regional death rates than other parts of the country, evidence indicated that rural women in these western states dealt with particularly long odds. Comparative state-by-state, rural-versus-urban records have not been preserved, but a retrospective Wyoming report detailed infant mortality rates for 1930. The data showed that for every thousand infants, fifty-five deaths occurred among urban infants compared to seventy in rural areas. Montana's rate was listed as fifty-two per thousand urban deaths and sixty-one per thousand rural deaths, with North Dakota at fifty-five per thousand for its urban population and sixty-three per thousand for rural residents. These numbers substantiated the concern that regional rural mortality rates consistently exceeded urban rates of death.[15]

Such data raised the question of causation. What was it about this region that brought about a reproductive crisis? Were there larger forces at work, or was this simply the result of individual women making poor choices or falling victim to a personal and private catastrophe? With the prevalence of female-centric care, why was the death toll higher—not lower—in the area?

By the mid-1800s women could purchase relatively effective contraceptive devices like condoms and diaphragms from mail-order catalogs.[16] Prophylactics would have been of great service to migrant mothers settling in areas where unsupported pregnancies (birth without the necessary structures like extended family and health care) were the norm by making it possible for them to time their pregnancies to when they could depend on a more extensive network of care. Unfortunately, the federal government passed the Comstock Act in 1873, which made the production, advertisement, and sale of any and all contraceptive or abortifacient devices illegal.[17] While some women, especially those in urban areas or from families that openly supported contraception, could still access tools to reduce fertility, rural women often obtained supplies via mail, which made securing devices or pharmaceutical preparations more difficult. Many mothers had no recourse except to endure repeated pregnancies.[18] After watching four of her young siblings die in infancy, Bertha Kummer Emmert quite possibly would have chosen to align her pregnancies with times when she resided near family, could physically sustain the burden of gestation, and was able to call upon a connected community of caregivers. Given the frequency of her pregnancies (she delivered her third baby about eighteen months after her second), it is likely that Bertha did not have access to any effective contraceptive devices.

Because the government restricted contraceptive information, Bertha faced a future of continual reproduction. If she made any attempt to prevent pregnancy, she did so in opposition to the official stance of the federal government. Pregnant with her third child and residing in Montana, she was following the guidance of those who claimed the authority to set policy and direct state and national aims. Unfortunately, those purposes did not adequately consider Bertha's happiness or health.

Western states, in collaboration with business and railroad interests, promoted settlement in the region, even though no official health-care infrastructure existed to provide a replacement for the female network of supportive care required for successful reproduction. According to Mary Hargreaves's masterful analysis of the region's history, dry farming was knowingly leveraged as an "organized effort to attract settlers into the region."[19] Governments assembled and disseminated their conclusions about potential settlement but quickly moved beyond their appropriate role as sources of data-based information to "blatant promotionalism."[20] Cooperation

between boosters and state agencies resulted in groundless publicity that enticed homesteaders and migrants to colonize and control
the northern plains and Rocky Mountain region for the benefit of
bureaucratic and institutionalized power.[21] This promotionalism dis-
counted the needs of settlers and newcomers in general and women
in particular. As federal and state governments worked to increase
settlement, they justified their actions as benefiting the public in the
belief that this regional development "served the general good—in
terms of the States' desire for increased wealth and the National
requirement for expanded production."[22]

Thus, the structure of western migrant settlement created a dangerous confluence of conditions for maternal and infant mortality.[23]
The government offered land and opportunity without planning for
the known needs of the women, men, and families who would, based
on grandiose and overblown state-sponsored promotion, relocate
to a region far different than anything they expected. Governments
had everything to gain in terms of workers and support staff to
enable economic growth, including the physical presence of Euro-
Americans to permanently occupy lands claimed by Native peoples.
Bertha Emmert and other mothers like her had everything to lose.

Conditions of Everyday Life

On a daily basis turn-of-the-twentieth-century mothers in Wyoming,
the Dakotas, and Montana performed strenuous, repetitive physical
tasks that, when conducted in an environment of geographic isolation, posed a strain to physiological systems already committed
to the high-calorie needs of childbearing. Women without indoor
plumbing hauled water by hand for cooking, washing dishes, drink-
ing (both for humans and animals), doing laundry, and watering the
garden. Even women in advanced pregnancy bucketed water multiple times throughout each day. Mothers also sewed clothes for the
family; cleaned the house and outbuildings; took care of livestock;
dug, planted, weeded, and harvested the garden; and then canned
or otherwise preserved surplus for the winter.[24]

A wide variety of materials could be ordered and delivered by rail, although in many cases the costs of getting to and from the nearest railroad stop added to the price of the goods and thus made these items too expensive for purchase.[25] Families also bought canned goods but usually reserved such treats for special occasions because of the price.[26] For example, two cans of tomatoes could be purchased for the same price as a pound of butter, and while the tomatoes provided important vitamins and nutrients, they fell far short of other similarly priced items in terms of caloric return.[27]

With few prepared foods available and hungry families to feed, mothers planned far in advance for meals and supplies. To prepare a chicken dinner, a woman hatched out chicks in the spring, guarded them from predators, and, when they finally reached full size, selected her victim. She then butchered, plucked, gutted, and cooked the bird at the conclusion of six months of work. Women also baked bread, milked cows, separated cream from milk, and churned butter. Most everything that families ate required at least six months of preparatory tending and thought. The basic act of keeping everyone fed involved an intensive cyclical process that demanded constant attention to detail.[28]

Residents of the Dakotas, Wyoming, and Montana also dealt with temperature extremes, especially in drought years. A typical winter might see the temperature drop to −20 degrees Fahrenheit, with summer heat blazing in excess of 100 degrees. High winds exacerbated the physical discomfort of such intense cold and heat, particularly for new residents in small dwellings with minimal protection. The threat of snow, blizzards, hail, tornadoes, wind, and rain placed an additional strain on women throughout all stages of their pregnancies and after delivery, as they performed tasks both indoors and outside in all weather conditions.[29]

Some women who engaged in this epic physical struggle saw friends and neighbors often—Lizzie Maclean and her whirlwind social schedule come to mind—and thus commiserated with and supported each other. Others, like Faye Hoven, who lived in a rural community thirty-five miles from Hobson, Montana, spent far more time alone. With a team and wagon as her only means of transportation, she did not often visit her nearest neighbors, who lived seven miles away. It is quite possible that she went for days with only her husband and children for company.[30] In a time when other women offered the sole source of reproductive information, Hoven and other isolated women were cut off from support and treatment for extended periods. Simple complaints, like bladder infections, vaginal tears, or chronic mastitis, when left untreated, became far more pressing and dangerous issues.

Many residents of the northern plains dealt with food scarcity as well. In 1915 average wheat yields in Montana stood in excess of twenty-six bushels per acre, but by 1919 some areas in the state were reporting harvest rates of fewer than three bushels an acre.[31] Such a dramatic drop in productivity meant that money was tight and some families—and certainly some pregnant women—rationed what little food and money they had.

A host of concomitant factors, including intense physical exertion, the absence of contraception, social isolation, limited food supplies, vitamin and nutrient deficiencies, financial limitations, irregular or nonexistent reproductive care, inadequate housing, unpleasant and even dangerous weather, frequent relocation, absence of family and community support, and a general sense of fear and instability created an environment in which mothers experienced one or more circumstances that jeopardized their health and their pregnancies.

While few women endured all of these threats simultaneously, most mothers in the northern plains and Rocky Mountains navigated their own unique constellation of these reproductive challenges. A relatively well-to-do woman like Laurentza Koch of Bozeman, Montana, did not worry as much about financial resources but still struggled to find care and desperately missed the presence of extended female kin networks.[32] The development and delivery of a healthy baby depended on a host of sequential factors, so women in the area, even those with ample financial resources, faced an elevated risk of mortality because of the combination of factors that often occurred simultaneously for those residing in the area.

A consistent lack of physical, psychological, and emotional support marked regional reproduction; examples include the inability to purchase varied foods like fresh fruits and vegetables that might offer necessary nutrients and vitamins, a shortage of funds needed to seek medical attention for chronic health issues, and the absence of social support networks that even excessive wealth could not purchase. Regular, low-level deprivation caused some mothers residing in the northern plains and Rocky Mountains to suffer from additional stress, impaired physical reserves, and eventual birth-related complications.[33] If scrubbing the house with water carried from the well, hauling wood or coal, lack of sleep, discomfort from inadequate living quarters, feeding and butchering animals, gardening, milking, dairy processing, and limited dietary variety did not deplete and drain a pregnant woman, distance from family, limited contact with friends, repeated relocations, monotony of tasks, and fear about the future probably did. What is startling is not the high numbers of women and infants who died in the northern plains and Rocky Mountains but rather the many mothers who found a way to perform all of the required tasks while maintaining the necessary reserves for a healthy infant and postpartum recovery.[34] The high death rates reported by the Montana Department of Health for 1911, the year of Bertha Emmert's death, occurred because western women died from a lack of basic care.[35]

Wyoming, Montana, and the Dakotas did not contain a strange airborne disease or a chronic condition brought on by overexposure to vast amount of sky. Instead, the specific causes of death for most of the birth-related fatalities represent a combination of related factors. Women, especially rural mothers in the northern plains and Rocky Mountains, faced unfortunate and somewhat unusual birthing odds, not because of one unique factor but as a result of the overlapping effects of isolation, physical and emotional stress, and absence of support. While any one of these conditions might have existed for other women—and in fact did exist for many women at this time—this combination of factors posed especially challenging circumstances.

Settling in rural Montana, Wyoming, or the Dakotas meant existing independently, without the necessary benefits of communal effort and empathetic care. These benefits resulting from the social safety net are difficult to measure in their presence but notable in death counts when absent. As Mary Hargreaves has explained, the "margin between success and failure," especially for families living in agricultural areas with low rainfall, was "very narrow."[36] With physical and emotional well-being inextricably linked, women's life satisfaction— their feelings of happiness and security—actually mattered to the health of their families. For mothers who could not, according to historian Nanci Langford, "abandon even temporarily [their] responsibilities," pregnancy, delivery, and nursing left area women "vulnerable and powerless."[37] Given the realities of women's lives, it is unsurprising, especially in hindsight, that the region experienced high mortality rates.[38]

Public Health Response

Maternal and infant death rates at the turn of the twentieth century presented enough of a concern to justify the creation of public health institutions, but epidemic disease posed a much more visible threat at the time. Smallpox in particular made its presence known with repeated outbreaks in Montana, leading the Montana legislature, just over a decade into its existence, to create the Montana State Board of Health in 1901.[39] The quartet of western states—Wyoming, North Dakota, South Dakota, and Montana—entered the union at nearly the same time: Montana and the Dakotas in 1889 and Wyoming in 1890.[40] Within a decade they each began establishing state infrastructure and delineating public health responsibilities, either through the creation of new public health entities (like Montana's State Board of Health) or by transitioning infrastructure already in place from territorial governments. North Dakota retained the structure of its

Territorial Board of Health upon statehood, and by 1893 the state legislature had tasked it with collecting vital statistics.[41] Similarly, Wyoming Territory established county health services in 1876, maintained the existing bureaucracy upon statehood, and reconstituted the department as the Wyoming State Board of Health in 1901.[42]

These health departments proved essential as the regional population expanded and residents and visitors moved to and through the region. By 1900 the area surrounding Butte, Montana, the largest metropolitan settlement in the region, had reached a population of forty-eight thousand. According to public health officer and historian Ellen Leahy, this increased settlement brought "all the conditions that spawned epidemics in eastern industrialized cities: sewage, crowding, and pollution."[43] Additionally, the relative ease and speed of railroad travel meant that swift transport of goods, people, and their diseases joined northern plains and Rocky Mountain states to the rest of the country.[44] The Dakotas, Wyoming, and Montana shared an individualistic, "self-made man" ethos, but residents were very much connected to the rest of the country and its bacteria, infectious diseases, and easily transmitted contagions. Western residents, still in the process of shaping their nascent state identities, encountered the competing demands of local government, state and federal control, and issues of public good and shared well-being.[45]

Educating both the general public and each state's legislative body about the need for public health services required a span of years, and over time health departments methodically gained the tools necessary to quantitatively assess the health conditions prevalent within state jurisdictions. In 1902, more than ten years after gaining statehood, the South Dakota Board of Health pleaded with the state legislature to pass necessary rules to secure and enforce reporting of births, deaths, and contagious diseases and to enforce vital statistics registration with both county and state offices to ensure complete data collection.[46] Like South Dakota, the Montana Board of Health, formed by statute in 1901, also struggled early in its existence to implement the laws necessary to achieve vital statistics registration.

It did not gain legislative imprimatur mandating centralized state recording and tabulation of population and mortality statistics until 1907, which meant a period of six years during which the inertia of institutional change resisted centralized information gathering.[47] Although legislative bodies in the region desired to provide basic public health services, legislatures only reluctantly proffered the necessary funding and statutory support.[48]

Advancing toward the goal of full vital statistics registration followed a similar pattern across the Dakotas, Wyoming, and Montana. First, health departments worked to pass statutes broad enough to cover the necessary reporting requirements, a task that required deliberation and patience while newly formed states addressed a host of governance and infrastructure issues. At times, getting it right required repeated trips to the legislature, as was the case in South Dakota. The legislature passed an initial measure that required a license for marriage but neglected to include in that law the recording of births and deaths. The South Dakota Board of Health publicized the matter and requested that the law be clarified to remedy the omission. Regional state legislatures, like South Dakota's, faced a multitude of issues and dealt with governing structures as they were able, fixing statutes and eventually granting health departments the tools necessary for vital statistics registration.[49]

Lest they celebrate their newfound statutory authority too freely, health departments indubitably dealt with a chronic scarcity of funding. In some cases the shortfall was so severe that departments almost ceased to function, dealing only with limited matters of the highest importance. Budgetary issues loomed so large in the initial years of the interim South Dakota Territorial Health Department that it failed to file reports from 1895 to 1900.[50] The department continued to struggle with inadequate legislative backup and insufficient funding, which resulted in reports that were, according to the department itself, "incomplete and insufficient to be of any value for statistics."[51] The matter required a number of years to rectify, and in South Dakota's case subsequent boards of health pleaded for more money and regularly apologized for the shoddy condition of the health department's records and activities. For a full decade— from 1900, when the department issued no report, until 1910— South Dakota's health department operated in near-crisis conditions bordering on "absolute chaos."[52] Such disarray put South Dakota's health department officials in the position of playing catch-up, both with their northern plains neighbors, who shared many of the same challenges, and with eastern colleagues who worked in states with an established tradition of public health infrastructure.

Motivated by the goal of improving public health and preventing unnecessary deaths, regional health departments also pushed for improvement out of a healthy sense of competition with other states in the area and across the country.[53] Birth registration officially began at the national level in 1902 with the passage of the Census Act, but the need to ensure that information was being recorded accurately slowed collection of data. The processes necessary for gathering legitimate data took time; the Census Bureau reported that only about two-thirds of the U.S. population had been accurately counted by 1915.[54]

Inaccessible and rural areas understandably lagged behind more urban areas in collecting reliable information. Women's clubs across the nation voluntarily helped with birth registration tests by assessing the completeness of a state's data collection, and Montana and Wyoming had thirteen and five women, respectively, at work on the issue. Compared to Iowa, with around eight hundred female volunteers, the western states were new to the game.[55]

The federal government stoked the flames of interstate competition when it created a death-registration area in 1910 and a birth-registration area for reporting states in 1915.[56] To be admitted, state health department officials in Wyoming, the Dakotas, and Montana worked to adopt the required legal language mandating birth and death registration and to satisfy the verification requirements put forth by the U.S. Census Bureau.[57] Only by 1933 were all states nationwide reporting at the accuracy level required by the Census Bureau for admittance to the registration area.[58]

Health departments sought Census Bureau approval as an indicator of meeting minimum standards of performance and a badge of legitimacy for their public health data. As late as 1926 South Dakota was still not in compliance with national vital statistics registration, a failure that rankled state officials.[59] Regional health departments continued to focus on interstate rivalries as a means of assessing progress, and as late as the 1930s Wyoming was still bemoaning its standing at the back of the regional pack for mortality statistics.[60]

Western state health departments, following the established pattern of their eastern neighbors, hired professional staff and adopted policies in line with routine health department protocol.[61] Officials in the Dakotas, Wyoming, and Montana pushed for data-based public health programs and campaigned for the registration of all births and deaths in their respective states. While each state began collecting mortality data soon after achieving official statehood status, they were concerned with verifying accuracy and routinizing procedures before publishing the results. Montana released its first partial statistics in 1907, North Dakota in 1911, South Dakota in 1920, and Wyoming only in 1924.[62]

As they organized and collected data, state governments became authoritative voices on maternal health, a realm previously governed entirely by women within the context of personal relationships. Newly arrived to the territory of reproductive health, officials in the northern plains and Rocky Mountains soon discovered—much to their collective chagrin—the frequency of deaths like Bertha Emmert's within their borders.[63]

Due to inaccuracies caused by the partial collection of data and a lack of familiarity with the process, early health department records do not carry the unquestioned veracity of later, more established data, but they still shed light on the heightened dangers to mothers giving birth in these sparsely settled states. While many residents acknowledged the riskiness of childbirth in turn-of-the-twentieth-century Montana, Wyoming, and the Dakotas, health department statistics revealed a surprisingly dire reproductive situation.[64] For example, the newly gathered data showed that Montana had the highest reported maternal death rates in the nation for the years 1911 through 1919. The findings were, as the Montana State Board of Health phrased it, "a distinct shock to our self-complacency."[65] The concern did not end at national boundaries, as the province of Alberta had the same troubles, with the highest infant and maternal mortality rates in Canada in 1921.[66] Canadian residents of the plains and Rocky Mountains experienced conditions similar to those that residents of the Dakotas, Wyoming, and Montana did, along with a remarkably high death rate for women and children during and immediately after birth. Montana's poor showing did not set it apart from its neighbors but instead indicated a regional condition that other states, still working to formalize their data collections procedures, had yet to verify.[67]

When assessing maternal death rates, it is essential to separate infant death from maternal mortality. The impact of a mother's death in childbirth affected public health differently than did the death of an infant; Bertha Emmert's passing and that of her newborn infant could be understood as different in multiple orders of magnitude. Pragmatically, infant death was managed within the framework of families and local communities and did not generate the kind of crisis that would unfold with the death of a mother, who left children without a caregiver and in need of state resources that were often nonexistent.

Infant death was a fairly regular event. Historian Janet Finn has calculated that in early 1900s Butte, Montana, "20% of live births might die before the age of 5, with half of that (50%) occurring in the first year," and "deaths of infants were daily occurrences as were deaths of toddlers as a result of accidents and injuries at home and in the streets."[68] Thus, while more infants than mothers died in the northern plains and Rocky Mountains, this statistic was following the general pattern. However, the high numbers of mothers who perished generated attention from agencies and the general public because of the tremendous impact the loss of these vital caregivers had on communities and civic culture. Children's deaths were unfortunately common, but the widespread demise of mothers who provided (with little recognition) so much essential cultural infrastructure prompted a rush to ascertain the details of this dangerous reproductive context. As state health departments struggled to enumerate birth rates and death rates and understand causes of mortality, health department staff discovered that doctors, midwives, and parents were resistant to the idea of state birth certificate registration. Turn-of-the-twentieth-century residents of these western states expected no interaction with officials or forms to be filled out regarding birth or death. These were private family matters seen as outside the purview of government agencies, so much so that public health officials found it necessary to actively train, inform, and at times threaten the population to encourage cooperation with the new vital statistics registration laws.[69]

The government's new reach into areas formerly the exclusive preserve of family and individual decision-making extended to defining the moment when state authority took precedence over individual privacy rights. The Wyoming State Board of Health took the position that many reported stillbirths were in fact living infants who were allowed to perish because they were "undesired." In the words of the health department, the absence of value on the part of parents was "no reason why the state should not lend [newborns] the protection of a vital statistics law."[70] Montana passed legislation stating that "no child that shows *any evidence of life* after birth shall be registered as a stillborn."[71] It seems possible that in the absence of effective contraception and with limited access to abortion, families overburdened with more children than they could support may have allowed weak newborns to perish as a last resort, an unfortunate means of family planning. While contemporary reproductive controversies struggle to define the point at which the state may become involved in a pregnancy, early health departments in the northern plains and Rocky Mountains presaged this argument by positing a clarification—and de facto extension—of state control by putting public health agencies in the position of determining birth as the point where the state claimed ownership and control of newborn citizens.[72]

Even with the necessary state statutes in place to enforce registration, officials still had to educate residents about the seemingly strange requirement to notify public health agencies about ordinary, and previously entirely personal, life events. A full five years after the new state laws on vital statistics registration were in place, a county physician in Glendive, Montana, placed a reminder in the local newspaper that "the obligation for report[ing] all births . . . is placed upon the physician or midwife" and then explained that if a physician or midwife failed to report the birth, then the responsibility fell to the parents or property owner where the birth occurred.[73]

The requirement to notify state government agencies about such personal matters as birth and death represented a marked departure from accepted practice that no doubt struck many as intrusive and bothersome. Wyoming state law required physicians or midwives to report and register all births they attended, but the Wyoming State Board of Health, a full decade after its formation, found it "impossible to compel the compliance with the law" as there was no funding for enforcement. The board requested subsequent legislatures to provide minimal funding so that midwives and physicians could receive "the payment of a small amount" upon registering each birth.[74] Evidently, the Wyoming State Board of Health decided that a carrot would be far more effective than a stick.[75]

In recognition of entrenched and widespread opposition to such reporting, health departments across the region made numerous claims that vital statistics registration served the common good. Fighting ongoing resistance, the Wyoming State Board of Health supported its case by informing state residents that registering births could aid in legal claims, as "many questions of inheritance, law or equity that may hinge on a correct birth or death record" could be resolved by reference to complete vital statistics documentation. The health department went so far as to compare human infants to puppies and livestock, stating that "the pedigreed dog is registered at birth—why not give the sweet little baby an equal chance?" and "the very people who often show a keen appreciation of registered stock, frequently betray an amazing lack of interest in registering the baby."[76] According to public health officials, completing birth documentation brought many benefits, among them "secur[ing] citizenship," "establish[ing] the right to vote," and allowing a person "to hold office" and secure title to land or possessions.[77]

State bureaucracies envisioned a fully documented future, and in that documentation-conscious world, children benefited from holding the proper credentials, like a birth certificate, which would be needed if one was to take part in civic life. Previously, individuals established their identity in relation to family and communities that vouched for them or, as sometimes happened in the American West, created an entirely new identity for themselves. With state governments in place, citizens established themselves and their legitimacy by reference to the state and through a demonstration of sanctioned documentation. In this quiet and unassuming way, health departments and vital statistics registration took on the role of making Americans, of granting individuals lawful standing based on their participation in birth registration.

Health departments recognized that, in addition to potential benefits accruing to registered inhabitants, the departments themselves depended on vital statistics information to perform the most basic of institutional functions. At its very inception, the North Dakota Board of Health informed the governor that accurate and complete vital statistics collection was "of the utmost importance" and "indispensable" to the work of the department.[78] The Wyoming State Board of Health explained that it depended on registrations "to know the actual increase of births over deaths, the effect of various occupations and sanitary conditions upon the health, vigor, and birth rate of our people. It is obvious, then, that the registration of births and deaths is the backbone of modern and efficient health work."[79]

In short, health departments saw many benefits for the general populace from vital statistics registration but recognized that the existence of public health efforts depended on convincing an unwilling citizenry to make previously private information available to bureaucratic institutions. It comes as no surprise that the transition to birth and death registration was a slow one, but, through consistent reminders and with the institutional might of the state, health departments made steady progress toward satisfactory record keeping.

The constellation of conditions in the northern plains brought to light the unfortunate and commonplace reality of frequent pregnancy-related death, both for mothers and for infants. With the development of state governments in the region, health departments became suddenly aware of the reproductive problems within their jurisdictions and, as a first step, attempted to collect data and calculate the extent of the problem. To their credit, health departments recognized the public health crisis that parturient women faced. Unfortunately, state governments did not make any inquiries of the most knowledgeable professionals at work on the issue—midwives and the mothers they served—about the nature of the problem, potential remedies, or simple preventative measures. Mothers like Bertha Emmert could have provided invaluable information if their input had been solicited.

The participation of state agencies in the previously personal event of birth marked a sea change in the cultural experience of childbirth. Instead of a personal decision about birth location, birth attendant, and postpartum care and assistance, the involvement of public health agencies moved childbirth from the private realm and made it the subject of state and national rhetoric. This was not necessarily a hindrance to women or a disadvantage for women's health, but it represented a dramatic change nonetheless and meant that mothers ceased to be the sole authority on childbirth. Even as they struggled to meet their own and national standards, public health departments in Montana, the Dakotas, and Wyoming annexed new territory with their foray into maternal health.

Bertha Emmert died in 1911 in the midst of Montana's inauspicious tenure as the national leader in maternal mortalities, but for her husband, daughters, and other family members, the grievous loss felt intensely personal. Her untimely death illustrated the cost, both individual and communal, that maternal mortality inflicted, from the sorrow of a husband and of children deposited at an orphanage to a community unable to care for its own and an extended family hundreds of miles away consumed with mourning.

6

Birth Goes Public

Health departments acknowledged the desperate reproductive situation for women in the northern plains and Rocky Mountains and searched for solutions to remedy the crisis. But destructive assumptions about women and their role in American culture—willing dismissal of their expertise and failure to solicit their opinions—institutionalized a damaging treatment of mothers and their bodies at the hands of health departments. Incalculable harm was visited on regional women, many of whom had made great sacrifices to be there, having taken leave of family and friends as they moved west with hope for a better future.

Charlotte Sykes left her home in Missouri and traveled by rail to Miles City, Montana, in 1902. There she climbed aboard a stagecoach for a fast trip to Ekalaka, in the far southeastern corner of the state. The journey took an interminable twenty hours yet was accomplished at such speeds that the decorations on Sykes's hat came loose, the flowers scattering, petal by petal, across the sagebrush and crescent grass of eastern Montana. By the time she arrived in Ekalaka, Sykes sported an entirely bare and unadorned chapeau.[1]

Determined to build an independent career for herself, Sykes taught school, one of the few options available for single women in early 1900s Montana. She quickly acclimated to the scarcity of women in the region but still found it noteworthy that eighty men showed up for a local dance and she was one of only three women among the male multitude. She married Peter Jensen in 1908, moved to his ranch, and became pregnant with her first child "in about three months." Sadly, "it was seven months before [she] saw another woman."[2]

Nearing the end of her pregnancy in the late fall of 1909 and living on an isolated cattle ranch, Charlotte Jensen made the decision to return to Ekalaka, about forty miles away, to await the birth of her first child. When labor began, she sent word to the local physician, but he refused to leave his poker game to attend her delivery, earning her lifelong antipathy. Fortunately, she safely delivered her baby with the help of a neighbor woman. Furious at the doctor's disregard for a patient in need of care, Jensen determined to avoid such a vulnerable situation in the future and, toward the end of her second pregnancy in 1913, returned to her family in Missouri. She birthed a second daughter there, this time with the support of female relatives.[3]

Similarly, Annie Knipfer took the train from Massachusetts to Baker, Montana, in 1919, to reunite with her fiancé. They married the day after she arrived and then traveled the forty-two miles to their ranch by wagon. Soon pregnant in rural Montana without any female connections, Knipfer arranged to deliver her first baby in Baker with the local physician. Concerned about the poor physical condition typical of many ranch women at the time, he required near-term pregnant mothers to stay in town for several weeks before delivery, a rare acknowledgment of the impact of rural lifestyles on women's reproductive health. Knipfer and her first child survived the delivery, but the doctor performed an instrument birth—the invasive and at times brutal use of forceps to move the infant along the birth canal. Understandably, Knipfer did not relish a repeat, and when she was well along in her second pregnancy, she bundled up her young daughter and traveled back to Massachusetts to be with her family for the delivery.[4]

Experiences like Jensen's and Knipfer's encapsulated the regional reproductive issues that the Montana State Board of Health, along with officials in the Dakotas and Wyoming, began working to publicize and remediate in the early 1900s. By the 1920s data collection by regional health departments had documented the threat posed by area reproductive conditions. Based on their own experiences and contact with other women, mothers already knew that their odds were not good, and health department efforts relative to pregnancy, delivery, and recovery did not immediately extend beyond validating the complaint that many women like Jensen and Knipfer had already made and acted upon. Birthing trips like Jensen's journey to Missouri and Knipfer's trek to Massachusetts, while potential solutions to the lack of care options in the rural West, represented an outlay of cash and a loss of women's labor at a time when their work often meant the difference between solvency and bankruptcy. For families that, like solo homesteader Lizzie Maclean's, absolutely depended on the woman's physical and fiscal contributions, leaving the state for childbirth might have been appealing and the preferable choice. However, the threat of starvation for the family left behind or bankruptcy prevented many women from relocating for childbirth.

The actual solution to the reproductive crisis women were facing rested on the issue of resources—having enough money to hire help during late pregnancy and the postpartum period, adequate food and rest, and the caring support of other women.[5] The reproductive problems that plagued women were not endemic to pregnancy but larger symptoms of scarcity that became evident during the taxing period of gestation, delivery, and nursing.[6] Julia Lathrop, director of the Children's Bureau from 1912 to 1921, presciently promoted the idea of preventing maternal exhaustion and advocated policies to protect the health of mothers and children instead of attempting partial, after-the-fact fixes that failed to address the root of the problem.[7] During her tenure at the Children's Bureau, Lathrop instigated data collection programs. One of the subsequent Children's Bureau studies, completed in rural Montana, documented the "flee-the-state" phenomenon evidenced by Jensen and Knipfer. Of the nearly five hundred mothers interviewed by the bureau's investigators, an astounding 23 percent made arrangements to leave the state and deliver in a situation where they could access a support network.[8]

The most sensible solutions to the reproductive crisis—like validating the overwhelming challenges posed by the regional geographic context and building on the reproductive expertise of existing female providers—required countercultural action that flew in the face of accepted beliefs about women's importance and capabilities.[9] Officials in Montana, Wyoming, and the Dakotas could have contacted community midwives already providing care across the region, sought their input in enhancing existing informal infrastructure, and offered the institutional support necessary to meet the needs of pregnant women and their families. Monies for midwives to travel to isolated women or funding for postpartum household help, while relatively minor in total dollar amount, could have returned dramatic and lifesaving benefits in mere weeks, especially since the existing network of midwives already had intimate and trusting relationships with women in their communities.

Unfortunately, health department officials were not so bold. The fact that circumstances beyond women's control caused the deaths of mothers and infants was a truth too challenging to countenance. If policies based on such a position were pursued, then public policies that promoted women's disempowerment and unequal access to wealth would have to be abolished. It was a critical moment for health department officials, and by partnering with the Children's Bureau they could have gained national support to quickly and substantively improve the reproductive context in the region. However, in a climate where such forthright truths were uncomfortable and inconvenient, health officials pursued other methods.[10]

The Sheppard-Towner Act

Representative Jeannette Rankin of Montana, the first woman elected to the U.S. Congress, found the early Children's Bureau results—

that infant and maternal deaths could be prevented—significant and introduced a bill in 1918 that acted decisively on this information. The bill, later called the Sheppard-Towner Maternity and Infancy Act after two of its cosponsors, found few congressional supporters, but the official enfranchisement of women in 1920 presented legislators with a wholly new voting bloc. Women's organizations like the League of Women Voters and the Women's Joint Congressional Committee claimed to be aligned by issue rather than along party lines, and they demanded passage of the Sheppard-Towner bill as a primary goal. Maternal and infant mortality rates in the United States continued to rank high relative to those of western European countries, and fear of punishment from women at the polls caused members of Congress to support the measure and pass the act in 1921 with a generous margin of support.[11]

The Sheppard-Towner Act provided federal funds to the states, which used the money to sponsor conferences on infant health, provide sterile birthing supplies in advance of home deliveries, pay for public health nurses, educate mothers about sanitation and hygiene, and disseminate information on maternity care. The Children's Bureau had had success in providing reproductive information—the bureau published *Prenatal Care* in 1913 and *Infant Care* in 1914—and, with Sheppard-Towner funding in hand, state health departments followed suit.[12] North Dakota's health department mailed out *Infant Care* pamphlets to parents when they filed a birth certificate, as well as to couples who completed marriage licenses. The department made the pamphlet available to physicians for distribution to prenatal patients and also handed pamphlets out at conferences and clinics.[13]

The Sheppard-Towner Act initially gave $5,000 to each state directly, along with another $5,000 if the state committed to matching a similar amount. The federal government allocated remaining funds according to a population-based calculation and funneled the monies through child welfare or public health divisions of state governments. Among the western states, Wyoming and South Dakota made use of the full funding available annually.[14] North Dakota also took Sheppard-Towner funding but struggled to allocate matching funds during some of the years the law was in effect.[15] Like other states in the region, Montana received Sheppard-Towner funds and used them in combination with state funds to distribute literature that taught mothers about maternal and infant health. In a two-year period the Montana Board of Health distributed 350,000 items in fulfillment of requests from around the state.[16]

Even this minimal collaborative attempt by state and national governments to deal with the ongoing deaths among mothers and children brought sharp and immediate opposition. Historian J. Stanley Lemons has described how the Sheppard-Towner Act "was assailed as a threat to the very institutions of the nation." The American Medical Association cuttingly derided the legislation as government overreach and vehemently opposed it. Criticized by antisuffragists, portrayed by conservatives as evidence of a "Bolshevist conspiracy against America," and resisted as contrary to the doctrine of states' rights, this seemingly moderate act to devote resources to the cause of women and children found few friends and an abundance of enemies.[17]

Sheppard-Towner represented a minimal commitment—in Montana it amounted to about $13,700 per year from 1921 to 1929—but the funds made an impact beyond the actual dollars spent. Prior to the act, federal, state, and local governments rarely addressed factors surrounding birth. The cascading effect of the Children's Bureau's work, begun in 1912, and the Sheppard-Towner Act, initially passed in 1921, marked not just the entrance of government into the arena of maternal and infant public health but the beginning of government attention to reproductive issues.

Sheppard-Towner failed to be renewed in 1929, much to the disappointment of its supporters. Although its sponsors originally intended the legislation to establish a permanent program, the American Medical Association (AMA) successfully lobbied to cancel funding for the act, thus ending its eight-year run. The AMA labeled the Sheppard-Towner Act a "socialist scheme," worked against its continuation based on opposition to state-sponsored health insurance, and successfully brought about its demise.[18] Over the years of Sheppard-Towner's existence, maternal and infant mortalities declined and supporters declared the act a success.[19] Like other states in the northern plains, Montana anticipated the demise of Sheppard-Towner monies and took steps to fund and continue some of the state programs initiated during its existence. In 1929 the Montana legislature approved the allocation of $18,800 in state funds for the Child Welfare Division of the State Board of Health.[20] When federal funding from Sheppard-Towner ceased in 1929, North Dakota ponied up $26,000 to support its Division of Child Hygiene, and the South Dakota legislature allocated funding specifically to adjust for the loss of Sheppard-Towner funds.[21]

The presence of federal funding earmarked for reproductive health from 1921 to 1929 helped to create public health programs that northern plains states continued and funded after the demise of Sheppard-Towner funding.[22] Even when a state's financial support for Sheppard-Towner funds was initially tenuous—as was the case in North Dakota when legislators reduced the total amount of state funding for the health department in favor of using Sheppard-Towner funds to perform work previously paid for with state dollars—a public health presence to deal with epidemic disease and address problems like high maternal and infant mortality rates came to be expected by state residents.[23] For nearly a decade Montana, the Dakotas, and Wyoming looked to functional state programs supported in part by Sheppard-Towner funding, and regional residents came to assume the importance of such work on the part of state governments. One can only imagine what a transformative impact sensible, women-friendly policies could have had over a similar span of time.

Long-Term Public Health Impacts

The Sheppard-Towner Act allowed state health departments to control the distribution of funds and set public health priorities. In short, the act boosted the power of new and sometimes struggling health departments in the region and made their allocation of resources and assessment of public health priorities far more significant to those residing in their jurisdictions.

The act amplified the methods used by state health departments at a time when the two main purveyors of public health information—the U.S. Children's Bureau and state health departments—operated under somewhat divergent motivations. Julia Lathrop directed the Children's Bureau at the national level until 1921 and pushed for birth certificate registration as a means of accurate information-gathering and subsequent action. For example, Etta Goodwin of the Children's Bureau explained that birth registration was a necessary precursor to public policy solutions: "You cannot find out why babies are dying unless you know what proportion of babies are dying."[24] For Children's Bureau staff, registration existed as a stepping-stone to constructive planning and implementation and also served as an impetus for action. State health departments focused on the role of birth registration as "the backbone of modern and efficient health work" and saw the collection of vital statistics as legitimate in and of itself, even without subsequent policy changes to address existing problems.[25]

The Children's Bureau pursued an egalitarian model in its projects and sought to collaborate with those it served, not dictate to them, in something of a reflection of how midwives worked with mothers. According to historian Alice Smuts, "Before beginning each study, the bureau won the cooperation of municipal officers, women's organizations, and local elites and created public interest in the study through the press and local clergy."[26] Children's Bureau staff recognized the importance of establishing trust with mothers, and bureau policy forbade interviewers from asking questions about "sensitive subjects" like "alcohol use," "venereal disease," and "illegitimacy."[27] At a time when state health departments used events, like contests at county fairs, to judge the "best" babies and encourage competition among mothers, Lathrop advocated health conferences as an avenue for helping mothers to gain information and develop camaraderie as they collectively sought to reduce reproductive mortality.[28] In line with the bureau's respectful treatment of mothers and their expressed needs, staff determined that at least forty-five thousand midwives actively practiced throughout the country. Sensing an opportunity to maximize the connections midwives maintained with birthing women, the bureau utilized midwives to facilitate the transfer of information to mothers.[29]

In the years immediately following their inception, regional health departments also dealt even-handedly with both midwives and physicians. These health departments addressed midwives and physicians jointly in official reports, referred to them in interoffice correspondence, and noted them in their minutes. Such mentions in early health department documentation in the Dakotas, Wyoming, and Montana indicated a measure of acceptance and equal standing. Initially, health department officials and staff treated midwives and physicians alike as legitimate practitioners.

Over time, however, a gradual shift occurred on the part of health departments; a subtle change in language revealed a significant reconception of the state's treatment of women, their bodies, and their children. Describing the difficulties in collecting birth registration data in 1912, the Wyoming Health Department recommended paying "physicians or midwives" a small fee to encourage cooperation with registration requirements and added that "in most cases *physicians* have cheerfully complied with the requirements of the law."[30] The board initially referred to both physicians and midwives as compilers of birth certificate information but then went on to state that "one of the greatest difficulties which the *physicians* meet with in properly making out the birth certificates is the failure of the parents to promptly name the new born child."[31] Weighing such a statement from the Wyoming Board of Health so heavily might seem excessive, but when it was followed by a clearer distinction— "In the case of births, when a physician is not employed the midwife or parents should make the report"—just four years later in 1916, the slowly growing but obvious preference for physicians over midwives is apparent.[32]

The use of this language could simply represent the effect of changing birthing preferences and not overt health department policy. However, as public institutions became far more present in the lives of residents by taking an authoritative stance in every birth and death through the legitimizing act of vital statistics recording, state health departments became more active policy makers and less passive recorders in the lives of northern plains residents. While some health department language could be interpreted as representative of a changing culture with a growing antimidwifery stance, it is important to note that health departments acted to promulgate and enforce particular behaviors and judgments across their range of responsibilities. Health department pronouncements and policies indubitably impacted public perception both covertly and through explicit statements that caused parents who employed midwives to feel second-rate compared to those who hired a physician. In 1930, when the North Dakota Department of Health described parents who sought midwifery care as those who "did not have competent and trained help" during birth, officials actively stigmatized the skill of professional midwives practicing in the state.[33]

Unwilling to elevate the status of women and in search of a more palatable solution in the face of embarrassing death rates in the northern plains and Rocky Mountains, public health departments looked to medical rhetoric, which railed against the evils of midwifery. Simultaneously, physicians positioned themselves as protectors of public health and painted midwives as purveyors of maternal death and destruction in order to reduce the number of practicing midwives and elevate the status of the medical profession.[34] Over time physicians gained public stature, the support of the public health bureaucracy, and the ability to implement restrictions on midwives through their public health connections. Public health officials found an organizing principle and a civilian enforcement arm in physicians, now aligned with the very registration requirements at which they previously fussed. Public health officials, in collaborating with physicians to suppress midwifery, contributed to the diminishment of the dominant reproductive profession.

Health departments, having thus allied themselves with physicians, became complicit in the attack on midwives. They began to take concrete steps toward reducing the services typically performed by midwives in an attempt to curtail their overall scope of practice. By 1920 South Dakota law had disallowed midwife-signed death certificates for stillbirths, and that same year the Montana Department of Health announced that both birth certificates and burial permits were now required for stillbirths of at least twenty-four weeks of gestation and that "certificates of death for stillborn children shall not be accepted from midwives."[35]

Such laws made physicians a part of the birth process even for those families who continued to hire midwives. If more than one health-care professional was required in the event of a stillbirth, the ease of hiring a single do-it-all individual—a physician—certainly appealed to parents, especially in conjunction with the abundance of propaganda against midwives. However, while a doctor could compile and complete the necessary forms, postpartum care, one of the most significant elements of successful recovery for mothers and infants, would not be under a doctor's purview. Additionally, as health departments published materials and sponsored public talks, they openly and regularly collaborated with physicians yet failed to utilize the services and knowledge of midwives in prenatal conferences, infant nutrition classes, or instruction in cleanliness.

Over time, health departments adopted the death-and-destruction theme of medicine in talking about childbirth, instead of the moderate tone and methods of midwifery, which focused on births as routine events. By 1931 the Wyoming Department of Health was lamenting the fact that "the laity has been taught through ages that reproduction and labor is a normal physiologic process" and that the only thing mothers feared was the pain of delivery. Exemplifying a perspective typical of physicians, the Wyoming Health Department suggested that mothers be taught to view pregnancy as "nine months of sickness," a topic assuredly included in instruction by public health staff and doctors alike, as they adopted the mantra of female deficiency and promoted the idea that women should harbor inordinate fear of the birth process and even of their own bodies.[36]

In the process of elevating physicians over midwives, health departments also directly cooperated with and publicly thanked local doctors. By 1924 the South Dakota Health Department was acknowledging the friendliness between department officials and physicians—"The cooperation and assistance of local doctors has been very helpful and greatly appreciated"—thus voicing a common sentiment across the region. But such gratitude was particularly striking in an environment where female health-care providers supplied the majority of delivery-related reproductive care and all of the postpartum support for mothers.[37] Expressing such overt appreciation for physicians who were still failing to shoulder the bulk of reproductive work, as well as neglecting to mention the multitude of acting midwives still serving in communities across the region, stands out as a calculated endorsement. The health department also recruited physicians to "lecture" women "on some subject pertaining to child care," a true turning point in elevating to the status of expert those who were least knowledgeable at the time.[38] Parturient women in Wyoming were required to obtain their physician's consent before attending or participating in health department classes about prenatal care and nutrition, as if the medical establishment owned mothers' bodies, controlled their pregnancies, and directed their intellects.[39]

The Effective Demise of Midwifery

Eventually and unsurprisingly, given the constant inundation of society with pro-physician rhetoric and the state health departments' denigration of midwifery, public opinion regarding midwives became openly negative. Although midwives were delivering the majority of infants at the turn of the twentieth century, over the next several decades their services were significantly reduced. In North Dakota midwifery services were effectively eliminated within thirty short years: midwives in the state attended the majority of births at the turn of the century, but by 1930 they were assisting at just 5 percent of deliveries.[40] Midwives discovered "that their work was despised by the medical profession and neither supervised nor supported by professional colleagues."[41] This opposition to midwives, especially among the medical and public health communities, became so strong that even nurses with midwifery training hid their background when working in medical circles to avoid the inevitable censure and disparagement.[42] The trend accelerated in the 1950s, when hospital birth became the widespread norm. By 1960 an entire generation had entered the world through the hospital portal under the supervision of physicians. After delivering uncountable generations throughout all of human history, midwives and their accumulated wisdom, as well as their long-tested and lovingly provided body of knowledge, were eliminated in a span of less than fifty years.[43]

What did this dramatic transition look like? How were so many skilled female reproductive practitioners encouraged to abandon their work and recede into the background? And how did communities in Wyoming, the Dakotas, and Montana that had so long depended on these women for their very survival ultimately fail to defend those who had served them so faithfully? Charting the removal of midwives is difficult, in large part because they never entered the historical record to begin with. Their demise was therefore a double erasure. However, the practice of Mary Kassmeier, the Fort Benton midwife who carefully documented her midwifery career in infant photographs, offers some rare insight into this commonplace character assassination.

Midwife Mary Kassmeier

Mary Catherine Reicks married Henry Kassmeier, eight years her senior, in 1903, just nine months after her twenty-third birthday. Mary grew up in Iowa, Henry claimed Nebraska as home, and after their marriage they remained in the Midwest for several years. Eventually the lure of land in Montana, as well as the encouragement of Mary's brothers already homesteading there, convinced them to relocate. By 1910 Mary and Henry had settled in Belt, Montana, with their two young children: Theresa, then four, and Rosie, two. Mary delivered the couple's third child, Herman, that same year.

Mary and Henry, like many other northern plains homesteaders, engaged in off-farm work to supplement their income. While they were living in Belt, Henry was employed at the area coal mine; he even relocated the family to Colorado for a brief period in 1913, when Mary gave birth to daughter Anna Marie. We do not know how Mary Kassmeier gained her knowledge of and experience with childbirth aside from her own deliveries, although family stories suggest that an older sister-in-law in Nebraska may have shared her specialized knowledge with Kassmeier. Regardless, when the family returned to Montana, Kassmeier began working as a midwife in Chouteau County.[44]

While we cannot conclusively identify the date when Kassmeier commenced active practice, the photo album documenting her midwifery work established the existence of a fully functional business by 1915, when she supervised about four or five births. Over the next two years the time she committed to midwifery significantly increased, with an estimated twelve births in 1917, fifteen in 1918, and a torrent of deliveries in 1919—twenty-four in all.

At the height of her practice Kassmeier attended about two births per month, and while that might seem like a small number, the actual time invested would have been substantial. If the mother called Kassmeier as soon as pains began and Kassmeier remained with the woman through the birth and then supervised the delivery of the placenta and initial nursing sessions, her time away from home could have extended to as many as two or three consecutive days for each birth. If she subsequently checked in on mother and infant in the following weeks, her midwifery work could have required every-other-day attention.[45] For each of the deliveries she supervised, Kassmeier monitored the normal course of labor, made

Fig. 21. Mary Kassmeier assisted at three of Winifred Burdick's deliveries. Burdick lost one child prior to 1922, and her four living children are pictured here. It is likely that Robert, the eldest, was delivered prior to the family's arrival in Montana. 2011-FK-054, Mary Kassmeier Album, Overholser Historical Research Center, Fort Benton, Montana.

routine adjustments (such as turning a breech baby), and directed the entire process from onset of labor to final cleanup. Kassmeier had an arrangement with St. Clare's, the Catholic hospital in Fort Benton, and delivered infants both in private homes and at the hospital.[46]

Kassmeier's services supported mothers' reproductive needs in a multitude of ways. She never learned to drive a car and so walked, took the short rail line, or hitched a ride to the births she supervised. A mother with a full slate of responsibilities, from laundry to cooking to gardening to childcare, could send for Kassmeier and depend on her to arrive prepared for a delivery and likely also carrying the ingredients for a tasty meal in hand. Kassmeier's ability to step in and direct household and family activities undoubtedly brought a sense of relief to her clients.

Mary Elizabeth Kelly
4 months 191

In addition to her knowledge of birth, Kassmeier utilized a voluminous pharmacopeia of plant-based treatments. She not only knew how to administer and prescribe necessary remedies but also harvested, prepared, and provided medicines as part of her practice. Comfrey, wild evening primrose, and wild raspberry each had specific delivery-related applications, from hastening labor to increasing the mother's milk supply, and Kassmeier undoubtedly put them to use, along with a tea of serviceberry bark, when called for, to help expel the placenta. Her knowledge base included a long list of useful herbs, such as wild mustard, for antiseptic uses and poultices; chamomile, used as a relaxant; kinnikinnick to treat bladder infections; coneflower to strengthen the immune system; white sage to ease menstrual cramps; and even the widely available willow. Those who were, like Kassmeier, of German heritage knew that willow, when combined with vinegar, created the effective painkilling combination we now identify as aspirin.[47] These treatments seem especially appealing and effective compared to common medical therapies of the era, which included bleeding (draining blood from the patient to remove "illness") and purging (achieved by administering calomel, a poisonous concoction of mercury, which Laurentza Koch's physician prescribed during her pregnancy). Mothers attended by Kassmeier could sit back and think only of delivering a baby—no small task but far more doable than managing the multiplicity of demands typically on the minds of rural women.

Like other midwives of the era, Kassmeier established connections to the families she served, and these connections did not end with the successful commencement of breastfeeding and maternal recov-

Figs. 22 and 23. Mary Kassmeier assisted at the births of two sisters: Mary Elizabeth Kelly and Anabel Kelly, born in Fort Benton in 1916 and 1917, respectively. Their mother, Mary Elizabeth Embleton Kelly, was born in Fort Benton in 1887, when Montana was still a territory. 2011-FK-015 and 2011-FK-025, Mary Kassmeier Album, Overholser Historical Research Center, Fort Benton, Montana.

ery. Rather, she developed relationships with families and returned, year after year, to celebrate and oversee the arrival of subsequent babies. When children contracted infectious diseases or fell victim to traumatic injury, families could share their grief with Kassmeier, who had been there at the child's birth and knew something of the energy and effort invested in each cherished infant.

Kassmeier, being a mother with a long list of domestic responsibilities of her own, managed the competing demands of caring for her own children, helping to bring other women's babies into the world, and maintaining relationships with the families of infants she delivered. Kassmeier's husband, Henry, required that his needs be met; he was not the helpful sort, and Kassmeier had to keep her own home in order while also attending births. When she began her midwifery work in Fort Benton in 1915, her daughters Theresa and Rosie were nine and seven, Herman was four, and Anna Marie was a one-year-old toddler. Herman and Anna Marie needed significant supervision, but Theresa and Rosie were able to provide at least rudimentary help during the five births that Kassmeier attended during her first year of practice. As Kassmeier's midwifery commitment increased, so too did the ages and abilities of her children. By 1919, while she carried on a bustling midwifery practice, thirteen-year-old Theresa was helping to direct domestic matters with the aid of her siblings, then eleven, eight, and five.[48]

While such responsibility required significant maturity on the part of Kassmeier's children and no small amount of hard work, it allowed Kassmeier to tend to home and family while simultaneously generating income and providing a meaningful service. Kassmeier did not maintain this pace indefinitely; she reduced her midwifery workload by about half in 1920, possibly in light of her own pregnancy. With the birth of Leonard, her fifth child, in 1921, she settled into a routine and averaged just under a dozen births each year through 1924—still a remarkable amount of work to integrate into the everyday needs of farm and family. With their father absent from time to time for work and their mother committed to sporadic,

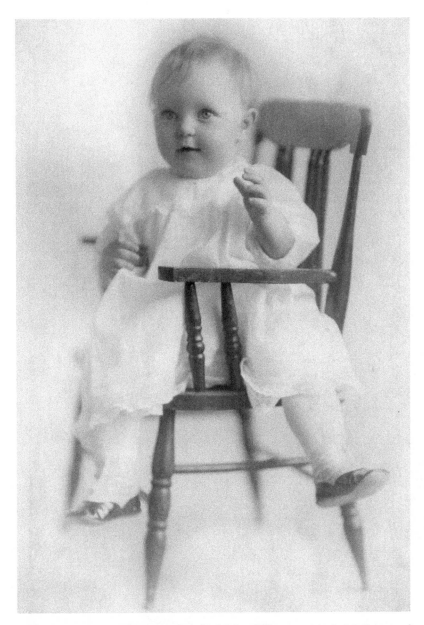

Fig. 24. Mary Kassmeier attended the birth of Florence Marie McGraw and likely spent time with the McGraw family two years later, when Florence died from "acute entero-colitis." 2011-FK-020, Mary Kassmeier Album, Overholser Historical Research Center, Fort Benton, Montana.

Fig. 25. Margeret and Dorothy Tailor's family postponed sending Mary Kassmeier a photograph for her album of babies she had delivered until they could provide a formal studio image. 2011-FK-051, Mary Kassmeier Album, Overholser Historical Research Center, Fort Benton, Montana.

time-intensive births, the Kassmeier children learned early on how to manage independently, with no small measure of pride.[49]

Later remembered by her grandchildren and extended family as a skilled healer, Kassmeier rarely talked about her central role in the Fort Benton community. Her midwifery work was common knowledge, but the daily evidence of her care—the mint tea she made, the nasturtium soap she crafted, or the rag soaked in vinegar that she administered to a child's sore throat—made a more immediate impression. She rescued grandchildren from the mean rooster in the chicken yard, cooked delectable meals on a wood stove, and cultivated a large garden. A resourceful and hardworking woman, she found great satisfaction in helping others, especially those who had as little as she did.[50]

Given her concern for children and desire to help, it is no surprise that Kassmeier willingly adjusted her fee for those struggling financially, thus forgoing a standard delivery charge and leaving it up to families to pay the amount they could afford.[51] Kassmeier's request for a picture no doubt soothed the self-respect of those without cash: they could, in some way, compensate her, even if they lacked the necessary funds. A number of the photographs in her album portray toddlers or young children, offering evidence that families remembered Kassmeier's request and provided the child's picture eventually, even if they could not afford a studio image immediately after the birth.

As might be expected, when parents and county officials became more familiar with, and less resistant to, governmental recording requirements, they complied more quickly with birth certifications. The birth certificates from Kassmeier's early deliveries—those from 1915 through 1920—indicate a time lag of up to several months from birth to certification. For infants born in 1921 and later, birth certificates were completed and signed anywhere from one to three days after the births.[52]

The demise of midwifery is sometimes perceived as occurring simultaneously with the shift from home births to hospital deliveries,

Fig. 26. Mary Kassmeier assisted at the births of Georgie (pictured here) and Patricia Wackerlin, siblings born two years apart at St. Clare Hospital. 2011-FK-091, Mary Kassmeier Album, Overholser Historical Research Center, Fort Benton, Montana.

with midwives delivering solely in homes and doctors taking over in hospitals. But Kassmeier's situation hinted at a more gradual, albeit short-lived, transition. From one-quarter to slightly more than one-half of the births that Kassmeier oversaw took place at St. Clare's, the Catholic hospital in Fort Benton.[53] While we do not know the nature of Kassmeier's business relationship with local doctors, the fact that various physicians signed birth certificates for her deliveries demonstrated that they certainly knew of her work and quite possibly collaborated with her.[54] Following a commonsense model, Fort Benton physicians might have engaged Kassmeier to attend births at the hospital, relying on her to direct routine deliveries and refer emergency situations to them. Alternately, in an era before admitting rights, mothers may have made their requests for a hospital delivery directly to Kassmeier. The specifics are uncertain, but the sparse record tells an indisputable narrative of an era of cooperation in Chouteau County and Fort Benton. Local physicians worked alongside Kassmeier and a long list of female providers to secure safe delivery for area infants and mothers. Midwives, doctors, and nurses knew each other and frequently interacted within the reproductive environment.

The intensely negative stance of the medical profession with regard to midwives might have remained a theoretical backgrounding to life in Fort Benton. It is possible that Kassmeier, after a decade of active work as a midwife, chose to quit assisting at deliveries, chose to cease her interactions with pregnant women, chose to leave the profession that gave her a sense of pride and meaning. As her family moved to farmland farther outside of Fort Benton, the conditions of her life may have dictated a change of lifestyle. But in 1925, with five children ranging in age from nineteen to four and increasingly able to tend to their own needs, Kassmeier might have been ready for an expanded practice, not a diminished one. Her records reveal that she attended an estimated fourteen births in 1924 but list only two in 1925 and one each in 1926 and 1927.

We are left wondering why such a consistent demand for her services seems to have evaporated.[55] Was her work a casualty of the

Fig. 27. Mary Catherine Reicks Kassmeier, born February 20, 1881, in Roselle, Iowa, is pictured here in the early to mid-1940s, when she was about sixty years old. 2011-FK-119, Mary Kassmeier Album, Overholser Historical Research Center, Fort Benton, Montana.

virulent antimidwifery campaign of the 1910s and 1920s? Did the dictates of the medical profession cause area doctors, who knew the expanse of her knowledge and had witnessed her skill in deliveries, to start seeing Kassmeier as a less qualified individual, instead of as a specialist in her own right? Did her years of experience alongside laboring women fade in the flood of professional literature suggesting an inherent faultiness of midwives?

It is quite possible—even likely—that Kassmeier had a congenial and mutually respectful relationship with area physicians. They might have regarded her as the colleague and knowledgeable specialist that she was. But it is also possible that slowly, over time, the national antimidwifery rhetoric and the desire for profit caused physicians to deride Kassmeier's services and remove her from the reproductive landscape to which she had brought such care and expertise.

Public Health Nurses

With the decrease in the numbers of practicing midwives in Montana, the Dakotas, and Wyoming, the scarcity of health-care providers became even more pronounced.[56] Francis Bradley, at the 1925 meeting of the Montana Medical Association, reported that the state had just "523 doctors to 555,000 people or 1 to more than 1611 persons, when the average for the country is 1 to every 726."[57] Health departments noted the disparity between desire for assistance and those willing to provide it, especially with the need for relationally based medical care growing as the number of practicing midwives was decreasing. To fill the interpersonal gap, state health departments, after playing an active role in ridding themselves of midwives, grudgingly began expanding the numbers of public health nurses.

The state of South Dakota offered to pay one-third the cost of county nurses, with individual counties covering the remaining two-thirds. The South Dakota Health Department also expanded the work of county nurses to focus on mothers and young children, sending out information about pregnancy and childbirth and sponsoring clinics and conferences.[58] In 1917 Montana enacted statutes that defined the duties of school and public health nurses, codifying much of what had been common practice prior to passage of the legislation.[59] Rules set forth clear lines of authority, requiring school nurses to serve under and report to the local superintendent of schools, with public health nurses reporting to and registering with the state health department, and county nurses following the direction of county commissioners. School nurses examined children, assessed the cleanliness of homes, and recommended quarantine procedures in the event of a communicable disease outbreak. Public health and county nurses conducted home visits and promoted education in sanitary procedures and hygiene. At times, public health and county nurses also served as school nurses, especially in sparsely populated areas.[60]

Home visits by public health nurses gave lonely or isolated mothers a chance to talk with someone about their children, express their concerns, and ask questions. One such public health nurse,

Mrs. John Anstice of South Dakota, reported that she "visited over six hundred homes and taught the mothers different methods of feeding, clothing and caring for their children" during 1928.[61] While women may have preferred a more consistent and less institutional remedy, mothers with a dearth of personal interaction might also have found some benefit in the mildly patronizing educational lectures and home visits.

Public health nurses also had to bend to the authority of physicians, as the health department demanded that they respond "to every call," despite the fact that they received firm direction "not to continue on a case unless a doctor [was] in attendance."[62] Health departments gave public health nurses the task of identifying public health and medical issues and then required that they encourage those in need of care to engage a physician. Similarly, school nurses were directed to examine all children in school, assess their "defects," and meet "discreetly" with parents to encourage them to consult a physician about the issue. The regulations stated that "the nurse must be careful not to advise the services of any one physician to the exclusion of other physicians."[63] In so doing, the health department acted in support of and as an enabler of the medical profession as a whole, advocating physician care in general while excluding reference to predominantly female local healers.

The cooperation of doctors and public health brought the state even further into the private lives of families. Parents now reported the details of births, the race and legitimacy of children, and the causes of death. Health departments also intervened in the lives of families: when children were absent from school without a "known cause," school nurses were directed to make a visit to the child's home and ascertain why they were missing.[64]

Bureaucracy Matters

The collaboration between physicians and health departments developed into a mesh of mutually agreeable arrangements. Physicians helped to collect vital statistics information, and they often served as county registrars, like the Fort Benton doctors who signed the birth certificates for most of the babies that Mary Kassmeier delivered. Health departments employed physicians, organized clinics and lectures featuring doctors, and compiled public health information that they furnished directly to medical organizations.[65]

Given the many ties between health departments and organized medicine, it is no surprise that the stature of midwives subsequently diminished. Without bureaucratic representation within the state-run infrastructure, professional midwives began to be considered second-class providers and eventually disreputable assistants. But the ousting of midwives from the work of reproduction represented more than a cozy institutional relationship between doctors and public health institutions. It was also evidence of the underlying dismissal of women in American culture. Midwives found themselves increasingly marginalized, even while holding both superior intellectual knowledge and the experience-based practical skills necessary in the birthing room. The fact that their practices were so easily diminished demonstrates the willingness of all parties involved—even the midwives themselves and the mothers they served—to believe that their work did not justify remuneration, public recognition, or institutional support.

The struggle itself was not with the presence of women in reproductive care, especially since female public health nurses were hired to fill the gap left by the removal of midwives. In fact, physicians and health departments depended on female nurses as a necessary part of the medical and public health infrastructure. The key difference was that nurses operated within the constructed medical and institutional hierarchy, putting in long hours and having little authority.[66] The idea of midwives working as *independent* agents offering care to pregnant women and their families proved untenable in American culture in the early 1900s, and even today the notion faces continued and virulent opposition from some physicians and public health officials.[67]

Isolated from each other by the absence of professional networks, targeted by the medical profession, and slowly downgraded by health departments, midwives rapidly decreased in number across the northern plains. With few young women seeing a future in the profession, practicing midwives remained only in those areas where medicine did not want to compete—in the most rural and isolated parts of the northern plains, in African American communities in the South, and in scattered Native American and Hispanic American populations.

Birth and death registration provided verifiable information about the reproductive context of the northern plains, but it also invited collaboration between the two stakeholders—health department professionals and medical doctors—least acquainted with women and their reproductive needs. The clear losers in the alliance of public health with the medical profession were not only midwives, who became subject to repeated public attacks and slurs upon their competency, but also women, families, and communities.[68] Mothers could no longer rely on female advocacy and control over the birthing process or access practitioners who prioritized their reproductive needs and requests. As the practice of midwifery dwindled, mothers lost more than an alternative to the dominant medical care paradigm. They faced the bewildering disappearance of solicitousness and the diminishment of relational value.

The Beginning of Midwifery's End

If we could somehow, with untold powers of historical memory, ask all reproductive care professionals across the northern plains and Rocky Mountains from the mid-1800s to the 1930s to step forward, a great host of regional inhabitants would emerge from the mists of the past. We would see Lizzie Maclean caring for her own stock with intense efficiency and then striding across the prairie to a neighbor's home to cook for a threshing crew or help with a birth. We would watch over the shoulder of the 1910 census taker as Anna Valleen, plying her trade in the midst of the boom-and-bust cycles of Butte, asked to be recorded as a "Professional Midwife."[69] Anna Hamalainen would hail us from Red Lodge, Montana, and point to babies, youth, and adults that she helped deliver in her more than thirty years of working as a midwife in the community.[70] Nurses at St. Clare Hospital in Fort Benton would smile and nod and explain that, even though they claimed membership in a rigid religious structure, they had found some measure of relative freedom in the expansive geography of the northern plains.[71]

We would recognize Mary Kassmeier juggling farm, family, and nearly full-time midwifery work, and Alice Susag would greet us as she set down her milking pail and began churning butter. Enmeshed in the relational tangle of western communities, these women were everywhere, from Malta, Montana, to Murdo, South Dakota, and from Bismarck, North Dakota, to South Pass City, Wyoming. Despite their presence, knowledge, and success, their work came, quietly and without fanfare, to a halt at the hand of health departments and medical organizations.[72]

The states of Montana, Wyoming, North Dakota, and South Dakota eliminated a vibrant regional practice of midwifery by forcing its gradual attrition. Quietly and incrementally, the state health departments cooperated with the medical profession to implement an entirely different framework for evaluating women, their skills, and their bodies. When Anna Hamaleinen passed away, she left behind no cohort of apprentice midwives to carry on her practice or share her expertise with the community. When Lizzie Maclean died, there was no crop of young mothers to fill her shoes, carry on her work, or add to her lifetime of reproductive wisdom. The experienced female elders so necessary for the support of young women faded into the background, their intimate and extensive knowledge deemed to be without value, their belief in female reproductive prowess denigrated as out of date and not worthy of preservation. Midwifery died a muted death, consigned to the silences of history by the conspiratorial vicissitudes of bureaucrats and doctors.

7

Maternity Homes and Motherhood

In a context of increasing attacks on their profession, female reproductive practitioners found diminishing niches of opportunity across the northern plains and Rocky Mountains. Attention to women's experiences reveals the infectious nature of the assumptions behind these attacks and the ways that destructive ideas mutated over time, becoming no less dangerous but continuing to control women and harm them and their families.

Catherine Walker's life spanned this difficult time in American history, and her approach to adversity embodied the attitude so common to women residing in the region. When she was just fourteen, a brutal tornado devastated her Minnesota hometown. During the onslaught, she sustained a deep facial laceration that a local physician stitched for her. Already interested in medicine, she found that the experience catalyzed her curiosity, and being a precocious, adventuresome teenager, she asked the doctor to take her on as an apprentice. Whether recognizing her natural talent or the value of a low-cost assistant, he agreed and immediately put her to work. For eight years she traveled with the doctor on his calls and quickly took on the responsibility of staying with laboring mothers during and after delivery. Eager to learn all she could, Walker soaked up an extensive medical education through this apprenticeship. When she married Russell Brodhead in 1893, she became Catherine Brodhead, an accomplished lay physician at only twenty-two years of age.[1]

In less than a decade Brodhead gave birth to four of her own children, and then she and Russell, like so many other western settlers, decided to move out of Minnesota. In 1907 Brodhead settled her family on a homestead south of Cartwright, North Dakota, where in 1911 she gave birth to a son, Wendell. Initially displeased by the barrenness of the Dakota prairie, she soon came to love the badlands she called home. The community venerated her healing skills, and pregnant women made use of her birthing expertise. She rode horseback "all over the country," and neighbors became accustomed to the sight of Brodhead astride her white horse on her way to a delivery.[2] Like other midwives of her era, she would "stay as long as needed" after a birth to help the mother recover, and she charged for her services on a sliding scale based on the family's resources, often accepting livestock or grain in lieu of cash.[3]

There being no physician to serve the area, Brodhead, according to local residents, "took the place of a doctor." The physician in the nearest town provided Brodhead with pharmaceuticals, which she then prescribed and administered to patients. When her husband found itinerant work out of state and left her to support their five children on her own, Brodhead, displaying the same resourceful ambition as she had at the age of fourteen, moved into the nearby town of Fairview, Montana, in 1928, and opened a maternity home.[4]

Maternity homes, also called lying-in homes or maternity hospitals, dotted the western landscape.[5] The rural town of Fairview, Montana, with a population nearing just six hundred residents in 1930, supported at least three lying-in hospitals: the Brodhead Maternity Home, along with small maternity hospitals like the Pominville and Berry Homes, operated by Hatty Pominville and Mattie Berry, respectively. These small businesses offered long-term on-site nursing and maternity care.[6]

Fairview, Montana, in the northeastern corner of the state, endured conditions similar to those of the larger northern plains and Rocky

Fig. 28. Catherine Brodhead, pictured here in the badlands where she worked, lived, and traveled. Courtesy of the Brodhead family.

Mountains region. For the difficult decades of the 1920s and 1930s, residents struggled with persistent drought.[7] Combined with the national economic crisis of the ensuing Great Depression, the drought made an already difficult environment that much more challenging.

Regional residents, faced with repeated crop failures in this largely agricultural region, eventually turned to the federal government for sustenance. According to historian Michael Grey, in the 1930s "60,000 families, a third of [North Dakota's] entire population, were dependent on county welfare boards. Between [North and South Dakota], half the population was on some form of relief and virtually everyone else qualified."[8] Extreme economic devastation characterized the region. Western historian Mary Murphy has explained how in the late 1930s "22 percent of the Montana work force was out of work, the highest unemployment rate of any state in the Union."[9]

The impacts to public health were legion, and while some conditions (like short-term hunger) could be remedied, the sustained nature of the crisis over a period of years meant that residents suffered from a number of health conditions that developed over time. The inability to afford care demoralized residents, as "many relief clients preferred not to be told the nature of their children's ailments, since they could do nothing about them."[10] The physical suffering brought about by economic conditions likely reduced fertility but did not eliminate it entirely, and without widespread access to contraception, women continued to conceive and grapple with health issues related to reproduction.

A host of federal agencies, including the Civilian Conservation Corps, the Bureau of Public Roads, the Public Works Administration, the Farm Security Administration, the U.S. Forest Service, and the Soil Conservation Service, directed work projects across the region.[11] It was these federal agencies that residents of the northern plains and Rocky Mountains, especially those residing in rural and poor areas, encountered. Federal employment opportunities certainly helped to alleviate some of the physical suffering associated with hunger, and some federal programs even went so far as to provide health care directly. In 1936 and 1937 Farmers Mutual Aid corporations were formed to provide basic care for residents of the Dakotas, and the Farm Security Association (FSA) created medical care cooperatives to serve residents of rural communities across the country.[12]

For pregnant women, government programs offered access to medical care but with certain caveats. Farmers Mutual Aid corporations and FSA medical care cooperatives adhered to the American Medical Association's guidance on care and demanded that certain standards be met, like requiring that reproductive care be provided exclusively by physicians.[13] The federal government's alignment with the AMA meant that other less expensive and potentially more effective providers, like midwives, could not serve women under the auspices of federal health-care programs. These AMA-approved guidelines "represented an unusually explicit government effort to monitor and modify medical practice for that period."[14]

Despite the lack of federal support for her work, Brodhead nevertheless continued to find a need for her services. She started her maternity home in rented quarters but soon purchased an imposing structure situated on a hill at the edge of town. The house had been constructed by a wealthy land speculator in 1911, and after his bankruptcy Brodhead purchased it. The large home's many sunny, well-lit rooms suited Brodhead's needs. She recruited her youngest son, Wendell, and his wife, Ruth, to assist with the business, and the extended Brodhead clan took up residence in the basement of the home. Maternity patients typically occupied the home's three bedrooms, and screens divided the dining and living rooms into separate patient areas as needed. While Brodhead saw to her patients' medical needs, Ruth did the cooking, laundry, and cleaning for the small facility, which housed from six to eight patients at a time.[15]

Women arrived in advance of their expected due dates and helped out with household work at the maternity home until their deliveries. Leon Brodhead, son of Ruth and Wendell Brodhead, remembered playing under the home's large oak table and being surrounded

Fig. 29. The Brodhead Maternity Home had a commanding view of the landscape from a hill just at the edge of town. The home still stands in Fairview, Montana, and has been renovated by its current owners. Courtesy of the Brodhead family.

by the ample knees and sturdy shins of maternity patients as they worked in the kitchen.[16] Sitting down and sharing stories with other women, even while peeling potatoes or chopping rhubarb, was likely a rare respite for these hardworking western women, and the companionship and support they gained surely made their delivery experiences all the more meaningful.

Fiercely protective of her clients, Catherine Brodhead made sure that mothers spent at least ten days recovering after delivery, often proclaiming that "these are women, not cows."[17] In the 1930s and 1940s the fee for an entire stay, including treatment, a bed, and meals, at the Brodhead Maternity Home ranged from thirty to forty dollars, although Brodhead always made arrangements for families without funds.[18] Her daughter-in-law Ruth remembered that Brodhead "gave the mothers and babies every minute they needed. She was on her feet constantly."[19] Community residents relied on Brodhead to be available at all hours of the day or night to tend their children in illness, help birth their babies, and watch over the elderly.

Brodhead's records, lovingly preserved by her family, showed that reproductive care made up at least two-thirds of her business, with the remainder including treatment of conditions like pneumonia, anemia, high blood pressure, and rheumatism. She also provided nursing care for those recovering from operations or strokes and even dealt with trauma, such as broken bones and even one patient, as noted in her records, who had been "shot through arm."[20] A practitioner who operated as both a midwife and a physician, Brodhead used pituitrin, a drug administered to hasten labor, and was trained in the use of forceps.[21] While she delivered infants for years on her own as a midwife, family history suggests that Brodhead modified her midwifery practice to enable the success of her maternity home. By calling local doctors for some deliveries, especially for families who could afford the charge, she allowed physicians to earn a substantial fee, usually around forty-five dollars and equal to or higher than her charge for the entire maternity stay. Brodhead's maternity home income only just met her basic living expenses, and to avoid losing her limited earnings, she likely adjusted her routine to ensure the support of local physicians. Maternity homes existed from around 1900 through the 1940s in the region, a relatively brief window of time. As a savvy business owner, Brodhead recognized her precarious position and took steps to protect her revenue.[22]

The proceeds from her maternity home supported Brodhead and provided a place where she could care for her extended family. She "always wore a dress and had a purse on her arm," and she loved to "jig" when the mood struck. While she may have looked back on her independent and possibly more remunerative midwifery days with longing, she no doubt recognized the change in reproductive care patterns and saw her work as worthy of respect. She chose to find happiness in a life surrounded by people who valued her skills, grandchildren who loved spending time with her, and a house where she could, as her family remembered, "mov[e] the table back" and dance on the hardwood floors.[23]

Brodhead did not experience overt opposition from the local medical establishment; she closed her maternity home in 1949 because of her own advancing age.[24] She died just five years later, in 1954, after a lifetime filled with generous caregiving. Over more than sixty years as a reproductive provider, Brodhead knew the value of loving presence and intentionally shared her skills with her family, her clients, and her community. As her grandson, Leon, remembered, "She was just there. She made sure I was taken care of."[25] Looking back on years of struggle and hours, days, weeks, and months filled with unending work, Brodhead had many reasons to feel sorry for herself. Instead, she chose to help others in a way that brought health and healing. In her time as proprietor of the Brodhead Maternity Home, she delivered more than one thousand babies, and her home came to stand as a totem for the Fairview community.[26]

Maternity Homes in the Northern Plains

Even though the unholy allegiance of health departments and medicine quickly toppled female dominance in reproductive care, women like Brodhead remained intimately involved in childbirth as maternity home operators. Maternity homes offered a transitional space from the female-dominated arena of midwifery care, still present in the minds of northern plains and Rocky Mountain residents in the late 1920s and 1930s, to the more rigid, physician-controlled space of the formal hospital.[27]

Maternity home owners, usually women, played an essential role in rural communities. Historian Dawn Nickel has explained that "small-town physicians, as well as patients, depended upon the availability of female proprietorships" across the region for basic medical care.[28] Women delivered at home in the 1800s, so there was little need for maternity hospitals before the turn of the twentieth century, but as mothers moved away from home birth in the 1900s, maternity hospitals became increasingly common.[29] A woman like Brodhead, with her vast experience providing reproductive care, could easily make space in her house for one or two patients. In fact, Brodhead's purchase of a building specifically suited to maternity home work required far more planning than was typical.

We do not know how many small hospitals like Brodhead's existed across the region.[30] Health departments in Montana, North Dakota, and Wyoming did not oversee maternity homes, though South Dakota did. By 1928 South Dakota inspectors had licensed ninety-nine lying-in homes, and in its annual report the South Dakota Health Department made note of the homes' particular value to residents in counties with few medical personnel.[31] The department's expanded count of 119 lying-in homes statewide in 1930 offered a sense of how widespread the institutions were in rural communities.[32]

South Dakota allowed midwives, nurses, and physicians to operate maternity hospitals, while also requiring that proprietors comply with notification and registration policies.[33] Standards required that lying-in homes maintain a certain level of cleanliness, be heated in winter, and provide laundered linens—all commonsense requirements. It is noteworthy that South Dakota law insisted that maternity home operators, many of whom claimed a lifetime of independent delivery experience, call physicians for all deliveries. Thus, South Dakota mandated for all maternity homes in the state the arrangement that Catherine Brodhead applied selectively. It is possible that Brodhead's shrewd practice—reducing her own level of control and total revenue in order to provide area physicians with a lucrative arrangement—may have been widely followed across the region.[34]

The timing and detail of South Dakota's maternity home registration efforts, especially in light of the move by physicians to eliminate competition from midwives, bears examination. Women needed time and space to recuperate from delivery. Midwives provided that service in the home; physicians were unwilling to provide it at all. However, it appears that, after critiquing the services of skilled female reproductive providers, the medical establishment, in cooperation with health departments, allowed those same women to operate maternity homes, with the stipulation that physicians also be guaranteed a steady and generous income.[35] By cooperating with medical providers, Brodhead carved out an important role for herself in a context where female reproductive expertise often garnered attack and women like Fort Benton midwife Mary Kassmeier saw practices years in the making evaporate under the onslaught of antimidwifery sentiment.

Individual midwives adjusted to the changing reproductive legal and social landscape and grudgingly accepted the futility of resistance; maternity home proprietors did not organize, demand recognition, or strike for more equitable pay. The relationship between doctors and maternity home owners has been characterized as one of "mutual dependence" and "egalitarian" in nature.[36] However, the fact that female proprietors failed to protest the arrangement should not be construed as agreement. Maternity home operators watched physicians arrive during the late stages of delivery and then depart, usually in just a couple of hours, during which time the home operator tended to the needs of the laboring mother, cleaned up from the birth, assisted the doctor, and then saw to other patients. The physician's approximately two-hour stint earned him the same compensation that the hospital proprietor collected for a full ten days of work, a situation more accurately described as the antithesis of egalitarianism.

Female maternity home owners worked in close contact with doctors, but proximity should not be equated with favor. Maternity home proprietors knew that "good relations with doctors and surgeons were imperative" and assiduously protected the remnants of reproductive employment that remained to them.[37] As they saw their incomes reduced and their livelihoods threatened, they might have felt a sense of shared purpose with physicians. It is just as likely, though, that they stewed inwardly, made the best of their limited circumstances, and, as a means of resistance, pushed the furniture back and danced on the hardwood floors.

While the true relationship between physicians and maternity home owners might never be decisively determined, we can conclude that proprietors filled a critical health-care gap. When physicians took over the work of reproductive care and moved childbirth out of the home, maternity hospital owners stepped forward to provide hands-on care, reproductive knowledge, and birthing space. In time, maternity homes, like midwives, also fell out of favor. In Montana only fifteen homes remained in 1933, in 1936 that number had dropped to seven, and by 1950 only two lying-in hospitals were operating in the state.[38]

Midwife to Doctor, Home to Hospital

As part of the incremental yet widespread removal of midwives like Mary Kassmeier, Lizzie Maclean, Anna Hamalainen, and even lay physicians like Catherine Brodhead from active practice, a two-phase process emerged. First, male doctors, endorsed by state institutions, replaced female midwives as the premiere birth assistants. This change addressed the type of provider but did not necessarily dictate location, and physicians continued to assist at home deliveries. The preference for doctors over midwives represented a victory for physicians but was incomplete. Doctors did not have carte blanche with pregnant women at home, as laboring mothers maintained the prerogative of summoning and dismissing the physician. Home-based birth, even with a male physician attending, allowed for some female authority. Ensconced in the home and still in control of the birthing environment, women monitored the activities and procedures performed. When female family members and friends lived nearby or traveled to be at the birth, they watched the doctor's actions and assessed his competence and diagnostic skills based on their own broad stores of reproductive knowledge. Physician interpretations and directives could be consistently questioned by the birthing mother, female relatives, neighbors, or friends, all of whom would likely consider themselves experienced in childbirth.[39]

Physicians continued delivering in mothers' homes during the first phase of the transition, but that practice transitioned to increasingly common hospital deliveries. In the hospital the physician stood at the topmost position in a clearly defined hierarchy, from which he could command nurses, restrict entry to the delivery room, and issue directives without challenge. Physicians found that hospital births simplified their routine: with centrally located obstetric patients the doctor attended to other duties and simultaneously managed two or more birthing patients. Able to provide consistent care to all of their patients while women labored in the hospital, physicians advised hospital delivery from a public health perspective, claiming that patients could receive better care from medical staff at the hospital.[40]

Physician convenience propelled the move to the hospital, but other constituencies found value there as well. For nurses, home care had a lingering association with domestic labor, so employment in hospitals carried higher status.[41] For women without family or friends nearby, hospital birth looked attractive. The hospital took care of the cleanup, nurses assisted with the new baby, and the mother temporarily escaped her domestic role.[42] Hospitals also gained an unlikely ally in the burgeoning availability of the automobile.[43] Access to transportation meant that women could travel to the hospital in the early stages of labor; they could go to the doctor at a centralized location that ensured the availability of medical attention. Urban women made the switch to hospital birth first, and rural women followed as hospital care became available in their local areas.[44]

Physician convenience, nursing employment patterns, women's preferences, and cultural changes cemented the transition from home birth to hospital delivery. In 1900 nearly all babies were born outside the hospital, but by the 1920s hospital birth was quickly becoming the norm for women in urban America.[45] Lacking continued contact with home birth, women of childbearing age relegated out-of-hospital delivery to the historic dustbin, unaware of the rapid transition to an unknown and untried practice of birth. The substitution of medical birth in a hospital ward for social birth in

Fig. 30. This 1929 photograph of nurses holding infants at the hospital in Rock Springs, Wyoming, captures the shift in childbirth practices from home to hospital across the northern plains and Rocky Mountains from 1890 to the 1940s. Sub Neg. 1772, Nurses with babies on steps, Rock Springs, 5-16-1929. Wyoming State Archives.

the company of friends and family was complete. American culture shifted from free range to industrial birth over the course of a few short decades.

These shifts—from midwife to doctor and from home to hospital—occurred in a messy hodgepodge influenced by local personalities, rural and urban demographics, and regional characteristics. The transition occurred from 1890 through 1940 across the Dakotas, Wyoming, and Montana; the reach of midwifery diminished, and increasing numbers of mothers delivered in hospitals. Given the number of unique factors impacting this change, it remained relatively easy to find seeming exceptions to this pattern. For example, midwives had all but ceased to practice by 1930 in South Dakota, but just across the state line in Powder River County, Montana, they continued to be the dominant reproductive care providers through the 1940s. While Montana, North Dakota, Wyoming, and South Dakota eventually adopted the physician-in-hospital model, these states' residents shifted to hospital births more slowly, especially in rural areas, as compared to many other parts of the United States. Regional circumstances delayed the eradication of midwifery and made possible the recollection and retrieval of the oral histories on which my research rests. A study of this nature in more urban regions of the country would not have been possible.

The Beast Beneath

In 1913 Lizzie Maclean toiled on a homestead held in her husband's name, and she could not vote in national elections. Just thirty years later Catherine Brodhead, with the deed to her maternity home in her own name and the ability to affect policy with her vote, operated in the midst of both expansions of and diminishments to female power.[46] Comparing their experiences shows how a consistent devaluing of women infects cultural practices and simultaneously evolves to colonize additional territory.

Lizzie Maclean moved through her daily round with confidence and boundless energy. Her drive to invest her efforts in the northern plains with meaning was not unusual, and her experiences revealed the ways that women worked, the scaffolding of emerging communities, and the formation of western culture. Maclean established a homestead and participated in an informal yet highly effective community infrastructure oriented around reproductive caregiving.

By recording the details of her own life and the lives of those around her in her diary, Maclean emerged from its pages as a complex, determined, and wryly sarcastic inhabitant of a beautiful but at times bleak landscape. In all of the tasks to which she set her hand and formidable will, she acted as a potent force. Even though the state had not seen fit to solicit her opinion on elections by allowing her to vote and no public health nurse educated her about cleanliness and sanitation, Maclean navigated the details of her life with a confidence based on her authority as a woman. She laid claim to her own common sense and served the reproductive needs of her community as a respected expert. Even though she lacked many of the rights that modern women enjoy, Maclean framed the world through an empowering, though essentialist, lens of reproduction.[47]

When pregnant women turned from family and midwives to physicians, power relationships shifted.[48] Catherine Brodhead's experience demonstrated this demotion in the span of just one lifetime. As a professional midwife, she practiced as the resident authority. When she dismounted from her white horse at a laboring mother's home, the family did not look behind her for the "real" expert. But as a maternity home owner just a few years later, she was forced to adjust her practice to suit not only her clients but the power of medicine.

The practice of midwifery ranks as one of the oldest and most established job titles in human history. That such a storied and venerated tradition could be supplanted in the northern plains and Rocky Mountains by seemingly inconsequential changes, including the mundane work of health department officials nagging residents about completing forms, demonstrates the potent impacts of devaluing women. The toxic habit of ignoring the opinions, voices, and skills of the female half of the population occurs in everyday events, consistently challenging areas where women hold power.

Adjusting to violations of space and personhood define the female experience. But at a specific time and place—at the turn of the twentieth century in the Dakotas, Wyoming, and Montana—women claimed reproduction as their purview, their right, and their domain. Because women like Maclean and Brodhead and their contemporaries embodied a practice of power but did not speak a language that acknowledged or valued it, they could not verbalize or protect this essential component of reproductive care.

Conclusion

What We Lost

Alice Susag and Mary Kassmeier lived nearly three hundred miles
from each other in northern Montana. Susag spent her days in the
open country of buttes, sage, and blowing grasses, with only occasional treks to town. Kassmeier embraced farm life, worked in a
hospital, and traveled on the Montague shortline railroad to visit
clients. Her world appeared cosmopolitan compared to Susag's, yet
both women dealt with a surprisingly similar reproductive reality:
they interpreted the world through the lens of productivity, from
setting hens to harvesting seasonal medicinal herbs. Women in all
stages of procreative capability populated their daily interactions:
young girls transitioning through puberty, new mothers haggard
from early-morning nausea, mature women with expanding families, and those demographically few who, in a state with a youthful
population, planned their days around farming and grandchildren
instead of marking potential pregnancies or worrying over multiple
miscarriages.

Susag and Kassmeier actively pursued financial stability for their
families, contributing income while simultaneously establishing
community ties. They invested in a social safety net that enriched
their lives and those of the people around them, and this safety net
could be called upon in the event of a devastating loss or economic

crisis. Their work did not take directly from the relational ecosystem in which they lived; they did not extract resources from the northern Montana soil. Instead, they found ways of creating. They helped to build something, producing vibrant communities, families, and identities.

Contributions like organizing community groups, teaching a bachelor neighbor how to bake bread, delivering butter, or sewing pretty new dresses for neighbor children helped people of the northern plains and Rocky Mountains move beyond bare survival and identify with, cultivate, and feel pride in their home. All across the Dakotas, Wyoming, and Montana, investments in caring, by both women and men, gave residents reason to hope, dream, and plan for a future, even in the midst of marginal cropland and scarce consumer goods.

The use of contextualized data helps to tease out some of these salient details and uncovers the buried realities of much of human history—the hidden portion that is so often female. Scientific number-crunching often marginalizes women and people of color, but data can also be leveraged to reveal patterns and demonstrate how women's economic, relational, and cultural contributions used reproductive caregiving as one of many tools to knit human experience into a social and caring pattern. These kinds of multifaceted connections birthed the American West.

From Lizzie Maclean and Alice Susag to Isabella Mogstad, Faye Hoven, and Lydia Keating, women performed the labor of reproduction for humans, livestock, and a geographic region. They took supportive and shrewd positions that enhanced both financial wellbeing and the health of the human ecosystem. Their work relied

Figs. 31 and 32. Julia Albright of Helena, Montana, pictured first with her husband and two of her children and then with her four children, visually demonstrates the physical presence of women's reproduction in the northern plains and Rocky Mountains. Pac 83-9-8, Edward and Julia Albright with Edna and Leola; Pac 83-9-9, Julia Reynolds Albright with her children. Montana Historical Society Research Center.

on reproductive expertise. They dealt with gestation, delivery, and postpartum recovery on a daily basis, weaving reproductive labor into the everyday routine of family, home, health, and economic survival. Mothers gained knowledge through routine life experiences of reproduction, like Mary Tinsley's multiple births and Idora Guthrie's miscarriage.

Reproduction includes acquainting children with their environment. Laurentza Koch, Pearl Johnson, Katie Adams, Peggy Czyzeski, and Beatrice Kaasch produced future generations *and* provided the interpersonal structure necessary for the development of American society. Reproductive activities made the northern plains and Rocky Mountains region a place to be from and a place to come home to. Women and mothers "made" citizens through tenderness and relationship. Theirs was an ecology of care connected to the land, the people, and the larger community.[1]

Native American women, violently removed from the spaces where they birthed and nourished their children, embodied geographically sensible and culturally nourishing reproductive practices. Existence in a challenging physical environment necessitated just the sorts of linkages between culture, landscape, and reproduction enacted in regional indigenous traditions. Ironically, subsequent settlers of the Dakotas, Montana, and Wyoming, while seeking to draw a clear line between themselves and the rightful Native inhabitants, adopted a practice with similar themes. Western women embraced elements of care; the particulars of their experience became intertwined in a grand snarl of life.

Past human experience was embodied in strains of connectedness, yet traditional methods of research often ignore the role of women and reproduction and thereby miss the truth of lived reality. Procreative events are not easily quantified. Data enumerate the patients seen or bushels harvested, but how can the value of an empathetic visit at a dying child's bedside be assessed? Does the difficulty of tabulation render the visit meaningless? To the contrary, relational and caring activities reside at the center of meaning and value. The difficulty of measurement should not deter us, as the study of reproduction contributes an essential complexity to studies of human history.

The sharing and exchange of resources based on individual human need allowed Euro-American settlers to colonize a harsh and unforgiving landscape without official public infrastructure.[2] The regional ethos of individuality has been taken out of context and made to stand as an emblem of American identity. At a time when the human species depends on collaborative human effort to solve daunting global problems, recognition of the full scope of migrant activity could inject a more balanced perspective. Excessive individuality did not define the region. Instead, residents of Montana, the Dakotas, and Wyoming, both male and female, depended on an ethic of exchange and sociability. Cynthia Jane Capron and Mary Zanto gave and received assistance; area midwives negotiated authority with the women who received their care.

The efforts of northern plains and Rocky Mountain midwives contributed intimacy, shared power, and negotiated authority to a region known for its emphasis on personal freedom and isolated individuality. Such actions of care have all too often been defined as nonessential. Even contemporary measures of gross domestic product consciously omit the value of caregiving, an essential human exchange whose value far outstrips the commodity production of pork bellies. Anna Hamalainen, Desiree Villian, Elizabeth Rae, Ethel Eide, and Erminia Maggini embodied the essential infrastructure of human culture. By working with mothers to make families, they constructed communities and forged a regional identity.[3]

In a time of mobility, poor nutrition, and scarce resources, death did happen; it was an all too frequent occurrence. A system that ignored the needs of all its citizens put many settlers in intolerable conditions, worked to the point of exhaustion, without the care of extended family. When mothers and infants at their most vulnerable died from those conditions, health departments and medical associations blamed women for their lack of knowledge and ignorance about sanitation. Contrary to the standard narrative, midwifery did not kill women. The scarcity of midwives did. The practice of ignoring women's needs and requests—pleas for more available care, demands for time to recuperate and heal—meant that women and infants perished. Bertha Emmert did not die because she lacked an informational pamphlet; she fell under the weight of a life without assistance, from the burden of childbearing without ample support.

When health departments took on the task of recording deaths and births, the state began to make citizens. Individuals no longer formed their identities solely through family, community, and national connections; vital statistics collection and recording took the lead in documenting personhood. The transition brought about some changes, and eventually reproductive death rates, especially among Euro-American populations in the northern plains and Rocky Mountains, declined.[4] But the change was accomplished by demonizing a system that offered uniquely pro-woman care—care that focused on improved nutrition, a reduction in physical depletion, and rest and recuperation for pregnant and postpartum mothers. As with most changes, the superintending of childbirth and death by state health departments brought a host of impacts. Reproductive policy became an important part of open discussions and benefited from its inclusion in public dialogue. But a particular concept of care suffered.

Childbirth and reproduction are initiated in the most private of acts and have far-reaching public and communal effects. Nations rely on citizens; culture depends on generativity. The demise of midwifery diminished the very actions that enhance well-being.[5] Getting the baby out of the uterus remains just a small part of the reproductive activity often termed "delivery." Integrating the child into the human community and celebrating nurturing are equally important. The history of childbirth and its particular details in the northern plains and Rocky Mountains tell a story of extracting babies in a mechanistic fashion not at all dissimilar from mining for copper or harvesting timber—a pattern of taking that entirely ignores connectedness and value.

The early twentieth-century attack on midwifery hurt the profession but did not end the need for generativity. A global community sharing authority and valuing other creatures as part of the ecology of care leads to generous abundance. Through an ethic of care, a community protects, as conservationist Aldo Leopold explained, the land's "capacity for self-renewal."[6] Childbirth is no different. The nation depends on the human species to self-renew through reproduction.

Childbirth is not simply a physical act. It is a social act, a cultural act, and an ethical act. It requires the give-and-take of conversation and demands a posture of listening and the exchange of both information and authority. Medicine willfully denied these realities in its aggressive colonization of the space of birth, and it effected the removal of women's legitimate ownership of and involvement in the intimate and personal act of procreation. The implications of this wrongheaded and unethical seizure continue to infect contemporary ideas and policies about women, the female body, and the process of childbirth. Ill-informed conclusions about midwives are even now being used to suggest ignorant policy changes, especially for midwives of color.[7]

I returned to eastern Montana to complete some of the final research for this book, and my oldest daughter decided to travel with me. My previous trips were characterized by hours behind the wheel, but on this journey she shared the driving and I soaked up the space and sky. The miles of western expanse, the grass-scented air, the bluffs that begged to be climbed, and the clouds piling up in the great blueness still remained, as did the memory of the women who had so recently and yet so long ago inhabited the northern plains.

I thought about what they taught me, about what I learned from the host of women in all those places across the Dakotas, Wyoming, and Montana. My task did not include monumental efforts like storming the Bastille or developing a fungus to biodegrade take-out containers but instead called for a practice far easier and simultaneously more challenging: to listen to and value women, care, connection, and kindness.

Fortunately, history is not determinism, and our inability to share power and negotiate authority in the past is just that: the past. Moving forward, we can do smart things more and foolish things less. We can resee the world with eyes that recognize women and the importance of empathy and kindness. We can emphasize care and value the most essential human act of reproduction.[8] In an age when caregiving is allocated so little value, Alice Susag, Mary Kassmeier, Pearl Johnson, Anna Hamalainen, Desiree Villian, and Martha Noble attest to the essential role of reproduction in maintaining human connections and raising happy and healthy members of future generations.

The diversity of human history is wide and deep, but we all, every one of us, share the experience of being born. We can make birth more than a bare-knuckled quest to survive. With an ear to the realities of the northern plains and Rocky Mountains, we can create systems and practices that listen to women, value caregiving, and celebrate birth.

NOTES

Introduction

1. The tendency to ignore reproduction, mothering, and childbirth is not
confined to the field of American studies or even the discipline of history. Archeologist Laurie Wilkie documents the academic "failure to
'see' motherhood" in her field. See Laurie Wilkie, *The Archaeology of
Mothering: An African-American Midwife's Tale* (New York: Routledge,
2003), xix. Molly Ladd-Taylor's classic text *Mother-Work: Women, Child
Welfare, and the State, 1890–1930* (Urbana: University of Illinois Press,
1994) also investigates this phenomenon.
2. A host of scholars laid the essential groundwork for questioning the
assumed western narrative. One quintessential text that stands as an
exemplar of this essential work is Susan Armitage and Elizabeth Jameson's edited volume *The Women's West* (Norman: University of Oklahoma
Press, 1987). Armitage and Jameson explicitly highlight these issues in
their introduction to that work.
3. Wilkie describes children as a "form of natural resource whose successful
transformation to adulthood ensures a society's continuation." This was
particularly true of my study period in the northern plains and Rocky
Mountains, where childbearing represented an important cultural and
economic activity critical to the region's development. Wilkie, *Archaeology
of Mothering*, 3.

4. Patricia Jasen investigates "what childbirth has been made to stand for" and documents the ways that cultural assumptions directed the interpretations of Native childbearing practices. Patricia Jasen, "Race, Culture, and the Colonization of Childbirth in Northern Canada," *Social History of Medicine* 10, no. 3 (1997): 383–400, quote at 383.

5. Marla Powers states that references to Native American reproductive practices employed "Western negative notions of female physiology," an example of constructed notions of birth at work. Marla N. Powers, "Menstruation and Reproduction: An Oglala Case," *Signs: A Journal of Women and Culture* 6, no. 1 (1980): 54–63, quote at 65.

6. The processes of reproduction and mothering are appropriately characterized as "socially constructed, fluid, and changing." Wilkie, *Archaeology of Mothering*, 11.

7. Ann Marie Plane, "Childbirth Practices among Native American Women of New England and Canada, 1600–1800," in *Women and Health in America: Historical Readings*, ed. Judith Walzer Leavitt (Madison: University of Wisconsin Press, 1999), 38–47, quote at 38.

8. Minnie Martin to Dr. Grace Raymond Hebard, January 29, 1927, 4, Folder 17, Box 25, Collection 40008, Grace Raymond Hebard Papers, American Heritage Center, Laramie, Wyoming.

9. Episiotomies, still performed with unnecessary frequency, involve incision of the sensitive flesh between the vagina and anus. Typically performed when the infant's head is crowning, episiotomies are subsequently stitched after delivery of the placenta.

10. Relocation Camp Report, 31, Folder 3, Box 1, Collection 4000036, Susan McKay Papers, American Heritage Center, Laramie, Wyoming.

11. Mary Melcher's research on reproduction in the Southwest offers another geographically based study as a point of comparison. See Mary Melcher, *Pregnancy, Motherhood, and Choice in Twentieth-Century Arizona* (Tucson: University of Arizona Press, 2012).

12. Sarah Carter offers a concise explanation of the central role of women in the American West in the introduction to her book *Montana Women Homesteaders: A Field of One's Own* (Helena MT: Far Country Press, 2009).

13. Tonia M. Compton, "'They Have as Much Right There as Bachelors': Provisions for Female Landowners in Nineteenth Century Homestead Legislation," paper presented to the Western History Association, Oklahoma City, October 2007, 1–2.

14. Frederick Jackson Turner's "Significance of the Frontier in American History," an essay penned on the occasion of the World's Columbian Exposition in Chicago in 1893, stands as a quintessential settler colonialist manifesto. Turner's interpretation of U.S. history rests on the idea that American settlement could "explain American development," as he stated in the first paragraph of that essay. Turner's work, like nearly all other accounts of the late 1800s, focuses entirely on the male endeavor of colonization. Philip Deloria has critiqued the staying power of ideas like Turner's, stating that American-ness continues to rest on "imagining and performing domination and power." Deloria points to race and gender as sites where such nation-making "play" occurs. Philip Deloria, *Playing Indian* (New Haven: Yale University Press, 1998), 186.

15. As Steven Conn relates in his book *History's Shadow: Native American and Historical Consciousness in the Nineteenth Century* (Chicago: University of Chicago Press, 2004), Native Americans were written out of the area's story. Under a settler colonial agenda, indigenous control and habitation did not fit the nationalistic metanarrative. White settlers refused to recognize Native peoples as historic forebears and relegated their existence to prehistory.

16. Patrick Wolfe points to the desire for land as the driver of settler colonialism. He lists a broad range of qualifying land uses, from agriculture to "forestry, fishing, pastoralism and mining." Patrick Wolfe, "Settler Colonialism and the Elimination of the Native," *Journal of Genocide Research* 8, no. 4 (2006): 387–409, quote at 395.

17. Lorenzo Veracini has charted the "progressive disappearance" of indigenous residents, followed by the "ultimate affirmation of settler control," with a final claim by settlers that they "have come to stay" and "will not return 'home.'" Lorenzo Veracini, *Settler Colonialism: A Theoretical Overview* (Basingstoke: Palgrave Macmillan, 2010), 6, 17, 53.

18. Neil Campbell, *The Rhizomatic West: Representing the American West in a Transnational, Global, Media Age* (Lincoln: University of Nebraska Press, 2008), 2.

19. I suggest that the central contribution of reproduction in the work of settler colonialism is along of the lines of Campbell's "fundamental critique of conventional representations," while cautioning against refashioning a replacement metanarrative that seeks to simplify the nuances of lived experience, especially that of women and their reproductive role in the

northern plains and Rocky Mountains. Neil Campbell, *The Cultures of the American New West* (Edinburgh: Edinburgh University Press, 2000), 9. Overly generalized narratives, as Campbell states, often "hide more than they explain" (15). We can explore and value Euro-American women's reproductive contributions while simultaneously recognizing the complexities and disconnectedness of their experiences in the American West.

20. Amy Kaplan has offered what must be recognized as a supremely cogent explanation of this idea, especially as she illuminates the role of gender and domesticity in settler colonialism. She explains that domesticity—and I include reproduction as a cultural signifier of home making—"makes Euro-Americans feel at home in terrain in which *they* are initially the foreigners." Amy Kaplan, "Manifest Domesticity," *American Literature* 70, no. 3 (1998): 581–606, quote at 591 (original emphasis).

21. Susie Walking Bear Yellowtail worked as a nurse on the Crow Indian Reservation beginning in the 1920s. Brianna Theobold's narration of Yellowtail's storied career as a health professional documented the potential for childbirth practices as sites of resistance. In both assisting women to give birth outside of Indian Health Service institutions and in bringing attention to coercive sterilizations, Yellowtail's activism highlighted the role of birth as both an important cultural moment and a place of colonial ideological attack. "Susie Walking Bear Yellowtail: 'Our Bright Morning Star,'" Women's History Matters (Montana Historical Society), May 6, 2014, http://montanawomenshistory.org/susie-walking-bear-yellowtail -our-bright-morning-star/; Brianna Theobald, "Nurse, Mother, Wife— Susie Walking Bear Yellowtail and the Struggle for Crow Women's Reproductive Autonomy," *Montana: The Magazine of Western History* 66, no. 3 (2018): 17–35; Gregory R. Campbell, "Changing Patterns of Health and Effective Fertility among the Northern Cheyenne of Montana, 1886– 1903," *American Indian Quarterly* 15, no. 3 (1991): 339–58.

22. Carter, *Montana Women Homesteaders*, 21.

23. Both males and female have a perineal region, commonly understood as the floor of the pelvis. For women, the word *perineum* often refers to the area between the vaginal opening and the rectum. While small perineal tears during delivery are common and usually heal swiftly, women who gave birth to extremely large babies, like Phelps's fourteen-pound

infant, often endured extensive ripping that should have received medical attention.

24. Quoted in Alice Boardman Smuts, *Science in the Service of the Children, 1893–1935* (New Haven: Yale University Press, 2006), 88–89.

25. Smuts, *Science in the Service of the Children*, 93.

26. These characteristics are true also for the Canadian province of Alberta, as pointed out in Dawn Nickel, "Dying in the West, Part 1: Hospitals and Health Care in Montana and Alberta, 1880–1950," *Montana: The Magazine of Western History* 59, no. 3 (2009): 25–45; and Dawn Nickel, "Dying in the West, Part 2: Caregiving in the Home and the Death of Daniel Slayton," *Montana: The Magazine of Western History* 59, no. 4 (2009): 3–23. Like the high mortality rates recorded in Montana, Alberta recorded striking levels of infant and maternal death in the early 1900s.

27. "Historical Decennial Census Population for Wyoming Counties, Cities, and Towns," Wyoming Department of Administration and Information, Division of Economic Analysis, accessed February 15, 2020, http://eadiv .state.wy.us/demog_data/pop2000/cntycity_hist.htm.

28. The federal census records did include a note indicating that "the [South Dakota] jump in population from 1890 to 1900 was due in part to the inclusion of residents of reservations (a total of 19,792 people) that were counted but not included in 1890 totals." Twelfth Census of the United States, February 1, 1901, Census Bulletin, Population of South Dakota by Counties and Minor Civil Divisions, 1. Dramatic growth also occurred in North Dakota, with an 1870 head count of 2,405 and a 1900 total of 319,146. Twelfth Census of the United States, January 23, 1901, Census Bulletin, Population of North Dakota by Counties and Minor Civil Divisions, 1.

29. 1920 Census, Montana, Number and Distribution of Inhabitants, 7.

30. 1920 Census, Montana, Composition and Characteristics of the Population, 26; 1920 Census, South Dakota, Composition and Characteristics of the Population, 30; 1920 Census, North Dakota, Composition and Characteristics of the Population, 30; 1920 Census, Wyoming, Composition and Characteristics of the Population, 2.

31. Elaine Lindgren's *Land in Her Own Name: Women as Homesteaders in North Dakota* (Norman: University of Oklahoma Press, 1991) lays out both the commonalities and individual differences in female homesteaders in

North Dakota. Carter's *Montana Women Homesteaders* presents similar detail for those settling in Montana.

32. The U.S. government created reservations in accordance with—and often reduced them in violation of—treaty agreements. Existing reservations in the area include the Fort Berthold Reservation, Turtle Mountain Reservation, Spirit Lake Reservation, and Standing Rock Reservation of North Dakota; the Cheyenne River Reservation, Crow Creek Indian Reservation, Flandreau Santee Tribal Lands, Lower Brule Indian Reservation, Pine Ridge Reservation, Rosebud Indian Reservation, Sisseton-Wahpeton Oyate Tribal Lands, Yankton Tribal Lands, and Standing Rock Indian Reservation of South Dakota; the Wind River Reservation in Wyoming; and the Fort Peck Indian Reservation, Rocky Boy Reservation, Northern Cheyenne Indian Reservation, Crow Indian Reservation, Fort Belknap Reservation, Blackfeet Indian Reservation, and Flathead Reservation in Montana. Information about sovereign tribes in the region, as well as the formation and location of reservations, can be located through state government websites (South Dakota, https://sdtribalrelations.sd .gov/; North Dakota, http://indianaffairs.nd.gov/tribal-nations/; Wyoming, http://www.wyo.gov/about-wyoming/wyoming-history; Montana, https://tribalnations.mt.gov/tribalnations).

33. Gary D. Libecap, "Learning about the Weather: Dryfarming Doctrine and Homestead Failure in Eastern Montana, 1900–1925," *Montana: The Magazine of Western History* 52, no. 1 (2002): 24–33.

34. Libecap, "Learning about the Weather," 32.

35. Mary Wilma Hargreaves shows how this pattern worked, with those "who could not make a heavy capital outlay" looking to less attractive areas. They were "encouraged to expand the agricultural frontier from the valleys and fringes of the Plains far back over the uplands." Mary Wilma M. Hargreaves, *Dry Farming in the Northern Great Plains, 1900–1925* (Cambridge MA: Harvard University Press, 1957), 19.

36. We have come to think of the word *doctor* as meaning just one type of practitioner, but in the 1800s and early 1900s many varieties and theories of medicine existed, including homeopathy, allopathy, osteopathy, and eclectics. Allopathic physicians are now seen as the dominant branch of the profession.

37. Nancy Schrom Dye, "History of Childbirth in America," *Signs* 6, no. 1 (1980): 97–108, quote at 98.

38. Sylvia D. Hoffert, "Childbearing on the Trans-Mississippi Frontier, 1830–1900," *Western Historical Quarterly* 22, no. 3 (1991): 272–88, quote at 274.

39. See chapter 7 for a detailed explanation of the final shift from midwives to allopathic physicians in hospitals. Mary Melcher states that "although some middle- and upper-class urban women in the northeastern United States had shifted from midwives to doctors in the late eighteenth and early nineteenth centuries, the long distances between ranches and towns, a lack of competent physicians in rural areas, and personal preferences and traditions meant that many western women, and especially minority women, relied on midwives up until the 1940s." Mary Melcher, "Times of Crisis and Joy: Pregnancy, Childbirth, and Mothering in Rural Arizona, 1910–1940," *Journal of Arizona History* 40, no. 2 (1999): 181–200, quote at 181.

40. With the entrance of women into the academy, the women's health movement in the 1970s and 1980s, and second-wave feminism's push to include the experiences women in official histories, scholars attempted to identify and describe midwives and the women they served. It is widely accepted that midwives played a critical role, but describing the nature of the part they played in U.S. medical, social, and cultural history has proven to be challenging. Historian Nancy Dye cautions that midwives can inadvertently be portrayed as "persecuted female protoprofessional[s]," a warning that I took to heart in assembling my research. It is important to recognize, though, that historical evidence establishes overt and systemic persecution of female midwives, and while researchers should be wary of victimizing them, we also have a responsibility to accurately reflect on the social conditions of their profession and their role in local communities. Dye, "History of Childbirth in America," 99.

41. Amy Nichols, interview by Larry Sprunk, August 11, 1974, Reeder, North Dakota, North Dakota Oral History Project, North Dakota State Archives, Bismarck, North Dakota (hereafter, ND Oral History Project).

42. Lulu Larson, interview by Bob Carlson, April 10, 1975, Valley City, North Dakota, ND Oral History Project.

43. Karolina Meidinger, interview by Bob Carlson, April 11, 1975, Valley City, North Dakota, ND Oral History Project.

44. Loretta Thompson, interview by Bob Carlson, December 19, 1975, Bismarck, North Dakota, ND Oral History Project.

45. Clara Ramey, interview by Larry Sprunk, July 6, 1974, Fort Yates, North Dakota, ND Oral History Project.

46. Lena Vanvig, interview by Larry Sprunk, July 23, 1975, Medora, North Dakota, ND Oral History Project.
47. This practice follows the method so powerfully explained by Susan H. Armitage, with Patricia Hart and Karen Weathermon, in their edited volume *Women's Oral History: The "Frontiers" Reader* (Lincoln: University of Nebraska Press, 2002). Two particularly relevant points from their work posit the "reconstruction" of the past, made possible through oral traditions, as well as the need to step back from the uniqueness of individual histories to identify larger trends and generalizable consistencies. Sherna Berger Gluck's "What's So Special about Women?," along with Susan H. Armitage's "The Next Step" and Susan H. Armitage and Sherna Berger Gluck's "Reflections on Women's Oral History: An Exchange"— all chapters in the referenced text *Women's Oral History*—reflect on this process.
48. Flora L. Bailey, "Suggested Techniques for Inducing Navajo Women to Accept Hospitalization during Childbirth and for Implementing Health Education," *American Journal of Public Health* 38 (October 1948): 1418–23, at 1420.
49. This observation, while not regularly noted in traditional histories, has been recorded by other historians, most notably Nanci Langford in her article "Childbirth on the Canadian Prairies: 1880–1930," *Journal of Historical Sociology* 8, no. 3 (1995): 278–302.
50. James C. Scott, *Seeing Like a State: How Certain Schemes to Improve the Human Condition Have Failed* (New Haven: Yale University Press, 1998), 2.

1. Birth in the Big Open

1. Details from Poughkeepsie, New York, newspaper clipping tucked inside Lizzie Maclean's diary. Maclean Diary, Collection 347, The History Museum, Great Falls, Montana.
2. Overview of Lizzie Maclean's early homestead work summarized from details in Maclean Diary.
3. Division of Indian Education, Montana Office of Public Instruction, *Montana Indians: Their History and Location*, accessed February 11, 2020, http://opi.mt.gov/Portals/182/Page%20files/Indian%20education/Indian%20education%20101/Montana%20indians%20their%20history%20and

%20location.pdf, which contains specific information on the Blackfeet tribe (5–14).

4. Maclean Diary, entries for spring and summer of 1915 with specific reference to the entry for June 23, 1915.

5. The allotment process deeded specific parcels of reservation lands to individual tribe members and made the remainder available to homesteaders. Division of Indian Education, Montana Office of Public Instruction, *Montana Indians*, with specific information on the Fort Peck Reservation and Blackfeet tribe at 56–61.

6. Alice N. Susag Diaries, entries for April 1918, MC 348, Montana Historical Society Research Center, Helena, Montana.

7. The emphasis on cleanliness came in part from the theory of scientific mothering. This philosophy, as described by archeologist Laurie Wilkie, promulgated the idea that "any woman, armed with proper information and common sense, was in a position to decide the best way to raise and care for her child." Ironically, it was this very emphasis on science that medical doctors subsequently used to "strip [women] of their authority as mothers," a process I describe in chapters 4 and 5. Wilkie, *Archaeology of Mothering*, 216.

8. Chapter 4 addresses regional standards and practices of cleanliness at the turn of the twentieth century in more detail. Information about sanitation can be found in a study sponsored by the U.S. Children's Bureau (Viola Isabel Paradise, *Maternity Care and the Welfare of Young Children in a Homesteading County in Montana* [Washington DC: U.S. Government Printing Office, 1919], 32–34) and in Mary Jensen Hill, *Powderville: A Personal History* (privately printed, 1994), 73–77.

9. The word *parturient* refers to the act of bringing forth young and is derived from a Latin root. It is one of just a few terms for childbirth, and while it is relatively unfamiliar to the general public, *parturient* is somewhat more accessible than *fructifying*, one of my favorite synonyms.

10. Catherine Scholten has described the social setting of childbirth as a "crowd of supportive friends and family." The midwife would direct the assemblage of women in "liberally fortif[ying]" the mother with alcohol, "provok[ing] laughter by making bawdy jokes," and putting the laboring mother at ease with stories of their own birthing adventures. Catherine M. Scholten, "'On the Importance of the Obstetrick Art': Changing Customs

of Childbirth in America, 1760 to 1825," *William and Mary Quarterly* 34, no. 3 (1977): 426–45, quote at 443.

11. Living History Farm manual (2018), Museum of the Rockies, Bozeman, Montana. Tinsley's pattern followed tradition. In colonial settlements on the North American continent, women birthed their first child in their early twenties and continued with pregnancies fifteen to twenty months apart. A woman could expect ten to fourteen pregnancies in the course of her reproductive life. Mothers nursed infants for one to two years and with serial pregnancies could experience two decades of uninterrupted nursing and pregnancy. Colonial women knew the energy demands of such constant caregiving, and the period of a woman's confinement after delivery represented an essential practice to ensure recovery to full health. Richard W. Wertz and Dorothy C. Wertz, *Lying-In: A History of Childbirth in America* (New York: Free Press, 1977).

12. Living History Farm manual (2018). This timeline assumes that Tinsley carried all pregnancies to term.

13. The Museum of the Rockies in Bozeman, Montana, moved Lucy Tinsley's log house from its original location to the museum grounds to serve as a living history farm. As a result, far more historical research exists about Lucy than her sister-in-law Martha. Living History Farm manual (2018), 5.

14. During the late 1700s and early 1800s, the average family included nine children. With a steady decrease in the birth rate, by 1900 that figure had fallen to an average of three children per family. Geoffrey Stone, *Sex and the Constitution: Sex, Religion, and Law from America's Origins to the Twenty-First Century* (New York: Norton, 2017). The actual number of children in each family varied widely, with women born earlier in this time period tending to deliver more children than women of the later period.

15. Langford, "Childbirth on the Canadian Prairies," 279.

16. Advancements in urine testing to detect pregnancy existed as early as the 1920s and became more accessible and precise through the 1950s and 1960s. The Boston Women's Health Collective included instructions in its first edition of *Our Bodies, Ourselves* to the effect that pregnancy could be accurately determined "as early as three weeks after conception." *Our Bodies, Ourselves* (Boston MA: New England Free Press, mimeographed copy, 1971), 77. Up until the 1970s, when the home pregnancy

test became available for over-the-counter purchase, women visited their doctor for early confirmation of pregnancy. Cari Romm, "Before There Were Home Pregnancy Tests," *The Atlantic*, June 17, 2015. Tests on the market today are accurate as soon as one to two weeks after conception.

17. Maclean Diary, entry for March 27, 1915.

18. Jane Lawrence, "The Indian Health Service and the Sterilization of Native American Women," *American Indian Quarterly* 24, no. 3 (2000): 400–419, quote at 413.

19. Lawrence, "Indian Health Service and the Sterilization of Native American Women," 413.

20. Laurentza Koch to her mother, n.d., Koch Family Papers, 1831–1912, #0652, Merrill G. Burlingame Special Collections, Montana State University, Bozeman, Montana.

21. Mail-order sources like Sears Roebuck stocked some less obvious contraceptive devices, such as douches, which were marketed as feminine hygiene products and also used by some as a postcoital rinse thought to reduce fertility and prevent conception. Laurel Thatcher Ulrich, *A Midwife's Tale: The Life of Martha Ballard, Based on Her Diary, 1785–1812* (New York: Vintage, 1991); Ann Hibner Koblitz, *Sex and Herbs and Birth Control: Women and Fertility Regulation through the Ages* (Seattle WA: Kovalevskaia Fund, 2014).

22. Stone, *Sex and the Constitution*, 154–62, 363.

23. Andrea Tone, *Devices and Desires: A History of Contraceptives in America* (New York: Hill & Wang, 2001).

24. Chapter 2 describes the formation of the Children's Bureau and its impact on public health in the early 1900s.

25. Quoted in Molly Ladd-Taylor, *Raising a Baby the Government Way: Mothers' Letters to the Children's Bureau, 1915–1932* (New Brunswick NJ: Rutgers University Press, 1986), 180–81.

26. Margaret Sanger, *Motherhood in Bondage* (1928; n.p.: Planned Parenthood of Northern Michigan, 2000).

27. Edna G. Cox McCann, interview by Diane Sands, May 5, 1983, Trout Creek, Montana, OH 655, Montanans at Work Oral History Project, Montana Historical Society Research Library, Helena, Montana (hereafter, MAW Oral History Project).

28. Pearl D. Johnson, interview by Diane Sands, June 9, 1982, OH 533, MAW Oral History Project.

29. Faye Hoven, interview by Laurie Mercier, March 30, 1982, OH 252, MAW Oral History Project.

30. Katie M. Adams, interview by Laurie Mercier, April 5, 1983, OH 492, MAW Oral History Project.

31. Hoven interview.

32. Physicians in urban hospitals were emphasizing prenatal care by the 1910s, and the Children's Bureau used its bureaucratic bully pulpit to encourage women to seek out prenatal care beginning in the 1920s. Wertz and Wertz, *Lying-In*, 140, 155. The date at which prenatal care came to be seen as normal in the northern plains and Rocky Mountains occurred sometime after that, as the regional culture of birth had shifted to physician-directed hospital birth by the 1940s and 1950s. Chapter 7 deals with this final transition in more detail.

33. Idora Z. Smith Guthrie Diaries, entry for September 14, 1905, MC 201, Montana Historical Society Research Library, Helena, Montana.

34. Idora Z. Smith Guthrie Diaries, entry for September 15 and 18, 1905.

35. Idora Z. Smith Guthrie Diaries, entries for September 17 to October 13, 1905.

36. Idora Z. Smith Guthrie Diaries, entry for October 14, 1905.

37. A lay physician provided medical care without the credentialed approval of an institution of higher learning or a state licensing process. Lay physicians often received training through an apprenticeship model, accumulating knowledge through varied life experiences and reading medical texts. As for rates of miscarriage, they remain difficult to track even in the contemporary era, in large part because many miscarriages occur early, often before a woman is even aware she is pregnant. Women in the late 1800s and early 1900s did not have access to any sort of at-home pregnancy test, and since they lacked conclusive evidence of conception, miscarriages, even those occurring later on in the gestational cycle, could be interpreted as a return of menses—a heavy period—instead of the end of a pregnancy. For a detailed exploration of how these factors impacted miscarriage reporting beginning in the 1970s, see Kevin Land and Ana Nuevo-Chiquero, "Trends in Self-Reported Spontaneous Abortions: 1970–2000," *Demography* 49, no. 3 (2012): 989–1009.

38. Tabulation of miscarriage cases by author based on Catherine Brodhead's maternity home patient ledger, covering the years 1930 through 1943. Ledger in the personal collection of the Brodhead family.

39. As a point of comparison, rates of miscarriage in the 2010s hovered around 15 percent. In other words, of ten "recognized pregnancies" (identified by ultrasound or pregnancy test), one to two ended via miscarriage in the first trimester. It is difficult to assess the impact of the constellation of physical, cultural, and geographic factors on northern plains and Rocky Mountain miscarriage rates, so contemporary findings offer only a suggestion of turn-of-the-twentieth-century miscarriage frequency. Judy Slome Cohain, Rina E. Buxbaum, and David Mankuta, "Spontaneous First Trimester Miscarriage Rates per Woman among Parous Women with 1 or More Pregnancies of 24 Weeks or More," BMC *Pregnancy and Childbirth* 17, no. 1 (2017): 437.
40. Koch to her mother, n.d.
41. See chapter 5 for a full discussion of regional mortality rates.
42. Nannie T. Alderson and Helena Huntington Smith, *A Bride Goes West* (Lincoln: University of Nebraska Press, 1942), 205.
43. Paradise, *Maternity Care*.
44. Paradise, *Maternity Care*, 10–12, 27–35.
45. For an example of a stillbirth experience, see Lillian Helena Mattson Lampi, interview by Laurie Mercier, June 23, 1982, OH 303, MAW Oral History Project. Lampi was married in 1917 and went to the hospital in the night when she delivered a stillborn baby.
46. Hoven interview.
47. Thelma "Peggy" Marie Dobson Czyzeski, interview by Laurie Mercier, May 21, 1982, OH 285, MAW Oral History Project.
48. Beatrice Kaasch, interview by John Terreo, November 16, 1989, Medicine, Health Care, and Nursing in Montana Oral History Project, Montana Historical Society Research Library, Helena, Montana.
49. Sophie Guthrie, interview by Kathryn Person White, August 1976, Columbus, Montana, OH 49-20, Archives and Special Collections, Maureen and Mike Mansfield Library, University of Montana, Missoula, Montana. Melcher also referenced this incident but added that Sophie Guthrie "ordered him out of the house because he told Mr. Guthrie not to listen to Sophie if she became hysterical." Mary Melcher, "'Women's Matters': Birth Control, Prenatal Care, and Childbirth in Rural Montana, 1910–1940," *Montana: The Magazine of Western History* 41, no. 2 (1991): 47–56, quote at 54.
50. Janet L. Finn, *Mining Childhood: Growing Up in Butte, Montana, 1900–1960* (Helena: Montana Historical Society Press, 2012).

51. Vina Stirling, interview by Laurie Mercier, September 3, 1981, OH 189, MAW Oral History Project.

52. Hoffert, "Childbearing on the Trans-Mississippi Frontier," 279–83.

53. Catherine Brodhead, the midwife, lay physician, and maternity home owner, vociferously advocated for at least a full ten days of rest for her patients, which indicates that some women might have had even shorter recoveries. Grayce Ray, "This Old House: Fairview Home Is Filled with History," *Williston (ND) Daily Herald*, April 5, 1987, 6c.

54. McCann interview.

55. Hoffert, "Childbearing on the Trans-Mississippi Frontier," 279.

56. Brett Lee Shelton, "Legal and Historical Roots of Health Care for American Indians and Alaska Natives in the United States," Henry J. Kaiser Family Foundation Issue Brief, February 2004, accessed January 10, 2019, https://www.kff.org/wp-content/uploads/2013/01/legal-and-historical-roots-of-health-care-for-american-indians-and-alaska-natives-in-the-united-states.pdf; Volney Steele, *Bleed, Blister, and Purge: A History of Medicine on the American Frontier* (Missoula MT: Mountain Press, 2005).

57. Nicola Kay Beisel, *Imperiled Innocents: Anthony Comstock and Family Reproduction in Victorian America* (Princeton: Princeton University Press, 1997).

58. Mary Zanto, interview by Laurie Mercier, April 28, 1982, OH 274, MAW Oral History Project.

59. Contemporary public health verbiage uses the term "sexually transmitted infections" (STIs), but public health professionals of the 1900s used the phrase "venereal disease" to refer to syphilis and gonorrhea.

60. Guthrie interview.

61. Frank B. Linderman, *Pretty-Shield: Medicine Woman of the Crows* (Lincoln: University of Nebraska Press, 1932); Robert H. Lowie, *The Crow Indians* (Lincoln: University of Nebraska Press, 1935).

62. Linderman, *Pretty-Shield*; Lowie, *Crow Indians*.

63. Judith Walzer Leavitt, *Brought to Bed: Childbearing in America, 1750–1950* (New York: Oxford University Press, 1986), 25.

64. Langford, "Childbirth on the Canadian Prairies," 281.

65. Langford, "Childbirth on the Canadian Prairies," 279.

66. Jodi Vandenberg-Daves, *Modern Motherhood: An American History* (New Brunswick NJ: Rutgers University Press, 2014), 71.

67. Hoffert, "Childbearing on the Trans-Mississippi Frontier."
68. Koch to her mother, n.d.; Guthrie interview; Melcher, "'Women's Matters.'"
69. Alice N. Susag Diaries, 160–62.
70. Maclean Diary, entry for June 1, 1915.

2. The Expertise of Women

1. Julia Lathrop's alma mater produced a retrospective of her life and work: "Julia Lathrop," Vassar College, 2005(?), http://vcencyclopedia.vassar.edu /alumni/julia-lathrop.html. Other significant works on Julia Lathrop include Miriam Cohen, *Julia Lathrop: Social Service and Progressive Government* (Boulder CO: Westview Press, 2017); and Jane Addams, *My Friend, Julia Lathrop* (New York: Macmillan, 1935).

2. "Julia Lathrop," Vassar College; Cohen, *Julia Lathrop*; Addams, *My Friend, Julia Lathrop*.

3. J. Stanley Lemons, "The Sheppard-Towner Act: Progressivism in the 1920s," *Journal of American History* 55, no. 4 (1969): 776–86; Paul Theerman, "Julia Lathrop and the Children's Bureau," *American Journal of Public Health* 100, no. 9 (2010): 1589–90; Dorothy E. Bradbury and Martha M. Eliot, *Four Decades of Action for Children: A Short History of the Children's Bureau* (Washington DC: U.S. Department of Health, Education, and Welfare, 1956).

4. "Chouteau Babes in U.S. Survey," *Ronan (MT) Pioneer*, August 17, 1917. This local newspaper referred only to Meigs and Paradise's arrival, but with thousands of square miles of prairie for the government staffers to canvass, it seemed plausible that a larger team collected data for the 1917 study. I included the full listing of participating staff according to the bureau's report.

5. Paradise, *Maternity Care*, 8.
6. Paradise, *Maternity Care*, 6.
7. Paradise, *Maternity Care*, 5–9.
8. Melcher, "'Women's Matters.'"
9. Sue Hart, "Gwendolen Haste: Giving Voice to the Homesteaders," *Montana: The Magazine of Western History* 57, no. 1 (2007): 3–13, quote at 12. While there may have been no simplistic medical remedy for intense reproductive stress and overwork, access to safe and reliable contraception would have made a life-changing difference for women of the era.
10. Nickel, "Dying in the West, Part 1."

11. Nickel, "Dying in the West, Part 1," 33.
12. Isabella Mogstad, interview by Laurie Mercier, March 17, 1982, OH 248, MAW Oral History Project.
13. Susie Clarke Huston, interview by Laurie Mercier, April 23, 1983, OH 519, MAW Oral History Project.
14. Hoven interview.
15. Among the Children's Bureau study participants, 46 birthed with the assistance of their husbands, 3 women delivered entirely alone, and physicians attended 129 births. The largest group—181 homesteading women—birthed with the assistance of friends, neighbors, and midwives. Paradise, *Maternity Care*, 27–35.
16. Zanto interview.
17. Chapters 4 and 5 detail medical and health department condemnations of midwives and their training.
18. Ethel Eide, interview by Larry Sprunk, December 10, 1974, Spartan, North Dakota, ND Oral History Project.
19. Zanto interview.
20. Lydia Keating, interview by Laurie Mercier, March 31, 1982, OH 255, MAW Oral History Project.
21. Women often selected midwives even when physicians were available. For example, Cynthia Jane Capron, a mother delivering in Wyoming in 1868, wrote that "I will have the best of care [during and after delivery] however for Mrs. Quain has had a great deal of experience. Mrs. Jordan had her in preference to the Dr. that was here then." Cynthia Jane Capron to her sister Mary, June 21, 1868, #1694, Folder 11, Box 1, Thaddeus H. Capron Family Papers, American Heritage Center, Laramie, Wyoming.
22. Maclean Diary, entry for May 13, 1915.
23. I have not been able to definitively locate the Hicks family in census data or birth registration records to determine Hicks's total number of births, but Maclean refers to the Hicks *children*, indicating that Hicks had given birth at least twice already.
24. Maclean Diary, entries for May 14–20, 1915.
25. Maclean Diary, entries for June 2–7, 1915.
26. Maclean Diary, entry for June 23, 1915.
27. Judy Barrett Litoff, *American Midwives: 1860 to the Present* (Westport CT: Greenwood Press, 1978).
28. "Julia Lathrop," Vassar College.

29. Maclean Diary, entries for July 5 and 8, 1915.
30. Accounting by the author based on the Maclean Diary.
31. Accounting by the author based on entries in the Maclean Diary.
32. Maclean Diary, entries for September 17–October 7, 1918.
33. Teton County History Committee, *Teton County: A History* (Chouteau MT: Chouteau Acantha, 1988), 331.
34. Teton County History Committee, *Teton County*, 437–38.
35. Annie Knipfer, interview by Kathy White, August 25, 1976, Billings MT, OH 49-28, Archives and Special Collections, Maureen and Mike Mansfield Library, University of Montana, Missoula, Montana.
36. Turn-of-the-twentieth-century men who worked as farmers or kept livestock would have had basic knowledge of the mammalian birth process from watching horses, cows, sheep, and pigs give birth.
37. Clara Ramey of Fort Yates, North Dakota, explained that she delivered her infant on her own before the doctor arrived. Clara Ramey, interview by Larry Sprunk, July 6, 1974, ND Oral History Project.
38. Both women and men dismissed these value-rich female activities, because women's contributions in westward settlement were forgotten or characterized as insignificant, not only by history but also in some cases by the women themselves. For example, Linda Peavey and Ursula Smith have shown that Pamelia Fergus supported her husband's mining ventures, making the family's relocation and subsequent success possible, yet at the end of her life she did not frame those accomplishments as noteworthy. Linda Peavey and Ursula Smith, "Women in Waiting in the Westward Movement," *Montana: The Magazine of Western History* 35, no. 2 (1985): 2–17. Unfortunately, many of these gendered perspectives on importance are still with us. Commenting on contemporary culture, classical historian and cultural critic Mary Beard asks, "How and why do the conventional definitions of 'power' . . . that we carry round in our heads exclude women?" Beard uses Charlotte Perkins Gillman's *Herland*, originally published in 1915, to show that the women who created a fully functioning and harmonious utopia with only females present "simply [did not] recognize their own achievements." Mary Beard, *Women and Power: A Manifesto* (New York: Liveright, 2017), 51–52.
39. Anne M. Butler, *Across God's Frontiers: Catholic Sisters in the American West, 1850–1920* (Chapel Hill: University of North Carolina Press, 2012), 80. These economic contributions were varied and far-reaching. For

example, women across the West raised the turkeys that adorned family dinner tables at Thanksgiving and Christmas. Hidden under the veil of women's work, the numbers of turkeys and the revenue generated were typically not counted, but some extant information is available. In Idaho the 1910 turkey production was calculated at $28,000, while in Montana, the population of turkeys in the state grew from 16,475 in 1910 to an astounding 86,867 by 1935. According to the U.S. Department of Agriculture in 1920, "80 percent of women [who lived on farms] kept care of poultry." Like women's earnings from reproductive care, dairy and poultry revenue was "not 'pin' or 'mad' money (though often described as such) but contributed directly to the family's economic base." Madeline Buckendorf, "The Poultry Frontier: Family Farm Roles and Turkey Raising in Southwest Idaho, 1910–1940," *Idaho Yesterdays* 37, no. 2 (1993): 2–8, quotes at 3, 4; Amy L. McKinney, "'There When We Needed Them': Harriette E. Cushman and the Birth of Montana's Turkey Marketing Cooperatives," *Montana: The Magazine of Western History* 65, no. 4 (2015): 41–54.

40. According to Laurie Mercier, "Women were 'economic linchpins' of Montana's farms and ranches," with the success of a farm or ranch "rest[ing] on the industriousness of the female partner." Laurie K. Mercier, "'You Had to Make Every Minute Count': Women's Role in Montana Agriculture," in *The Montana Heritage: An Anthology of Historical Essays*, ed. Robert R. Swartout Jr. and Harry W. Fritz (Helena: Montana Historical Society Press, 1992), 134. Kathryn McPherson has found that "bachelors failed to 'prove up' their homesteads more frequently than did married men," which she interpreted as testament to the critical economic contributions of women. Kathryn McPherson, "Was the 'Frontier' Good for Women? Historical Approaches to Women and Agricultural Settlement in the Prairie West, 1870–1925," *Atlantis* 25, no. 1 (2000): 75–86, quote at 76. It is possible that Euro-American and Native American women alike provided core income and nutrition. Elizabeth Fenn has applied a similar analysis to Native women who cultivated, stored, and traded essential nutrients for tribes residing across the West. She explains that maize was the primary item of exchange for Mandans and Assiniboines, as part of a trade network that supplied a vast quantity of important calories in the form of squash, corn, and beans to other Native American groups. Fenn's description includes a nutritional explanation of how essential corn was

to Native peoples—even and especially those who did not grow it—by helping them to avoid protein poisoning. It is likely that Mandan women who cultivated food plants filled a similar role to that of settler women like Maclean and Susag by performing an essential community, caloric, and civic service in their stabilizing role that met nutritional needs *and* enabled trade and reciprocity. Elizabeth A. Fenn, *Encounters at the Heart of the World: A History of the Mandan People* (New York: Hill and Wang, 2014).

41. Kristin Burnett, "Obscured Obstetrics: Indigenous Midwives in Western Canada," in *Recollecting: Lives of Aboriginal Women of the Canadian Northwest and Borderlands,* ed. Sarah Carter and Patricia McCormack (Edmonton AB: AU Press, 2011), 165.

42. Linderman, *Pretty-Shield;* Lowie, *Crow Indians.*

43. Unsigned introduction to the Susag Collection, Folder 1, Box 1, MC 348, Alice N. Susag Papers, Montana Historical Society Research Center, Helena, Montana; Marilyn Waring, *If Women Counted: A New Feminist Economics* (San Francisco: HarperCollins, 1988); Maclean Diary, entries from September 10–11, 1914; Joan C. Tronto, *Caring Democracy: Markets, Equality, and Justice* (New York: New York University Press, 2013).

44. MHS introduction to the Susag Collection; Waring, *If Women Counted;* Maclean Diary, entries from September 10–11, 1914; Tronto, *Caring Democracy.*

45. Unsigned introduction to the Susag Collection; Waring, *If Women Counted;* Maclean Diary, entries from September 10–11, 1914; Tronto, *Caring Democracy.*

46. Anthropologists document these kinds of human relationships, especially in light of Marcel Mauss's work, as a "mechanism by which individual interests combine to make a social system, without engaging in market exchange." Marcel Mauss, *The Gift: The Form and Reason for Exchange in Archaic Societies* (New York: Norton, 1990), xiv.

47. Maclean meticulously recorded all of her receipts and included the detail in her diary. Examples of these monetized exchanges are described in Maclean Diary, entries for June 10, 1915, April 26, 1916, and March 19 and 20, 1917.

48. Evidence of these types of behaviors is scattered throughout Maclean's diary and can also be found in regional oral histories and reminiscences of early settlers. Maclean Diary, entries for December 8, 1915, January

16, 1918, and October 7, 1918. Alice Susag's daily routine reflected a similar contextualized economy. On September 15, 1917, she and Oswald traveled to see a neighbor about renting a field and received a gift of garden vegetables. The Susags stayed to dinner, thus using a meal to build relationships that most likely enhanced both their professional and personal exchanges. Just as they returned home that evening, Mrs. Stenson arrived to purchase butter. Susag subsequently reported a visit from the Hanson family, followed by the appearance of Mr. Stenson to look at their horses. More horse trading, possibly initiated by the supper and gifted vegetables, took place the next evening, followed by a shared meal and Mrs. Stenson's arrival to buy some eggs. Susag walked to the Stenson place to deliver butter, and when she returned, two neighbors, Mrs. McMullen and Mrs. Campbell, appeared in search of eggs. Susag Diary, 70, 72, and entries for April 29, May 9, and June 20, 1917, Alice N. Susag Papers.

3. Midwives among Us

1. P. M. Dunn, "Louise Bourgeois (1563–1636): Royal Midwife of France," *Archives of Disease in Childhood: Fetal and Neonatal* 89, no. 2 (2004): F185–87.

2. According to some estimates, only 6 percent of the French population could read in 1475. The French literacy rate had increased to 19 percent by 1550, making Bourgeois unusual for her era. Max Roser and Esteban Ortiz-Ospina, "Literacy," Our World in Data, last updated September 20, 2018, https://ourworldindata.org/literacy.

3. Wendy Perkins, *Midwifery and Medicine in Early Modern France: Louise Bourgeois* (Exeter: University of Exeter Press, 1996); *The Guardian* (UK), December 13, 1993; *Journal of Nurse-Midwifery*, July–August 1981; *Midwives Chronicle & Nursing Notes*, January 1971.

4. Burnett, "Obscured Obstetrics," 165.

5. Dunn, "Louise Bourgeois (1563–1636)," F186.

6. The French literacy rate increased to 29 percent in 1650. Roser and Ortiz-Ospina, "Literacy." Women's literacy was particularly important for the spread of midwifery knowledge, and it increased from 14 percent in the late 1600s to 27 percent in the late 1700s. James Van Horn Melton, *The Rise of the Public in Enlightenment Europe* (Cambridge: Cambridge University Press, 2001), 81–82.

7. Government-run programs in Europe supported vigorous maternal and infant health and served national aims by ensuring healthy population growth. Judith Pence Rooks, *Midwifery and Childbirth in America* (Philadelphia: Temple University Press, 1997), 13–15. More information about the development of midwifery in Europe can be found in P. A. Kalisch, M. Scobey, and B. J. Kalisch, "Louyse Bourgeois and the Emergence of Modern Midwifery," *Journal of Nurse Midwifery* 26, no. 4 (1981): 3–17.

8. Data gathered from the 1900 and 1910 censuses shows that many settlers in the northern plains and Rocky Mountains came from countries with long-established traditions of midwifery. In 1900, 69 percent of settlers in Montana, North Dakota, South Dakota, and Wyoming came from Germany, Norway, England, Sweden, Ireland, Denmark, Scotland, Austria, Switzerland, France, and Wales, with that figure dropping slightly to 68 percent in 1910. These percentages include both those directly emigrating from these places, as well as those whose families had arrived in previous generations but who identified as "foreign white stock." The Canadian practice of midwifery was strongest among French migrant populations, so only French Canadians have been included in this count. Thirteenth Census of the United States, vol. 6, U.S. Bureau of the Census, 1913, 929, 930, 933. For information on the history of midwifery in Europe, see Rooks, *Midwifery and Childbirth in America*; and M. Joyce Relyea, "The Rebirth of Midwifery in Canada: An Historical Perspective," *Midwifery* 8, no. 4 (1992): 159–69. For history specific to Canada and Germany, see Karen Scheuermann, "Midwifery in Germany: Its Past and Present," *Journal of Nurse Midwifery* 40, no. 5 (1995): 438–44.

9. Rooks, *Midwifery and Childbirth in America*, 13–15.

10. Twelfth Census of the United States, roll 911, page 16B, U.S. Bureau of the Census, 1901; advertisement in the *Anaconda Standard*, November 28, 1889.

11. Butte City Directory, 1899 and 1904; Helena City Directory, 1891, both accessed at Ancestry.com, *U.S. City Directories, 1821–1989* (Provo UT: Ancestry.com Operations, 2011); advertisements in the *Helena Independent*, June 26, 1892, February 25, 1894; advertisements in the *Anaconda Standard*, December 25, 1897, October 14, 1899, October 30, 1899, November 26, 1899; advertisement in the *Butte Inter-Mountain*, May 3, 1902; "Butte News," *Anaconda Standard*, February 10, 1903.

12. Twelfth Census of the United States, roll 911, page 39B, U.S. Bureau of the Census, 1901; Butte City Directory, 1904; advertisements in the *Anaconda Standard*, October 14, October 30, November 26, 1899.

13. Butte City Directory, 1900; Thirteenth Census of the United States, vol. 6, U.S. Bureau of the Census, 1913.

14. Arlene Harris, daughter of Aino "Anna" Hamalainen Puutio, wrote a description of her mother's work, "An Early-Day Montana Midwife," which is held by the Carbon County Historical Society in Red Lodge, Montana. Harris also authored an article, "Midwife Aino," published in *Missoula Borrowed Times*, September 1, 1974.

15. Bertha Wallace record: Butte City Directory, 1902. Martha Noble record: "Another Suit Begun," *Anaconda Standard*, December 11, 1889. Julie Moe records: Butte City Directories, 1900, 1905, 1906. Ellen Thomas records: "Midwife Is in Jail on Murder Charge," *Daily Missoulian*, June 1, 1913; 1881 Wales Census, RG 11, Pience 5295, folio 49, page 22, GSU roll 1342274; Twelfth Census of the United States, roll 914, page 7B, U.S. Bureau of the Census, 1901; Thirteenth Census of the United States, roll T624_836, page 1B, U.S. Bureau of the Census, 1913; Fourteenth Census of the United States, roll T625_976, page 6A, U.S. Bureau of the Census, 1921. Rose Brown records: advertisement in the *Anaconda Standard*, November 26, 1899; Butte City Directory, 1902; Twelfth Census of the United States, roll 915, page 12B, U.S. Bureau of the Census, 1901. Bertha Watmer records: Butte City Directory, 1910; advertisements in the *Butte Inter-Mountain*, March 25, August 26, December 16, 1902.

16. Twelfth Census of the United States, U.S. Bureau of the Census, 1901; Thirteenth Census of the United States, U.S. Bureau of the Census, 1913; Butte City Directories, 1900–1910.

17. Hilda Peterson, interview by Larry Sprunk, October 4, 1974, Fort Ransom, North Dakota, ND Oral History Project.

18. Mona Leeson Vanek, *Behind These Mountains, Volume 1: People of the Shining Mountains Where the Clark's Fork River Churns* (Colville WA: Stateman-Examiner, 1986).

19. McCann interview, 29.

20. Leona Lampi's *At the Foot of the Beartooth Mountains: A History of the Finnish Community of Red Lodge, Montana* (Coeur d'Alene ID: Bookage Press, 1998), 59, 186, describes the midwifery community of Red Lodge, as does Shirley Zupan and Harry Owens's *Red Lodge: Saga of a Western Area* (Red

Lodge MT: Carbon County Historical Society, 1979), 120, 124–26, 181, 376–78. Liiza Honkala's records: "Old Time Resident Dies Yesterday," *Carbon County News* (Red Lodge MT), March 13, 1946; Twelfth Census of the United States, roll 909, page 15B, U.S. Bureau of the Census, 1901; Fourteenth Census of the United States, roll T625_967, page 8B, U.S. Bureau of the Census, 1921. Hilma Ylenni's records: Red Lodge City Directory, 1917, accessed in Ancestry.com, *U.S. City Directories, 1821–1989*; Fourteenth Census of the United States, roll T625_967, page 6A, U.S. Bureau of the Census, 1921; Fifteenth Census of the United States, roll 1252, page 3A, U.S. Bureau of the Census, 1931. Agnes Rahkola's records: Fourteenth Census of the United States, roll T625_967, page 9A, U.S. Bureau of the Census, 1921; Birth Record, roll/fiche number SC-1610, vol. 1001, 1890, Swedish Church Records Archive, Johnanneshov, Sweden.

21. Anna Kjas's records: Sixteenth Census of the United States, roll T627_2226, page 1A, U.S. Bureau of the Census, 1943. Mary Jenkins's records: Fourteenth Census of the United States, roll T625_967, page 1A, U.S. Bureau of the Census, 1921. Gertrude White's records: Bozeman City Directory, 1908, 1914, 1925, accessed at Ancestry.com, *U.S. City Directories, 1821–1989*; Thirteenth Census of the United States, roll T624_832, page 1B, U.S. Bureau of the Census, 1913; Fourteenth Census of the United States, roll T625_970, page 13B, U.S. Bureau of the Census, 1921.

22. Verona Barnes's records: Chouteau County Directory, Gold Butte, 1911, accessed in Ancestry.com, *U.S. City Directories, 1821–1989*; Twelfth Census of the United States, roll 910, page 2B, U.S. Bureau of the Census, 1901; Thirteenth Census of the United States, roll T624_830, page 1B, U.S. Bureau of the Census, 1913; Fourteenth Census of the United States, roll T625_977, page 4B, U.S. Bureau of the Census, 1921. Percy Clauton's records: Twelfth Census of the United States, roll 915, page 4B, U.S. Bureau of the Census, 1901; Thirteenth Census of the United States, roll T624_837, page 7B, U.S. Bureau of the Census, 1913; Fourteenth Census of the United States, roll T625_974, page 5A, U.S. Bureau of the Census, 1921. Viola Ebaugh's records: Fourteenth Census of the United States, roll T625_974, page 13A, U.S. Bureau of the Census, 1921. Mary Robertory's records: Fourteenth Census of the United States, roll T625_974, page 4A, U.S. Bureau of the Census, 1921. Inga Johnson's records: Fifteenth Census of the United States, roll 1257, page 9A, U.S.

Bureau of the Census, 1931; Eva Hallam Solberg, *Looking Back Again: Life Stories from the Prairies of Montana* (privately printed by the author, 2008). Nancy Lease's records: Twelfth Census of the United States, roll 932, page 7A, U.S. Bureau of the Census, 1901; Thirteenth Census of the United States, roll T624_831, page 11A, U.S. Bureau of the Census, 1913; Fifteenth Census of the United States, roll 1254, page 1A, U.S. Bureau of the Census, 1931. Borghild Ronning's records: advertisement in *Producers News*, January 17, 1919; U.S. Passport Application, issued September 14, 1920, Collection Number ARC 583830, series M1490, roll 1357, National Archives and Records Administration (NARA), Washington DC; Fourteenth Census of the United States, roll T625_975, page 7B, U.S. Bureau of the Census, 1921.

23. Information about Cornelia Mowatt can be found in an advertisement in the *Fergus County Argus* (Lewiston MT), February 28, 1900; and the Lewistown City Directory, 1910, accessed in Ancestry.com, *U.S. City Directories, 1821–1989*. The 1920 census lists comparative population figures for Montana towns; see "Population: Montana," Fourteenth Census of the United States, U.S. Bureau of the Census, 1921, 2 and 16.

24. Living in an urban area did not cause women to claim the title of midwife. Instead, trained midwives who needed to support themselves independently tended to gravitate to urban areas where a large enough clientele existed to support full-time midwifery work. Single or widowed women who named midwifery as their profession probably did so because the income from reproductive services supported their families and constituted the main source of household revenue. For example, Catherine Carruthers of Fort Benton, Montana, emigrated from Ireland and listed herself as a midwife and head of her household. Twelfth Census of the United States, roll 910, page 19B, U.S. Bureau of the Census, 1901. For many women in the northern plains and Rocky Mountains, midwifery served as a means to receive compensation for the work of mothering. Because the labors of domesticity were typically uncompensated and often unrecognized, some individuals attending births saw their midwifery services as an extension of women's work instead of as an independent profession. For a look at this perception see Wilkie, *Archaeology of Mothering*, xx.

25. Sarah Deer, *The Beginning and End of Rape: Confronting Sexual Violence in Native America* (Minneapolis: University of Minnesota Press, 2015);

Linderman, *Pretty-Shield*; Alma Hogan Snell, *Grandmother's Grandchild: My Crow Indian Life*, ed. Becky Matthews (Lincoln: University of Nebraska Press, 2000); Fred W. Voget, *They Call Me Agnes* (Norman: University of Oklahoma Press, 2001); Felix S. Cohen, *Handbook of Federal Indian Law* (Washington DC: U.S Government Printing Office, 1945); Shelton, "Legal and Historical Roots of Health Care for American Indians and Alaska Natives in the United States." Brianna Theobold's *Reproduction on the Reservation: Pregnancy, Childbirth, and Colonialism in the Long Twentieth Century* (Chapel Hill: University of North Carolina Press, 2019) offers an important analysis of Native American reproduction in the region. Additional resources on Native birthing and reproductive practices include Valerie Shirer Mathes, "A New Look at the Role of Women in Indian Society," *American Indian Quarterly* 2, no. 2 (1975): 131–39; and Freda Ahenakew and H. C. Wolfart, eds., *Our Grandmothers' Lives: As Told in Their Own Words* (Regina SK: Canadian Plains Research Center, 1998). Sylvia Van Kirk, in her book *Many Tender Ties: Women in Fur-Trade Society, 1670–1870* (Norman: University of Oklahoma Press, 1980), has provided multiple examples of Native birthing practices; Jennifer Finley's *To Be Women and Salish* (Pablo MT: Heartlines, 2013) describes the midwifery work of a Sack woman in the Bitterroot Valley of the late 1800s; and Sarah Preston's "Competent Social Behavior within the Context of Childbirth," *Papers of the Thirteenth Algonquian Conference*, vol. 13 (Ottawa ON: National Museums of Canada, 1982), 211–17, explores the conditions and cultural traditions surrounding childbirth in Cree society. Gregory R. Campbell's "Changing Patterns of Health and Effective Fertility among the Northern Cheyenne of Montana, 1886–1903," *American Indian Quarterly* 15, no. 3 (1991): 339–58, explains that "frequent child deaths among Northern Cheyenne families promoted fertility for fear of not having any surviving offspring. In a situation of repeated cycles of pregnancy and lactation, major demands would be made upon maternal nutritional intake[,] promoting chronic malnutrition. Thus women would tend to give birth to underweight babies, increasing the risk both of infant and childhood mortality. Therefore, a perpetual cycle of high fertility coupled with high infant mortality would result, producing biologically stressed, but reproductively active women, and infants at high risk for contracting an infectious disease and dying" (355).

For an examination of Navajo practices, both in and outside of the hospital, see S. J. Kuntz, "A Survey of Fertility Histories and Contraceptive Use among a Group of Navajo Women," *Lake Powell Research Bulletin* 21 (1976): 1–70; and R. Cruz Begay, "Changes in Childbirth Knowledge," *American Indian Quarterly* 28, no. 3–4 (2004): 550–65.

26. Shelton, "Legal and Historical Roots of Health Care for American Indians and Alaska Natives in the United States," 7.

27. Shelton, "Legal and Historical Roots of Health Care for American Indians and Alaska Natives in the United States."

28. Cohen, *Handbook of Federal Indian Law*, 12. The involvement of the federal government in Native health care did not stop with confinement to reservations. As the U.S. government looked for ways to get out of its treaty commitments, or to "terminate its legal obligations to tribes" in the words of the federal government, it enacted policies in the 1950s and 1960s that offered incentives for Native Americans to relocate away from tribal lands to large urban centers. For Native Americans enduring impoverished conditions on rural reservations, the potential for work and health care in American cities offered a way forward, and more than 160,000 Native Americans relocated as part of the Bureau of Indian Affairs (BIA) program. Participation in the BIA relocation program did not make Native Americans ineligible for Indian Health Service (IHS) services, but it did move them away from reservation clinics and effectively severed their access to health services provided by the federal government. The BIA relocation program was therefore highly successful in reducing the federal government's treaty obligations, but the policy's impact extended far beyond the reach of IHS dollars spent. Office of Urban Indian Health Programs, "History," Indian Health Service, https://www.ihs.gov/urban/history/.

29. Rooks, *Midwifery and Childbirth in America*, 17–22; Maryland Young Pennell and Paula Stewart, *State Licensing of Health Occupations* (Washington DC: National Center for Health Statistics, 1968); "State Examines," *Wyoming Tribune*, June 10, 1908.

30. State endorsement of midwifery in some European nations did not indicate the absence of conflict between or among physicians and practicing midwives. See Louise Bourgeois, *Midwife to the Queen of France: Diverse Observations*, ed. Alison Klairmont Lingo (Toronto: Iter Press, 2017), for an explanation of the cultural climate of the era; see especially 16–17 for

physician responses to midwives and 36–37 regarding competition among midwives. The differences in treatment of midwives across cultures varied for a host of reasons, including beliefs about women and childbirth, the state's provision of health care, and the power of physicians. Texts like Helaine Selin's *Childbirth across Cultures: Ideas and Practices of Pregnancy, Childbirth and the Postpartum* (New York: Springer, 2009) describe birth practices and practitioners from Tibet to Tanzania and add important context for the ways that cultures and nations managed, controlled, or supported human reproduction.

31. Florence Kassmeier Wilmes, interview by author, July 6, 2017, Fort Benton, Montana; Mary Kassmeier Photo Album, held by the Overholser Historical Research Center, Fort Benton, Montana.

32. County records of birth registration in Montana, the Dakotas, and Wyoming are private and not available to the public. As an example, Montana law (the Montana Code Annotated, or MCA) allows only certain family members (e.g., spouses, children, and parents) to obtain certified copies of birth certificates (50-15-121 MCA, 37.8.126 ARM). While a multitude of birth certificates can be located in online genealogical services, those documents are generally uploaded by family members able to obtain original copies. In the early 1900s a hardworking Chouteau County employee recopied county birth certificate information into a paving-stone-size hardbound ledger and listed the "name of attendant" in a separate column. Personal identifying information was listed separately from the names of midwives, nurses, and physicians, which enabled me to make a highly unusual count without violating birth certificate privacy rules.

33. "Fort Benton Doctors," Joel F. Overholser Files, Overholser Historical Research Center, Fort Benton, Montana (original source unknown). A number of physicians traveled through Fort Benton in its early years, seeing patients sporadically. Beginning with Roswell Tibbitts in 1867, the town claimed regular medical attention from resident physicians. Will Turner arrived in 1874 and stayed until his death in 1889. Francis Atkisson settled in Fort Benton in 1881 to partner in Turner's practice and retired in 1910. James Murphy set up a regular practice in 1910 and served the community for the next fourteen years. Carl Bassow worked in the area from 1916 until 1945, overlapping with J. Kaulbach, who practiced from 1914 to 1945. Evon Anderson, who worked in Fort Benton

from 1925 to 1962, rounded out the main group of doctors who assisted at deliveries in the county.

34. Journalist Tom Lutey's research substantiated this work arrangement. Women like Elizabeth Rae, he wrote, "teamed with doctors, though often they worked alone." Tom Lutey, "Pioneering Nurses: Old Stories of Nursing in Montana Hard to Find," *Bozeman Daily Chronicle*, March 1, 1998.

35. Lutey, "Pioneering Nurses."

36. Lutey, "Pioneering Nurses." More information about Elizabeth Rae can be found in the Livingston City Directory, 1904 and 1925, accessed in Ancestry.com, *U.S. City Directories, 1821–1989*; as well as in the Twelfth Census of the United States, roll 913, page 19A, U.S. Bureau of the Census, 1901; and the Fourteenth Census of the United States, roll T625_974, page 18A, U.S. Bureau of the Census, 1921.

37. Paradise, *Maternity Care*.

38. Eide interview.

39. Harris, "Early-Day Montana Midwife"; Harris, "Midwife Aino."

40. Harris, "Early-Day Montana Midwife"; Harris, "Midwife Aino."

41. Charley and Persis Hanson, interview by Larry Sprunk, November 25, 1975, Turtle Lake, North Dakota, ND Oral History Project.

42. Additional examples of the types of trade goods that midwives took in payment for delivery services include those that Catherine Brodhead received: chickens, grain, and weaner pigs. Mary Mercer, "Grandma Brodhead an 'Angel of Mercy,'" *Sidney (MT) Herald*, October 1, 1989, 3B, 8B.

43. Irvine Loudon, *Death in Childbirth: An International Study of Maternal Care and Maternal Mortality, 1800–1950* (Oxford: Clarendon Press, 1992), 307.

44. Nichols interview.

45. Larson interview.

46. Vanvig interview.

47. Eide interview.

48. A. Gretchen McNeely, "From Untrained Nurses toward Professional Preparation in Montana, 1912–1987" (DNSc diss., University of San Diego, 1993).

49. Augusta E. Ariss, *Historical Sketch of the Montana State Association of Registered Nurses and Related Organizations* (Butte MT: Conventions of the Nurses Association, 1936), 27.

50. Montana Nurses Association, *Nursing in Montana* (Great Falls MT: Tribune Printing, 1961).

51. Barbra Mann Wall, "Unlikely Entrepreneurs: Nuns, Nursing, and Hospital Development in the West and Midwest, 1865–1915" (PhD diss., University of Notre Dame, 2000).

52. Todd L. Savitt and Janice Willms, "Sisters' Hospital: The Sisters of Providence and St. Patrick Hospital, Missoula, Montana, 1873–1890," *Montana: The Magazine of Western History* 53, no. 1 (2003): 28–43.

53. Ariss, *Historical Sketch.*

54. Elizabeth Douglass and Susan Douglass (Erminia Maggini Eide's great-granddaughter and granddaughter), email correspondence with author, August 13, 2015.

55. Douglass and Douglass email.

4. The Practice of Birth

1. D. Mark Anderson, Ryan Brown, Kerwin Kofi Charles, and Daniel I. Rees, "The Effect of Occupational Licensing on Consumer Welfare: Early Midwifery Laws and Maternal Mortality," unpublished draft, November 2016, subsequently published as "Occupational Licensing and Maternal Health: Evidence from Early Midwifery Laws," *Journal of Political Economy* 128, no. 11 (2020): 4337–83.

2. Anderson et al., "Effect of Occupational Licensing on Consumer Welfare."

3. Anderson et al., "Effect of Occupational Licensing on Consumer Welfare."

4. Barbara Ehrenreich and Deirdre English published an important text titled *Witches, Midwives, and Nurses: A History of Women Healers* (New York: Feminist Press, 1973) as part of second-wave feminism's incursion into traditionally male academia. Their book demonstrates some of the ways female healers were characterized as witches in order to remove them from powerful cultural positions, despite evidence showing that traditional female healers often incorporated a more "humane, empirical" practice than other health-care providers of the era (4).

5. This chapter provides an overview of a deeply researched history of medicine as it relates to women and reproduction. A number of full-length, peer-reviewed texts investigate this past with nuance and rigor, and the reader will gain tremendous benefit from perusing any one of the many classics in the field. The realities of medical malfeasance in the treatment of puerperal fever, the development of medicine's position of power and respect in American culture, as well as comprehensive coverage of all facets of health care and societal assumptions receive insightful treatment

in the following list of standard-bearing texts: Charlotte G. Borst, *Catching Babies: The Professionalization of Childbirth, 1870–1920* (Cambridge MA: Harvard University Press, 1995); Leavitt, *Brought to Bed*; Judith Walzer Leavitt, ed., *Women and Health in America: Historical Readings* (Madison: University of Wisconsin Press, 1984); Litoff, *American Midwives*; Catherine M. Scholten, *Childbearing in American Society: 1650–1850* (New York: New York University Press, 1985); Helen Varney and Joyce Beebe Thompson, *A History of Midwifery in the United States: The Midwife Said Fear Not* (New York: Springer, 2015); Wertz and Wertz, *Lying-In*; and Jacqueline H. Wolf, *Deliver Me from Pain: Anesthesia and Birth in America* (Baltimore: Johns Hopkins University Press, 2009). For an analysis of reproductive history from a public health framework, see Robyn L. Rosen, ed., *Reproductive Health, Reproductive Rights: Reformers and the Politics of Maternal Welfare, 1917–1940* (Columbus: Ohio State University Press, 2003), which covers topics from pregnancy-as-disease to contraception. The field of public health became one in which Progressive-era women found space to develop policy based on maternalism and claims of women's particular ability to care for the nation's domestic matters.

6. Ehrenreich and English include examples of antimidwifery claims in *Witches, Midwives, and Nurses*, as do the classic texts listed in the previous notes. Leavitt's previously cited work, as well as her article "'A Worrying Profession': The Domestic Environment of Medical Practice in Mid-19th-Century America," in *Sickness and Health in America: Readings in the History of Medicine and Public Health*, ed. Judith Walzer Leavitt and Ronald L. Numbers (Madison: University of Wisconsin Press, 1978), offers context for these types of reactions to midwifery. Additionally, specific examples can be found in Litoff, *American Midwives*, 29–30, 64–90.

7. Wertz and Wertz, *Lying-In*, 51–54.

8. An Anaconda, Montana, physician known as Dr. Harding represented just such a situation. The local newspaper described him as "shady," and although he did not follow licensing procedures, no enforcement action was taken against him and his practice was "tolerated by the citizens and by the courts." *Anaconda Standard*, July 21, 1893.

9. Richard Wertz and Dorothy Wertz detail one of the most complete overviews of the dangerously limited scope of medical training focused on reproductive issues; see Wertz and Wertz, *Lying-In*, 58–76.

10. Todd L. Savitt, "'The Days of Traveling Pill Peddlers Are Done': The Establishment of Montana's Board of Medical Examiners," *Montana: The Magazine of Western History* 70, no. 4 (2020): 21–25.

11. Richard Harrison Shryock, *Medical Licensing in America, 1650–1965* (Baltimore: Johns Hopkins Press, 1967), 105. Shryock explains that "the view that 'practical' men need not be carefully trained and licensed was long an obstacle to the development of a learned profession in this country" (105–6).

12. Volney Steele's *Bleed, Blister, and Purge* fully describes typical regional medical treatments of the era.

13. William G. Rothstein, *American Physicians in the Nineteenth Century: From Sects to Science* (Baltimore: Johns Hopkins University Press, 1972). Richard Shryock states that "many general practitioners, prior to 1900, had received a mediocre education at best," and he goes on to describe the evolution of the licensing process. Shryock, *Medical Licensing in America*, 105. For a fabulous examination of the laborious and time-consuming nature of the licensing process in the northern plains region, see Savitt, "'Days of Traveling Pill Peddlers Are Done.'"

14. The histories of the American Medical Association and the American College of Obstetricians and Gynecologists are available at the groups' websites: https://www.ama-assn.org/about/ama-history/ama-history and https://www.acog.org/about, respectively. Initial publication of the *American Journal of Obstetrics and Diseases of Women and Children* occurred in 1868, with articles covering topics from the anatomy of the placenta to diarrhea in infants. The first issue can be accessed through the HathiTrust Digital Library at http://babel.hathitrust.org/cgi/pt?id=mdp.39015030741626&view=2up&seq=17.

15. Borst, *Catching Babies*, 101–6; Litoff, *American Midwives*, 50–51; Wertz and Wertz, *Lying-In*, 55.

16. Leavitt, *Brought to Bed*, 76–78.

17. As previously noted, Wertz and Wertz in *Lying-In*, 58–76, offer one of the most complete overviews of the dangerously limited scope of medical training focused on reproductive issues. Leavitt describes the typical medical training for obstetric practice and documents that medical students frequently trained only with mannequins and thus had no experience with live women and little informed knowledge of the birth process. Leavitt, *Brought to Bed*, 42–63. Borst in *Catching Babies* addresses the

same constellation of issues as other scholars of reproductive history but with a particular eye to contrasting the aggressive professionalization of medicine with the absence of formal occupational structure in midwifery. Wolf in *Deliver Me from Pain*, 20–23, pays particular attention to the role of anesthetic technologies.

18. Shryock, *Medical Licensing in America, 1650–1965*.
19. Margot Edwards and Mary Waldorf, *Reclaiming Birth: History and Heroines of American Childbirth Reform* (Trumansburg NY: Crossing Press, 1984), 4–5. Multiple in-depth explanations have been published detailing the status of women's reproductive functions as pathology. Edwards and Waldor's *Reclaiming Birth* covers the most salient elements of the argument in just two pages.
20. One of the most complete sources for understanding the evolution of scientific training and subsequent pronouncements on the female body is Londa Schiebinger's *Nature's Body: Gender in the Making of Modern Science* (Boston: Beacon Press, 1993). This classic text methodically details a deep context for the relevant scientific philosophies and concomitant practices, and it covers the evolution of thought about femaleness and women from Aristotle through the contemporary era. Additionally, Thomas Laqueur's "Orgasm, Generation, and the Politics of Reproductive Biology," in *The Making of the Modern Body: Sexuality and Society in the Nineteenth Century*, ed. Catherine Gallagher and Thomas Laqueur (Berkeley: University of California Press, 1987), 1–41, offers a beautifully concise overview of the changing ideas about maleness and femaleness, reproduction, sexuality, and the role of childbearing in society. The application of these ideas to the specific American context are addressed in Leavitt, *Brought to Bed*; her discussion of social childbirth begins on 36. Wertz and Wertz's *Lying-In* devotes the first twenty-eight pages to women's social practice of childbirth. Wolf, *Deliver Me from Pain*, 14–20, also reviews the history of social birth, as does Litoff in *American Midwives*, 3–17.
21. Litoff, *American Midwives*, 3–17.
22. Leavitt, *Brought to Bed*, 41; Wertz and Wertz, *Lying-In*, 77–90.
23. Leavitt, *Brought to Bed*, 50–59, 142–54; Litoff, *American Midwives*, 64–90; Wolf, *Deliver Me from Pain*, 13–104; Wertz and Wertz, *Lying-In*, 65–67.
24. Janet Bogdan, "Care or Cure? Childbirth Practices in Nineteenth Century America," *Feminist Studies* 4, no. 2 (1978): 92–99.
25. Leavitt, *Brought to Bed*.

26. Londa Schiebinger, "Skeletons in the Closet: The First Illustrations of the Female Skeleton in Eighteenth-Century Anatomy," in *The Making of the Modern Body: Sexuality and Society in the Nineteenth Century*, ed. Catherine Gallagher and Thomas Laqueur (Berkeley: University of California Press, 1987), 42–82. Schiebinger demonstrates the ways that eighteenth- and nineteenth-century science used women's anatomy as a means to devalue them and place the female form as subordinate to the male. She refers specifically to the impact of this scientific thinking on midwifery (70).

27. Mary Poovey, "'Scenes of an Indelicate Character': The Medical 'Treatment' of Victorian Women," in *The Making of the Modern Body: Sexuality and Society in the Nineteenth Century*, ed. Catherine Gallagher and Thomas Laqueur (Berkeley: University of California Press, 1987), 137–68. Poovey makes the point that "the silenced female body can be made the vehicle for any medical man's assumptions and practice because its very silence opens a space in which meanings can proliferate" (152).

28. Bogdan, "Care or Cure?"; Scholten, "'On the Importance of the Obstetrick Art.'"

29. M. Steen, "Risk, Recognition and Repair of Perineal Trauma," *British Journal of Midwifery* 20, no. 11 (2012): 768–77.

30. E. D. Hodnett, S. Downe, and D. Walsh, "Alternatives versus Conventional Institutional Settings for Birth," *Cochrane Database of Systematic Reviews*, no. 8 (2012), article no. CD000012, https://doi.org/10.1002/14651858.CD000012.pub4. As Faith Diorgu explains, "studies have indicated that the supine-lithotomy position is associated with a number of negative consequences. This position promotes loss of control, narrows the pelvis and makes it difficult for the baby to descend." Faith Diorgu and Mary Steen, "Mothers' and Healthcare Stakeholders' Views and Experiences of Birthing Positions and Perineal Injuries during Childbirth in a Low-Resource Setting in Nigeria," *Evidence Based Midwifery* 16, no. 3 (2018): 94–100, quote at 95.

31. C. Racinet, "Positions maternelles pour l'accouchement" [Maternal positions during parturition], *Gynécologie Obstétrique & Fertilité* 33, no. 7–8 (2005): 533–38.

32. William Dewees, one of the leading obstetric proponents of the pregnancy-as-a-disease approach in the 1800s, acknowledged the frequency with which forceps caused debilitating genital injuries to women

and reminded his students to be sure that "no part of the mother is included in the locking of the blades." Quoted in Scholten, "'On the Importance of the Obstetrick Art,'" 444.

33. Mary Poovey addresses the importance of women's silence in "'Scenes of an Indelicate Character.'" Additionally, the following texts make reference to the power differential between women and doctors, as well as the cultural imperative for female silence: Borst, *Catching Babies*; Leavitt, *Brought to Bed*; Leavitt, *Women and Health in America*; Litoff, *American Midwives*; Scholten, *Childbearing in American Society*; Wertz and Wertz, *Lying-In*; and Wolf, *Deliver Me from Pain*.

34. Schiebinger, "Skeletons in the Closet," 72.

35. Wertz and Wertz, *Lying-In*, 91–106.

36. Poovey, "'Scenes of an Indelicate Character.'" Poovey offers invaluable analysis of the scientific and medical discussion about the central role the uterus played in defining women as reproductive creatures. Her work demonstrates the ways that medical assumptions about the female body served to place doctors in the position of overseeing women's reproductive functions. She states that medicine's interpretation of the female body resulted in "an image of woman as always lacking and needing control— whether that control be exercised by the obstetrician, superintending her lying-in, or by the consulting physician, monitoring the disorder that makes her what she is" (147). Poovey carefully delineates the process by which science and medicine actively sought to exercise control over women's bodies, in both practice and theory.

37. Litoff, *American Midwives*, 22. While consistently referring to delivery as a dangerous activity, physicians emphasizing the perils of childbirth became more prevalent in the early decades of the twentieth century as attacks on the profession of midwifery increased.

38. Leavitt, *Brought to Bed*; Wertz and Wertz, *Lying-In*, 1–28; and Litoff, *American Midwives*, 3–17, document the routine and social nature of female reproduction before physician domination of delivery.

39. Medical training and physician perceptions included an emphasis on childbirth as erratic and lacking in consistency, as covered in Wertz and Wertz, *Lying-In*; Leavitt, *Brought to Bed*; Borst, *Catching Babies*; and Laurel Thatcher Ulrich, "Martha Moore Ballard and the Medical Challenge to Midwifery," in *Sickness and Health in America: Readings in the History of Medicine and Public Health*, ed. Judith Walzer Leavitt and

Ronald L. Numbers (Madison: University of Wisconsin Press, 1978), 72–84.

40. Scholten, "'On the Importance of the Obstetrick Art'"; Wertz and Wertz, *Lying-In*; Litoff, *American Midwives*; Borst, *Catching Babies*; Leavitt, *Brought to Bed*; Bogdan, "Care or Cure?"; Charles D. Meigs, *Introductory Lecture to the Class of Midwifery in the Jefferson Medical College, Delivered Wednesday, October 9, 1854* (Philadelphia: T. K. and P. G. Collins, 1854), 8; Judith Walzer Leavitt, "'A Worrying Profession': The Domestic Environment of Medical Practice in Mid-19th-Century America," in *Sickness and Health in America: Readings in the History of Medicine and Public Health*, ed. Judith Walzer Leavitt and Ronald L. Numbers (Madison: University of Wisconsin Press, 1978), 145–60; and Ulrich, "Martha Moore Ballard and the Medical Challenge to Midwifery."

41. Steele, *Bleed, Blister, and Purge.*

42. Wertz and Wertz, *Lying-In*, 58–76; Leavitt, *Brought to Bed*, 42–63; Borst, *Catching Babies.*

43. Scott, *Seeing Like a State*, 315–16.

44. Dunn, "Louise Bourgeois (1563–1636)"; Perkins, *Midwifery and Medicine in Early Modern France.*

45. Scott has described a hypothetical apprenticeship model for just such a situation that mirrored the actual practice of midwifery. New practitioners were trained in a process in which certain responses were "largely acquired through practice (often in formal apprenticeship) and a developed feel or knack for strategy." Scott, *Seeing Like a State*, 315–16.

46. J. K. Gupta, A. Sood, G. J. Hofmeyr, and J. P. Vogel, "Position in the Second Stage of Labour for Women without Epidural Anaesthesia," *Cochrane Database Systematic Reviews*, no. 5 (2017), art. no. CD002006, http://doi .org/10.1002/14651858.CD002006.pub4.

47. Vanvig interview.

48. Interestingly, part of the evolution of allopathic medicine involved abandoning a mentorship model, in which students learned by assisting experienced physicians, and moving toward a school-based structure. Rothstein, *American Physicians in the Nineteenth*, 85–87. This transition in medical education allowed for greater consistency of training but also eliminated the opportunity to learn by apprenticeship.

49. Wertz and Wertz, *Lying-In*, 133.

50. Scholten, "'On the Importance of the Obstetrick Art.'"

51. Wertz and Wertz, *Lying-In.*
52. Meigs, *Introductory Lecture to the Class of Midwifery*, 8.
53. The status of physicians also received a boost from concerns about infant feeding. A number of cultural changes—like migrant women working long hours, an increasing focus on sexualized marriages, and breasts being seen as sexual and in need of preservation—caused a decrease in the frequency of breastfeeding, which led to women with lower milk production and increased need for supplemental feeding. In an era without consistently safe milk supplies, infant deaths became a public health issue, especially in larger cities. Jacqueline Wolf's text looks at these changes and points to pediatricians and other doctors as having an elevated role in ensuring a safe milk supply for infants. Jacqueline H. Wolf, "Don't Kill Your Baby: Public Health and the Decline of Breastfeeding in the Nineteenth and Twentieth Centuries," *Journal of American History* 90, no. 1 (2003): 250–51.
54. Steele, *Bleed, Blister, and Purge.*
55. Wilkie, *Archaeology of Mothering*, xviii. Significantly, evidence does not exist to show that each and every male physician of the era sought an expanded role for his services. Quite to the contrary, it is assumed that individual doctors, especially those less steeped in the professions' antimidwifery rhetoric, followed a potentially different method of practice.
56. Wertz and Wertz, *Lying-In*; Leavitt, *Brought to Bed*; Borst, *Catching Babies*; Shryock, *Medical Licensing in America.*
57. For a concise overview of birth rates from the late 1700s through the 1900s, see "Family," *The First Measured Century*, PBS, http://www.pbs .org/fmc/book/4family9.htm.
58. Wertz and Wertz, *Lying-In*, 55–65; Litoff, *American Midwives*, 64–90; J. Whitridge Williams, "Medical Education and the Midwife Problem in the United States," *Journal of the American Medical Association* 58, no. 1 (1912): 1–7.
59. Litoff, *American Midwives.*
60. DeLee quoted in Loudon, *Death in Childbirth*, 322–23.
61. Loudon, *Death in Childbirth*, 322.
62. Organized medicine sought to criticize midwifery as vocally and frequently as possible, so examples of these attacks can be found in medical journals and newspapers of the era. Some of the common examples are chronicled in Wertz and Wertz, *Lying-In*, 55–65; and Litoff, *American Midwives*, 64–90.

63. Nicholson quoted in Litoff, *American Midwives*, 77.

64. Mississippi bureaucrat quoted in Litoff, *American Midwives*, 78.

65. Clipping without headline, from a Harlem, Montana, newspaper, November 23, 1911, in the collections of the MonDak Heritage Center, Sidney, Montana, likely to be "Midwife System Is Attacked: Would Put Obstetrics in Hands of Physicians," *The Enterprise* (Harlem MT), November 23, 1911, per Newspapers.com.

66. The research of Charlotte Borst in *Catching Babies* eloquently demonstrates the role that class played in the widespread elimination of mainstream midwifery care in the United States. Using birth practices documented in the state of Wisconsin, Borst follows the evolution of midwifery, general practice physicians, and obstetric specialists and shows that class was a distinct criterion that pregnant women used to select a birth attendant. The use of a medical doctor indicated higher social standing and reflected the mother's intention to consciously imbue her choice of birth attendant with a marker of upward mobility.

67. Lucy Russell, interview by Larry Sprunk, August 11, 1976, Medora, North Dakota, ND Oral History Project.

68. Scott, *Seeing Like a State*, 7.

69. Lisa F. Stinson, Matthew S. Payne, and Jeffrey A. Keelan, "Planting the Seed: Origins, Composition, and Postnatal Health Significance of the Fetal Gastrointestinal Microbiota," *Critical Review of Microbiology* 43, no. 3 (2017): 352–69, http://doi.org/10.1080/1040841x.2016.1211088.

70. Paradise, *Maternity Care*.

71. Paradise, *Maternity Care*, 33.

72. Thompson interview.

73. Leavitt, *Brought to Bed*, 154–70; Wertz and Wertz, *Lying-In*, 109–31.

74. Leavitt, *Brought to Bed*, 154–70; Wertz and Wertz, *Lying-In*, 109–31.

75. Since we now know that infants receive their mother's infection-fighting antibodies through the placenta and breast milk, the role of the birth attendant in infection is clear. Given that the infant was only just recently submerged in the mother's system, her bodily fluids pose a relatively minor risk to the infant. Furthermore, Leavitt explains that physicians were more likely to cause puerperal fever than midwives: "Inappropriate forceps use and the careless administration of ether and chloroform introduced serious lacerations and breathing disorders that otherwise might not have developed. Perhaps even more significant, physicians

often carried puerperal fever, which was potentially disastrous, to birthing women. Because their medical practices included attending patients
with communicable diseases, doctors were more likely than midwives
to bring with them on their hands and on their clothing the agents of
infection." Judith Walzer Leavitt, *Brought to Bed: Childbearing in America,
1750–1950* (1986; New York: Oxford University Press, 2013), 57.

76. Paradise, *Maternity Care*, 33.

77. Jennifer J. Hill, "Midwives in Montana: Historically Informed Political Activism" (PhD diss., Montana State University, 2013), appendix C,
"Puerperal Fever in Montana, 1921–1925," 184–86. It is possible that
the rate of puerperal fever deaths nationwide (usually around 75 percent of all maternal deaths) differs from the rate in Montana (around
50 percent) because a higher number of midwifery-assisted deliveries
occurred in the region. Even while the specific cause of this lower fatality
rate from puerperal fever cannot be determined, we can conclude that,
while women in the northern plains and Rocky Mountains died from
childbirth-related causes all too frequently, those reasons for death were
less often attendant-caused infection.

78. Leavitt, *Brought to Bed*, 154–70 (this and all subsequent citations are from
the original 1986 edition); Wertz and Wertz, *Lying-In*, 109–31.

79. From the 1850s through the 1940s the profession of medicine struggled,
especially in certain parts of the country, to contain puerperal fever. The
eventual use of antibiotics to successfully treat these types of infections
saved countless lives. Leavitt, *Brought to Bed*, 154–70; Wertz and Wertz,
Lying-In, 109–31.

80. Susan E. Cayleff, *Wash and Be Healed: The Water-Cure Movement and
Women's Health* (Philadelphia: Temple University Press, 1987), 8, examines the element of social class with regard to medical providers and
suggests some of the rationale for women's decision to give birth in a
hospital setting.

81. Judith Walzer Leavitt, "Birthing and Anesthesia: The Debate over Twilight
Sleep," *Signs* 6, no. 1 (1980): 147–64, quotes at 148.

82. Henry Smith Williams, *Twilight Sleep: A Simple Account of New Discoveries
in Painless Childbirth* (New York: Harper & Brothers, 1914), 91.

83. Leavitt, *Brought to Bed*, 134–35; Leavitt, "Birthing and Anesthesia." Jacqueline Wolf devotes an entire chapter of *Deliver Me from Pain* (44–72)

to examining the development, dangers of, and subsequent popularity of twilight sleep.

84. Poovey, "Scenes of an Indelicate Character." Poovey's essay explores the role that doctors' fear played in the ways they responded to and sought scientific control over the female body.

85. Because national tabulation of public health statistics did not occur until well into the twentieth century, a complete analysis of midwifery rates versus physician rates cannot be compiled. However, Leavitt explains that "if the hospitals were safer for childbirth, maternal mortality rates should have begun to decrease as more women entered the hospitals; in fact, the death rates stayed the same or even increased in the years when women began going to the hospital to give birth." Leavitt states that increasing mortality rates among women delivered by physicians in hospitals were a reality that doctors were "not eager to admit . . . even among themselves." Leavitt, *Brought to Bed*, 183. Other scholars have documented varied evidence that indicates the relative safety of midwifery-assisted delivery in comparison to that of doctors in the late 1800s and early 1900s; see Wolf, *Deliver Me from Pain*, 16–17; Litoff, *American Midwives*, 108; and Wertz and Wertz, *Lying-In*, 162–65.

86. Joan Jensen, *Calling This Place Home: Women on the Wisconsin Frontier, 1850–1925* (St. Paul: Minnesota Historical Society Press, 2006), 163.

87. Melcher, "'Women's Matters,'" 53.

88. A multitude of studies, including the econometrics examination of midwifery referenced at the beginning of this chapter, conclude that midwives achieved lower rates of maternal and infant death than did physicians. For example, Anderson et al. state that "contemporary studies provide strong evidence that mortality rates were higher among mothers attended by a doctor than among mothers attended by a trained midwife." Anderson et al., "Effect of Occupational Licensing on Consumer Welfare."

89. The legacy of medicine's malicious propaganda against midwives is still with us. The study I encountered in 2017 was made widely available and, as of this writing, has been cited more than twenty times. Turn-of-the-twentieth-century campaigns against midwives became an international export and are currently being used to critique traditional practices of midwifery around the world, as exemplified in David J. Phillips, "Licensing Midwives Saves Lives," *Chicago Booth Review*, March 2, 2017.

It is critical that we examine the medical profession's attempts to rewrite our shared reproductive past. Yet, in exploring and acknowledging the duplicitous history that was foisted on the American public, we must also avoid heralding historical midwives as untarnished feminist icons or as warmhearted but ignorant do-gooders. Some contemporary natural birth proponents paint all midwives, regardless of experience, as heroes in the fight against misdirected misogyny, an effort that ignores elements of racism present *within* midwifery. For further examination of this topic, see Christa Craven and Mara Glatzel, "Downplaying Difference: Historical Accounts of African American Midwives and Contemporary Struggles for Midwifery," *Feminist Studies* 36, no. 2 (2010): 330–58.

90. The ability to speak for other women and to stand in their stead could have been performed by men; after all, biology and identity were not destiny. But in turn-of-the-twentieth-century America gender was powerful. A male physician deeply desirous of understanding the female experience of birth could do so, but cultural barriers made this technical potential a pragmatic impossibility.

5. Death in the West

1. Marriage certificate of Albert Kummer and Elisabeth Krieg, as well as record of children born to the marriage, in the personal collection of Marie Melton, Bertha Kummer Emmert's granddaughter.
2. Manifest of Alien Passengers for the Commissioner of Immigration, April 19, 1903, Massachusetts, Passenger and Crew List, available through Ancestry.com.
3. Marie Melton, interview by Jennifer Hill, August 25, 2016, Bozeman, Montana.
4. Melton interview; "Accident and Fire at Brewery," *Broadwater Opinion* (Townsend MT), November 30, 1911, 2; "Fire and Explosion," *Broadwater Opinion*, December 2, 1911. According to the family, the coworker who saved George was his nephew, John Reeg.
5. "Accident and Fire at Brewery," *Broadwater Opinion*, 2; "Fire and Explosion," *Broadwater Opinion*.
6. "Accident and Fire at Brewery," *Broadwater Opinion*, 2; "Mrs. Geo. Emmert Passes Away," *Townsend Star*, December 23, 1911.
7. Bertha Emmert death certificate, Emmert infant birth certificate, personal collection of Marie Melton, Bertha Kummer Emmert's granddaughter.

8. Melton interview.

9. Melton interview.

10. Melton interview.

11. To offer some local context, Townsend, Montana, a town of only 759 residents in 1910, reported the deaths of two infants and one young married woman in the first four months of 1912, just after Bertha's death. In a year when nine local men died of age-related causes and six men perished in a mining accident, women's deaths were not the numerical leader in Townsend but did occur with some regularity. *Townsend Star*, January 20, 1912.

12. For Native birthing and reproductive practices, see chapter 3's note 25.

13. Hoffert, "Childbearing on the Trans-Mississippi Frontier," 284–85.

14. Montana State Board of Health, *Eleventh Biennial Report of Montana State Board of Health, 1921 and 1922* (Helena MT, 1922), 7. It is important to note that women in other countries may have experienced maternal and infant mortality rates similar to those of northern plains mothers. While we cannot determine that women in Montana, the Dakotas, and Wyoming faced worse odds than their rural counterparts on a global scale, we do know that their reproductive situation was far more dangerous than that of women residing in eastern and more urban parts of the United States.

15. "Report of the State Board of Health, 1935–1936," Wyoming State Archives, Cheyenne, Wyoming. Additionally, Dawn Nickel's two-part series "Dying in the West" cites sources that put the rural infant mortality rate at "twice or more than the city rates." Nickel, "Dying in the West, Part 1," 29–30.

16. Tone, *Devices and Desires*; Janet Farrell Brodie, *Contraception and Abortion in Nineteenth-Century America* (Ithaca NY: Cornell University Press, 1994).

17. John D'Emilio and Estelle B. Freedman, *Intimate Matters: A History of Sexuality in America* (New York: Harper and Row, 1988); Tone, *Devices and Desires*.

18. Brodie, *Contraception and Abortion*.

19. Hargreaves, *Dry Farming in the Northern Great Plains*, 220.

20. Hargreaves establishes how overly inflated publicity, coordinated by states and railroads, "acquired status as a public good." Thus, settlers searching for objective information obtained data from states in the region, thinking they were gaining fact-based resources, while states simultaneously

worked with railroads to promote increased settlement that served state needs but did not necessarily benefit settlers. Hargreaves, *Dry Farming in the Northern Great Plains*, 275.

21. Hargreaves, *Dry Farming in the Northern Great Plains*, 275.

22. Hargreaves, *Dry Farming in the Northern Great Plains*, 540.

23. Indubitably, some of these same conditions existed for migrants settling in states like Wisconsin and Minnesota decades earlier but on a different order of magnitude. There was not one determinative condition unique to the northern plains and Rocky Mountains but rather a number of factors that, taken together, combined to create a more highly stressed reproductive environment. For example, the issue of crop production, a matter of concern for residents of the northern plains and earlier settlement areas alike, was exacerbated by the lower annual rainfall totals in Montana, the Dakotas, and Wyoming. While Wisconsin and Minnesota averaged more than thirty inches of precipitation per year, settlers farther west in the northern plains and Rocky Mountains could expect little more than fifteen inches annually, with some areas experiencing even more arid conditions. Historical rainfall and temperature information can be obtained from the climate summaries offered by the National Oceanic and Atmospheric Administration (NOAA), https://statesummaries.ncics.org.

24. This listing of routine tasks performed by turn-of-the-twentieth-century northern plains and Rocky Mountain women was compiled by the author from North Dakota and Montana oral histories, held by the North Dakota State Archives, Bismarck, North Dakota, and the Montana Historical Society Research Center in Helena, Montana. Children, another segment of the population whose valuable work is often overlooked, also helped with these tasks.

25. See Dale Martin, *Ties, Rails, and Telegraph Wires: Railroads and Communities in Montana and the West* (Helena: Montana Historical Society Press, 2018) for information on the impact of railroads in Montana and the larger region.

26. M. Hill, *Powderville*.

27. In 1913 the average price of butter across the country was thirty-eight cents per pound, and a can of tomatoes went for sixteen cents. While the cost of butter in Butte, Montana, was the same as in the rest of the country, canned tomatoes (which had to be transported via railroad)

cost an additional 12 percent per can over the national average. United States, Bureau of Labor Statistics, "Retail Prices, 1913 to December 1919: Bulletin of the United States Bureau of Labor Statistics, No. 270," *Retail Prices* (February 1921).

28. Data on annual food preparation performed by turn-of-the-twentieth-century northern plains and Rocky Mountain women compiled by the author from North Dakota and Montana oral histories, held by the North Dakota State Archives and the Montana Historical Society Research Center.

29. Information on weather conditions and travel restrictions affecting turn-of-the-twentieth-century northern plains and Rocky Mountain women compiled by the author from North Dakota and Montana oral histories held by the North Dakota State Archives and the Montana Historical Society Research Center.

30. Hoven interview.

31. Libecap, "Learning about the Weather."

32. Koch to her mother, n.d.

33. Irvine Loudon, demographer and social historian, has assessed the host of factors that cause mortality and morbidity and concluded that "malnutrition associated with poverty does indeed increase the risk of dying in childbirth." Loudon, *Death in Childbirth*, 379–80.

34. It is important to note that much of the daily routine, like food preparation and cleaning tasks, would be similar for urban women but in a somewhat different order of magnitude. For women residing in or near a town or city, ladies' groups and church activities offered regular social connections, food supplies could be more regularly purchased, and help could be hired in times of great need or in cases of emergency.

35. Historian Nanci Langford has established a similar rationale for Canadian women of the era; see Langford, "Childbirth on the Canadian Prairies," 279.

36. Hargreaves, *Dry Farming in the Northern Great Plains*, 8.

37. Langford, "Childbirth on the Canadian Prairies," 279.

38. This phenomenon affected women just to the north in Canada, as well as in Montana, the Dakotas, and Wyoming. Kathryn McPherson has shown that "high rates of infant and maternal mortality persisted" in western Canada, as women there faced situations similar to those that northern plains and Rocky Mountain mothers experienced. Kathryn McPherson,

"Was the 'Frontier' Good for Women? Historical Approaches to Women and Agricultural Settlement in the Prairie West, 1870–1925," *Atlantis* 25, no. 1 (2000): 75–86, quote at 77. The desperation felt by mothers of the region impacted families and communities, and it is likely that turn-of-the-twentieth-century women dealt with the symptoms of postpartum depression on a regular basis. In some cases, though, women suffered even more acutely. The *Butte Miner* reported in 1883 that a mother had died after being hospitalized with what was termed "puerperal insanity." Committing women to an asylum after giving birth, as was the case for Minnie McAuliff, who was confined to an institution after each of her three children were born, and for Laura Reynolds, committed just two weeks after the birth of her baby, did not reduce mothers' feelings of despair and misery; instead, it reminded area women of additional perils they could face. *Butte Daily Miner*, August 17, 1883; *Anaconda Standard*, May 11, 1893. The Centers for Disease Control and Prevention (CDC) estimates postpartum depression to occur in 10 to 20 percent of mothers. For a full report on the risk factors and treatments for postpartum depression, see "Reproductive Health: Depression among Women," CDC, last updated May 14, 2020, https://www.cdc.gov/reproductivehealth/depression/index.htm.

39. Ellen Leahy, "'Montana Fever': Smallpox and the Montana State Board of Health," *Montana: The Magazine of Western History* 53, no. 2 (2003): 32–45, esp. 33.

40. For a brief history of the region's transition to statehood, see "Wyoming History," State of Wyoming, accessed February 26, 2016, http://www.wyo.gov/about-wyoming/wyoming-history; and "Summary of North Dakota History: Statehood," State Historical Society of North Dakota, accessed February 26, 2016, http://history.nd.gov/ndhistory/statehood.html.

41. "State Department of Health," State Historical Society of North Dakota Archives, accessed May 30, 2018, http://history.nd.gov/archives/stateagencies/health.html.

42. Jim Donahue, ed., *Wyoming Blue Book: Guide to the State Government and Municipal Archives of Wyoming* (Cheyenne: Wyoming State Archives, Department of Commerce, 1991), vol. 5, part 2, 432.

43. Leahy, "'Montana Fever,'" 36.

44. Leahy, "'Montana Fever,'" 35.

45. Ellen Leahy has discussed how epidemic disease forced area residents "to find tenuous balancing points between action and reaction, personal liberty and the common good, and state and local responsibility." Leahy, "'Montana Fever,'" 45.

46. *Biennial Report of the State Board of Health of South Dakota, for the Years 1901–1902* (Aberdeen SD: News Printing Company, 1902), 12, held by Department of Health, State Board of Health Reports, Annual 1890–1923, Box 7170A, State Archives of the South Dakota Historical Society, Pierre, South Dakota.

47. "Fourth Biennial Report of the State Board of Health of Montana," 1907–8, held by the Montana Historical Society Research Center, Helena, Montana.

48. State health departments could follow the lead of the U.S. Children's Bureau, which also pushed birth certificate registration as a means of accurate information gathering and subsequent action. Parker and Carpenter, "Julia Lathrop and the Children's Bureau."

49. Summary of health department process based on department reports from North Dakota (held by the North Dakota State Archives, Bismarck, North Dakota), South Dakota (held by the State Archives of the South Dakota Historical Society, Pierre, South Dakota), Wyoming (held by the Wyoming State Archives, Cheyenne, Wyoming), and Montana (held by the Montana Historical Society Research Center, Helena, Montana).

50. *Biennial Report of the State Board of Health of South Dakota, for the Years 1901–1902*, 12.

51. *Biennial Report of the State Board of Health, State of South Dakota, 1904–1905* (printed as "1904–1905," which was crossed out and "1903–1904" written in) (Aberdeen SD: News Printing Company, 1905), 3.

52. *Biennial Report of the State Board of Health of the State of South Dakota, 1908–1910* (Sioux Falls SD: Mark D. Scott, Printer and Binder, 1910), 5.

53. As early as 1890 the South Dakota Board of Health noted that "other States all around us have laws [requiring registration of births and deaths] relating to these very vital subjects. Our State is settled by as intelligent a class of people as any of our sister states can claim, and we are derelict in these matters which concern us vitally." *Second Annual Report of the State Board of Health of South Dakota, December 1, 1890* (Pierre SD: Free Press, 1890), 9.

54. Birth Registration in the United States, n.d., Box 23, 4-0-1 Birth Registration, RG 102, Records of the Children's Bureau, Central File, 1914–1920, 3-5-1-1 to 4-0-1-1, National Archives and Records Administration, College Park, Maryland.

55. Progress Made in Birth Registration Test in Cooperation with General and State Federations of Women's Clubs and the Association of Collegiate Alumnae and Other Women's Organizations, March 9, 1916, Box 24, 4-0-1-1 Progress in Birth Registration, RG 102, Records of the Children's Bureau, Central File, 1914–1920, 4-0-1-1 to 4-2-0-2-2.

56. Vital Statistics, U.S. Center for Health Statistics, 71, accessed June 1, 2018, https://www.census.gov/prod/2/gen/96statab/vitlstat.pdf.

57. To be admitted to the registration area, states like South Dakota had to include specific language in health department codes and meet accuracy benchmarks in their data collection. State of South Dakota, *Seventh Biennial Report of the State Board of Health, for the Period July 1, 1924, to June 30, 1926* (Mitchell SD: Mitchell Publishing, 1926), 5.

58. Vital Statistics, U.S. Center for Health Statistics, 71.

59. State of South Dakota, *Seventh Biennial Report of the State Board of Health, State of South Dakota, for the Period July 1, 1924, to June 30, 1926*, 5.

60. Wyoming State Health Department, Eleventh Biennial Report, 1931–33, 18, Wyoming State Archives, Cheyenne, Wyoming.

61. Leahy, "'Montana Fever,'" 35. Children's Bureau staff were largely college-educated white women, like Julia Lathrop, and state health departments pulled from a similar pool and also hired male staff, directors, and physicians. Ladd-Taylor, *Raising a Baby the Government Way*.

62. Reports of the state boards of health for Montana, North Dakota, Wyoming, and South Dakota, held by the Montana Historical Society Research Center, North Dakota State Archives, Wyoming State Archives, and State Archives of the South Dakota Historical Society.

63. Mortality rates also became a national issue. Children's Bureau head Julia Lathrop pushed President William H. Taft to address this public health crisis, which he did in his 1912 State of the Union address. Parker and Carpenter, "Julia Lathrop and the Children's Bureau," 64.

64. It is important to note that, as archeologist Laurie Wilkie has pointed out, "white, middle-class, and elite America had constructed mothering as an exclusive site of white privilege and entitlement." Wilkie, *Archaeology of Mothering*, 212. The great majority of public concern during this period

focused on the deaths of Euro-American mothers, while multitudes of more marginalized women struggled with even worse reproductive challenges. Thus, for the women this text focuses on, motherhood was simultaneously a privilege and also a locus of oppression.

65. Montana State Board of Health, *Eleventh Biennial Report of Montana State Board of Health, 1921 and 1922*, 7. From 1911 through 1919, a total of 7,888 Montana infants and 1,000 mothers died. For this period the infant mortality rate in Montana averaged 86 deaths per 1,000 births; the maternal mortality rate in the state averaged just under 11 deaths per 1,000 births. Health departments focused primarily on collecting Euro-American data, so it is likely that mortality figures did not include Native American infant and maternal deaths. In later years, when more complete statistics were collected, mortality rates for Native American populations were typically higher. This is not surprising since the conditions that plagued settler women—like lack of food, poor access to health care, and physical and emotional stress—were even more pronounced in Native communities. For a more extensive discussion of mortality data, see J. Hill, "Midwives in Montana."

66. Nickel, "Dying in the West, Part 1."

67. The Children's Bureau discovered that infant deaths were nearly all preventable, and it pointed to lack of sanitation, inadequate nutrition, and feeding issues as the main factors. Ladd-Taylor, *Raising a Baby the Government Way*, 20.

68. Finn, *Mining Childhood*, 20–21.

69. Summary of typical responses to registration laws compiled by the author from Montana, North Dakota, Wyoming, and South Dakota health department reports.

70. Health Department Report, Wyoming State Board of Health, 1911–12, 31, Wyoming State Archives, Cheyenne, Wyoming.

71. Board Minutes, 1920, 139, Folder 1-3, Box 1, Montana State Board of Health Records, 1920–38, RS 238, Montana Historical Society Research Center, Helena, Montana.

72. Leslie Reagan, *When Abortion Was a Crime: Women, Medicine, and the Law, 1876–1973* (Berkeley: University of California Press, 1997); James Mohr, *Abortion in America: The Origins and Evolutions of National Policy, 1800–1900* (New York: Oxford University Press, 1978).

73. *Yellowstone Monitor* (Glendive MT), January 4, 1912.

74. Wyoming State Board of Health, "Health and Sanitation during the Past Two Years," 1911–12 report, 71, Wyoming State Archives, Cheyenne, Wyoming.

75. Eventually the Wyoming registration law established the payment of twenty-five cents per certificate to the midwife or physician who completed each form. Wyoming State Board of Health, "Health and Sanitation during the Past Two Years," 1911–12, 71.

76. Wyoming State Board of Health report, 1911–12, 31–32; Wyoming State Board of Health report, 1915–16, 18–19, both in Wyoming State Archives, Cheyenne, Wyoming.

77. Wyoming State Board of Health report, 1915–16, 18–19.

78. *Fifth Biennial Report of the State Board of Health to the Governor of North Dakota*, dated December 1, 1898 (Bismarck ND: Tribune State Printers and Binders, 1899), 7, held by the North Dakota State Archives, Bismarck, North Dakota.

79. Wyoming State Board of Health report, 1915–16, 18–19.

6. Birth Goes Public

1. M. Hill, *Powderville*, 47.

2. M. Hill, *Powderville*, 50–51.

3. M. Hill, *Powderville*, 51.

4. Knipfer interview.

5. Anthropologists have documented the ways in which various cultures provide care and value supportive relationships. The most abundant regional example can be found in the Native American tradition of gifting ceremonies. The mythology behind such exchanges is discussed in Robyn Wall Kimmerer, *Braiding Sweetgrass: Indigenous Wisdom, Scientific Knowledge, and the Teachings of Plants* (Minneapolis MN: Milkweed Editions, 2015).

6. These issues were particularly salient for turn-of-the-twentieth-century women, as they were often dependent on their male partners. Few employment opportunities existed, and those that did were often frowned upon. For example, Mary Ducello, a resident of eastern Montana in the early 1900s, was abandoned by her husband and left with two young children to care for without any source of income. She took one of the only jobs available to her: as a housekeeper for a cattle ranch. Despite her desperate need for employment and universal approval of her stellar

managerial and cooking skills, members of the community continued to look askance at her employment. M. Hill, *Powderville*, 34–35.

7. Parker and Carpenter, "Julia Lathrop and the Children's Bureau."

8. Paradise, *Maternity Care*. The decision to relocate and deliver in more amenable circumstances, usually closer to female relatives and delivery assistance, presented certain difficulties. Travel was not cheap, either in terms of time or money. To avoid traveling too close to their expected due dates, women might have to leave the state for several months, and the travel costs could be in the neighborhood of $150 (11). In a time when a good horse could be purchased for $85, spending nearly twice that amount on delivery-related costs would have put a serious dent in a family's resources. Women who could not afford or did not want to travel so far or stay away so long often considered relocating to town. Mary Stephenson lived near Circle, Montana, and when she was pregnant with her first child in 1910 and 1911, she "thought it would be better to be living with some friends in Glendive." Mary Stephenson, interview by Laurie Mercier, October 29, 1981, OH 209, MAW Oral History Project.

9. The assumed hierarchy of value placed women's needs, experiences, and perceptions as secondary to men's. For example, Charlotte Jensen remembered the sting of her parents paying for violin lessons for her less responsible brother but not for her. She, like so many other women, "learned early on that special privileges were to be accorded to males." M. Hill, *Powderville*, 55.

10. In defense of health department staff, those courageous enough to consider the logical removal of impediments to women's ability to support themselves had only to look to Julia Lathrop's work at the Children's Bureau to see how such innovative strategies might be received. The organized opposition to and pushback against the Sheppard-Towner Act demonstrated widespread opposition to such ideas. Parker and Carpenter, "Julia Lathrop and the Children's Bureau"; Lemons, "Sheppard-Towner Act."

11. According to Lemons, "Sheppard-Towner Act," the maternal mortality rate in the United State fell from 67:1,000 to 62:1,000 when the act was in effect—an important decrease that still put the United States well behind nations like New Zealand (with a rate of 35:1,000) and England (at 31:1,000).

12. These publications were requested by all sorts of mothers—including poor, working-class, and farming women—and the bureau sent out 1.5

million copies from 1914 to 1921. Ladd-Taylor, *Raising a Baby the Government Way*, 2.

13. The North Dakota Health Department reported that by 1930 the department had annually distributed nearly thirty thousand copies of *Infant Care*, a tidily countable quantity that lacked any associated data on how women interpreted or used the information or whether they even desired it in the first place. The South Dakota Health Department published a variety of similar texts, including *Food and Nutrition, Prenatal Care, Care during the Lying-In Period, Infant Care, Child Care*, and *Control of Communicable Disease*, as well as copies of *Mother's Book* mailed to mothers upon the department's receipt of a birth certificate. Item no. 3074800101, report, 1926–30, State Health Department, Reports to the State Health Officer, Series no. 30748, Folder 1, Box 1, Division of Child Hygiene, State Department of Public Health, North Dakota State Archives, Bismarck, North Dakota; Ninth Biennial Report, South Dakota Department of Health, 1927–29, 8, State Archives of the South Dakota Historical Society, Pierre, South Dakota.

14. Ninth Biennial Report, Wyoming State Health Department, 1927–29, 5, Wyoming State Archives, Cheyenne, Wyoming; Seventh, Eighth, and Ninth Biennial Reports of the South Dakota Board of Health, 1924–30, State Archives of the South Dakota Historical Society, Pierre, South Dakota.

15. Item no. 3074800101, report, 1926–30, [North Dakota] State Department of Health.

16. Montana State Board of Health, *Fifteenth Biennial Report of Montana State Board of Health, 1927 and 1928* (Helena: Montana Historical Society Research Center, 1929).

17. Lemons, "Sheppard-Towner Act," 779.

18. Lemons, "Sheppard-Towner Act," 781; Kimberley S. Johnson, *Governing the American State: Congress and the New Federalism, 1877–1929* (Princeton: Princeton University Press, 2007).

19. Data demonstrating the act's effectiveness included 183,252 health conferences, 2,978 prenatal care centers, contact with 4,000,000 infants and 700,000 pregnant mothers, 3,131,996 home visits, and the distribution of 22,020,489 pieces of literature. Lemons, "Sheppard-Towner Act."

20. Montana State Board of Health, *Fourteenth Biennial Report of Montana State Board of Health, 1929 and 1930* (Helena: Montana Historical Society Research Center, 1930).

21. Item no. 3074800101, report, 1926–30, [North Dakota] State Department of Health; "Ninth Biennial Report of the South Dakota State Board of Health, July 1st, 1928, to July 1st, 1930," 45, State Archives of the South Dakota Historical Society, Pierre, South Dakota.

22. Lemons, "Sheppard-Towner Act."

23. Item no. 3074800101, report, 1926–30, [North Dakota] State Department of Health.

24. Goodwin quoted in Parker and Carpenter, "Julia Lathrop and the Children's Bureau," 67.

25. Wyoming State Board of Health, report, 1915–16, 18–19.

26. Smuts, *Science in the Service of the Children*, 87.

27. Smuts, *Science in the Service of the Children*, 87. In contrast to the Children's Bureau approach, the tone of regional health departments leaned toward "demanding" that statistics collection procedures be altered, as well as to the shifting of blame for the poor condition of state data. *Biennial Report of the State Board of Health of South Dakota, for the Years 1901–1902*, 12. The North Dakota State Board of Health acknowledged that "the collection of vital statistics is in a very unsatisfactory condition" and justified the situation by pointing the finger at cities and counties that "make reports" it suggested were "of little value." *Biennial Report of the State Board of Health to the Governor of North Dakota for the Years 1901 and 1902* (publication date of 1902), North Dakota State Board of Health Biennial Reports, State Historical Society of North Dakota Archives, 12. The South Dakota State Board of Health was not immune to this attitude and excused its lack of results, lamenting that "it has been impossible for this board to gather vital statistics." *Biennial Report of the State Board of Health of South Dakota, for the Years 1901–1902*, 12.

28. Parker and Carpenter, "Julia Lathrop and the Children's Bureau," 72. For an exploration of Better Baby contests, see Meghan Crnic, "Better Babies: Social Engineering for 'a Better Nation, a Better World,'" *Endeavour* 33, no. 1 (2009): 12–17.

29. Bradbury and Eliot, *Four Decades of Action for Children*.

30. Wyoming State Board of Health, "Health and Sanitation during the Past Two Years," 1911–12, unpaginated portion (emphasis added).

31. Wyoming State Board of Health, "Health and Sanitation during the Past Two Years," 1911–12, 31–32 (emphasis added).

32. Wyoming State Board of Health, "Health and Sanitation during the Past Two Years," 1915–16, 18–19, Wyoming State Archives, Cheyenne, Wyoming.

33. Item no. 3074800101, report, 1926–30, [North Dakota] State Health Department, 1.

34. Loudon, *Death in Childbirth*, 32.

35. Board Minutes, 1920, Montana State Board of Health Records, 1920–38, 139; "Fifth Biennial Report of the South Dakota State Board of Health, July 1st, 1920, to June 30th, 1922," 12, State Archives of the South Dakota Historical Society, Pierre, South Dakota.

36. Wyoming State Board of Health, Eleventh Biennial Report, 1931–33, 8, 16.

37. See chapter 3 for a full discussion of the quantity of reproductive care women were providing.

38. Sixth Biennial Report of the South Dakota State Board of Health, 1923–24, 7, State Archives of the South Dakota Historical Society, Pierre, South Dakota.

39. Wyoming State Board of Health, Eleventh Biennial Report, 1931–33, 8.

40. Item no. 3074800101, report, 1926–30, [North Dakota] State Health Department.

41. Loudon, *Death in Childbirth*, 305.

42. Loudon, *Death in Childbirth*, 321.

43. Wertz and Wertz, *Lying-In*, 133. However, midwives remain the dominant reproductive care provider in much of the contemporary world. See, for example, Midwives Alliance of North America (MANA), https://mana.org/.

44. Wilmes interview; Kassmeier/Kassmier family interview by author, Fort Benton, Montana, July 6, 2017; Thirteenth Census of the United States, vol. 6, U.S. Bureau of the Census, 1913.

45. Conclusions based on author's analysis of the Mary Kassmeier Photo Album. Each photo in the album was identified by name, and research was performed to determine whether a birth certificate or other identifying information had been made available by family members on genealogical research sites. When available, birth certificate data (such as date of birth, parents' names, location of birth, and birth attendant) were entered into a database. This database was then used to sort, search, and draw conclusions about the specific details of Mary Kassmeier's midwifery practice.

46. Conclusions based on author's analysis of the Mary Kassmeier Photo Album.

47. Based on family recollections of Kassmeier's herbal knowledge and plant-based remedies, Mary Kassmeier's great-grandson compiled a detailed listing of plants available in the Golden Triangle (the area north of Great Falls that includes Fort Benton) and used by Kassmeier. C. Sedlak, email correspondence with author, August 20, 2018.

48. Wilmes interview; Kassmeier/Kassmier family interview; conclusions based on author's analysis of the Mary Kassmeier Photo Album.

49. Wilmes interview; Kassmeier/Kassmier family interview.

50. Wilmes interview; Kassmeier/Kassmier family interview.

51. Wilmes interview; Kassmeier/Kassmier family interview.

52. Analysis performed by the author by calculating the average number of days between a birth and the filing of the birth certificate for early births (1915–20) versus later births (1921 and thereafter); Mary Kassmeier Photo Album.

53. Conclusions based on author's analysis of the Mary Kassmeier Photo Album. The individual in each photograph in the album was identified by name, and research was done to determine whether a birth certificate or other identifying information had been made available by family members on genealogical research sites. Full demographic details were located for half of all the photographs and results extrapolated from that data. It is possible that the birth certificates for which additional information was not available could have been heavily weighted to home births, which would mean that Kassmeier's hospital work made up only 25 percent—not 50 percent—of her practice.

54. Conclusions based on author's analysis of the Mary Kassmeier Photo Album. Birth certificate data include the signature of the individual filing the form, most typically a midwife, doctor, county registrar, or parent.

55. Sadly, Kassmeier's daughter Theresa died at the age of twenty-one, and her death may have had additional impacts on the family that influenced Kassmeier's midwifery practice. Even if Kassmeier temporarily ceased her midwifery work around the time of Theresa's illness and death, the question remains as to why she did not return to her established community practice sometime in the following years.

56. "Wanted in Montana: Public Health Nurse," *Broadus Examiner*, July 18, 1919, states that much death and disease could be prevented by rural

communities banding together to support a public health nurse in their area.

57. Francis S. Bradley, "Why a Child Welfare Division in the State Board of Health?," *Northwest Medicine* 25, no. 3 (1926): 147–50, quote at 147.

58. Sixth Biennial Report of the South Dakota State Board of Health, 1923–24, 5.

59. Ninth Biennial Report of the Montana State Board of Health, 1917–18, Montana Historical Society Research Center, Helena, Montana.

60. "Regulations Governing the Use of School Nurses," Minutes, Montana State Board of Health, RS 238, Folder 2, Box 1, Montana State Board of Health Records, Montana Historical Society Research Center, Helena, Montana.

61. Ninth Biennial Report of the South Dakota Health Department, 1927–29, 8, State Archives of the South Dakota Historical Society, Pierre, South Dakota.

62. Regulations Governing County and Public Health Nurses, Montana State Board of Health Records, 1913–20, 71, RS 238, Folder 1-2, Box 1, Montana Historical Society Research Center, Helena, Montana.

63. Regulations Governing County and Public Health Nurses, Montana State Board of Health Records, 1913–20, 70.

64. Regulations Governing County and Public Health Nurses, Montana State Board of Health Records, 1913–20, 70.

65. Item no. 307480101, report, 1926–30, [North Dakota] State Health Department.

66. Loudon, *Death in Childbirth*, 300.

67. Loudon, *Death in Childbirth*, 321.

68. As multiple historical studies have shown, "there is no doubt that the properly trained midwife produced results as good if not better than the physician." Loudon, *Death in Childbirth*, 32.

69. Butte City Directory, 1900; Thirteenth Census of the United States, vol. 6, U.S. Bureau of the Census, 1913.

70. Arlene Harris, "Midwife Aino," *Missoula Borrowed Times*, September 1, 1974.

71. Rugged topography limited communication and travel, and the sisters were often left to make independent and at times weighty decisions on their own. As they developed a habit of independent action, religious sisters across the northern plains found themselves gaining confidence

and, after making many policy decisions, taking on a large portfolio of projects for which they had primary authority. Butler, *Across God's Frontiers*, 311.

72. As health officials slowly gained a data-based sense for the conditions in their jurisdictions, they began to consider and request other kinds of useful information about residents. By 1926 Dr. Hazel Bonness, the director of the Division of Child Welfare in Montana, was aware that her department did not have a count of practicing midwives, so she contacted the Children's Bureau to inquire about information they might have about practicing Montana midwives. Dr. Hazel Bonness to Dr. Blanche Haines, May 11, 1926, Box 331, 11-28-1 Official Correspondence, RG 102, Records of the Children's Bureau, Central File, 1925–28, 11-26-2 to 11-28-1, National Archives and Records Administration, College Park, Maryland. In an interesting twist, birth certificates asked for the mother's and father's occupations, mother's full maiden name, number of children she had, and her birthplace, enabling a greater understanding of demographic characteristics. Recording of details about the mother especially helped to facilitate subsequent genealogical and historical research that would otherwise have been impossible, as women tended to disappear from the historical record upon marriage. While health departments were complicit in subjugating mothers' reproductive expertise, they also enabled the entry of women into the historical record in ways that were not previously possible.

7. Maternity Homes and Motherhood

1. Mercer, "Grandma Brodhead an 'Angel of Mercy'"; Leon Brodhead, interview by author, December 10, 2018, Sidney, Montana; Renee Sundheim, interview by author, December 10, 2018, Sidney, Montana; Ray, "This Old House"; Mary Barr, "Early Day Medical Care," *Fairview (MT) News*, Centennial Edition, April–May 1977. While the "Angel of Mercy" article by Mary Mercer in the *Sidney Herald* stated that Brodhead was born in 1874 and began working at the age of twelve, calculations in this chapter are based on a birth year of 1871, a more accurate date according to the Brodhead family.

2. Mercer, "Grandma Brodhead an 'Angel of Mercy.'" In equine circles, horses that appear to be white are traditionally referred to as "gray" because they usually have black skin and white hair. No documentation

exists to determine if Brodhead's steed was truly white, with white skin and white hair, or was more accurately a gray.

3. Mercer, "Grandma Brodhead an 'Angel of Mercy.'"

4. *Courage Enough: Mon-Dak Family Histories* (Richland County MT, 1975), 156; Brodhead interview.

5. Existing scholarship on maternity homes is relatively thin, but sources on maternity homes of this era include the following: Polly Aird, "Small But Significant: The School of Nursing at Provo General Hospital, 1904–1924," *Utah Historical Quarterly* 86, no. 2 (2018): 102–27; Carolyn Carson, "Maternity Care in the Progressive Era: The Elizabeth Steel Magee Hospital," *Pittsburgh History* 77, no. 3 (1994): 116–28; Regina Kunzel, *Fallen Women, Problem Girls: Unmarried Mothers and the Professionalization of Social Work, 1890–1945* (New Haven: Yale University Press, 1995); Loretta Hefner, "The National Women's Relief Society and the U.S. Sheppard-Towner Act," *Utah Historical Quarterly* 50, no. 3 (1982): 255–67; Marian Morton, "Go and Sin No More: Maternity Homes in Cleveland, 1869–1936," *Ohio History* 93 (Summer–Autumn 1984): 117–46. These texts deal with maternity homes in urban areas, which usually existed to assist unmarried mothers during pregnancy and delivery. Maternity homes in the northern plains served a much different purpose and thus deserve documentation in their own right.

6. Barr, "Early Day Medical Care"; Brodhead interview.

7. Mary Murphy, *Hope in Hard Times: New Deal Photographs of Montana, 1936–1942* (Helena: Montana Historical Society Press, 2003), 38–45.

8. Michael R. Grey, *New Deal Medicine: The Rural Health Programs of the Farm Security Administration* (Baltimore: Johns Hopkins University Press, 1999), 42.

9. Murphy, *Hope in Hard Times*, 85.

10. Murphy, *Hope in Hard Times*, 44.

11. Murphy, *Hope in Hard Times*, 55. See Jason Scott Smith, *A Concise History of the New Deal* (New York: Cambridge University Press, 2014), for more context on New Deal programs across the United States.

12. Grey, *New Deal Medicine*, 49.

13. Grey, *New Deal Medicine*, 86–87.

14. Grey, *New Deal Medicine*, 86.

15. Ray, "This Old House"; Brodhead interview.

16. Brodhead interview.

17. Quote recalled in Ray, "This Old House."
18. Ray, "This Old House"; Mercer, "Grandma Brodhead an 'Angel of Mercy'";
    Brodhead interview.
19. Quoted in Ray, "This Old House."
20. Catherine Brodhead ledger, private collection of the Brodhead family.
    The Brodhead family generously allowed me access to the ledger, which
    contained the names of patients, conditions for which they were treated,
    and dates admitted. After comparing the ledger information to other
    sources to verify its validity, I entered the data contained therein and
    then drew conclusions based on that information.
21. Catherine Brodhead ledger; Brodhead Maternity Home pharmacy
    receipts, private collection of the Brodhead family.
22. Brodhead interview; Sundheim interview; Brodhead Maternity Home
    income/expense summary, private collection of the Brodhead family; Ray,
    "This Old House." Maternity homes first came to my attention when I
    was searching county histories to locate local midwives and noticed refer-
    ences to numerous women who were proprietors of these establishments.
    While common in the region in the early 1900s, maternity homes have
    received little academic attention, and, especially with the digitization
    and searchability of historic newspapers, could be a fascinating topic of
    research. In addition to listings of them in county histories, maternity
    homes can be discovered by reviewing historic newspapers, as proprietors
    frequently placed advertisements for their lying-in hospitals.
23. Sundheim interview.
24. Brodhead interview; Ray, "This Old House."
25. Brodhead interview.
26. Mercer, "Grandma Brodhead an 'Angel of Mercy.'"
27. Nickel, "Dying in the West, Part 1," 40–42.
28. Nickel, "Dying in the West, Part 1," 40.
29. Nickel, "Dying in the West, Part 1," 39.
30. As of this printing, no one has undertaken a full-scale investigation of
    maternity homes in Montana, Wyoming, and the Dakotas, but such a
    project would fill in some essential gaps in our understanding of rural
    health care. (See note 22 above for an explanation of how such research
    could be accomplished.) The practice of housing small private hospitals
    in residences—instead of in a publicly funded structure—was more prev-
    alent in the American West than other areas of the country, according to

Nickel, "Dying in the West, Part 1," which makes a prospective study of this nature even more important from a regional perspective.

31. "Eighth Biennial Report of the South Dakota State Board of Health, July 1st, 1926 to July 1st," 1928, 43–44, State Archives of the South Dakota Historical Society, Pierre, South Dakota.

32. "Ninth Biennial Report of the South Dakota State Board of Health, July 1st, 1928 to July 1st, 1930."

33. "First Biennial Report of the State Board of Health and Medical Examiners, State of South Dakota, July 1st, 1912, to June 30th, 1914," State Archives of the South Dakota Historical Society, Pierre, South Dakota; "First Biennial Report of the State Board of Health and Medical Examiners, State of South Dakota, 1912–1914," 53, State Archives of the South Dakota Historical Society, Pierre, South Dakota. Perhaps given its tumultuous start, the South Dakota State Board of Health issued reports that appeared to be duplicates but actually contained some textual differences. In this case, both versions of the report referred to maternity homes.

34. "Seventh Biennial Report of the South Dakota State Board of Health, July 1st, 1925 to July 1st, 1926," State Archives of the South Dakota Historical Society, Pierre, South Dakota.

35. "First Biennial Report of the State Board of Health and Medical Examiners, July 1st, 1912, to June 30th, 1914," State Archives of the South Dakota Historical Society, Pierre, South Dakota. The initial legislation allowed physicians and midwives to obtain a license, but by 1925 the state had begun requiring that doctors be called for all deliveries. "Seventh Biennial Report of the South Dakota State Board of Health, July 1st, 1925 to July 1st, 1926."

36. Nickel, "Dying in the West, Part 1," 42.

37. Nickel, "Dying in the West, Part 1," 42.

38. Nickel, "Dying in the West, Parts 1," 40–42.

39. Leavitt, "'Worrying Profession.'"

40. Susan Smith and Dawn Nickel, "From Home to Hospital: Parallels in Birthing and Dying in Twentieth-Century Canada," *Canadian Bulletin of Medical History* 16, no. 1 (1999): 49–64, esp. 53–54.

41. Smith and Nickel, "From Home to Hospital," quote at 55.

42. Leavitt, *Brought to Bed.*

43. Litoff, *American Midwives.*

44. Smith and Nickel, "From Home to Hospital." In an effort to tackle linger-
    ing issues of class, private hospitals catered to wealthy women by offering
    elite birthing environments. Private nurses, well-appointed rooms, and
    access to the latest anesthesia marked the upper-class birthing suite
    as distinctly different from hospitals serving poor and disadvantaged
    women (55). The idea of death as a hospital experience followed a similar
    trajectory to that of birth. Hospitals, at least up until the 1940s, were
    not seen as places for people to die, and administrators discouraged the
    admittance of terminally ill patients. Nickel, "Dying in the West, Part 1."
    Eventually, though, just as with birth, death moved to the hospital from
    1900 to 1950. Hospitals advertised the benefits of a warm and caring
    atmosphere with the added bonus of medical personnel and technology.
45. Wertz and Wertz, *Lying-In*, 133.
46. Robbie Davis-Floyd, *Birth as an American Rite of Passage* (Berkeley: Uni-
    versity of California Press, 1992). Without midwives, maternity home
    proprietors, and older female neighbors and friends on hand to initiate
    mothers into the meaning and practice of motherhood, new institutions
    developed rituals and practices to perform this important cultural func-
    tion. By the 1910s and 1920s and with the assistance of public health
    professionals, retailers and department stores made a dramatic entrance
    into the process of making mothers, and these entities cemented their
    influence on patterns of consumer behavior through the 1930s and
    1940s. As an offshoot of the Children's Bureau's educational efforts,
    Baby Weeks helped to spread awareness about birth and motherhood.
    Public health workers, department stores, and doctors organized the
    first Baby Week events in Chicago in 1914. The Children's Bureau did
    not mandate particular dates of observation but did supply some of the
    content and recommended topics for communities that observed the
    event from 1916 through 1918. Baby Week presentations included doctors
    and nurses offering information on the care and feeding of infants, as
    well as retailers promoting mothers' purchases of infant-related items.
    In the same way that doctors cooperated with health departments, they
    also worked with retailers. Historian Cheryl Lemus's research has detailed
    how stores "invited physicians to lecture on prenatal care, hired nurses to
    advise prospective mothers, and trained sales staff in the latest medical
    advice and findings." Cheryl Lemus, "Save Your Baby, Save Ten Percent:
    National Baby Week, the Infants' Department, and the Modern Preg-

nant Woman, 1905–1925," *Journal of Women's History* 25, no. 3 (2013): 165–87, quote at 165. By framing motherhood as a performed behavior, physicians and retailers communicated the message that mothers should look outside of themselves to meet expert standards and demonstrate their fitness for parenting. Urban health departments, store owners, and doctors cooperated to construct the consumerism-oriented mother by establishing the expectation that each mother should demonstrate her skills "as a patient and as a consumer" (166).

47. Jennifer Henderson, *Settler Feminism and Race Making in Canada* (Toronto: University of Toronto Press, 2003). Henderson's work examines the essentialist role of the mother and credits the state with granting authority to women according to their domesticity. My argument aligns with Henderson's in recognizing women's categorization as reproducers but differs on the issue of power. While Henderson sees the role of mother as one of "authority in the family" at that time in history, my research examines women's ability to exercise power and decision-making in childbirth, an arena where they lost significant ground from the mid-1800s through the 1940s (31).

48. Lemus, "Save Your Baby, Save Ten Percent," 172. Physicians became the experts on childbirth, and mothers came to defer even to salesclerks as the official source on how to shop and provide for their infants. According to Lemus, specialist expertise was not a new phenomenon, but especially in the realm of reproduction, while women remained responsible for pregnancy, delivery, and childrearing, they were "no longer the authorities" (179).

Conclusion

1. John Muir, renowned environmental philosopher, famously posited this idea when he explained that "when we try to pick out anything by itself, we find it hitched to everything else in the Universe." John Muir, *My First Summer in the Sierra* (Boston: Houghton Mifflin, 1911), 211.

2. It is important to note that Native Americans successfully inhabited the region for thousands of years, all without public health infrastructure. Indigenous practices of communal support offer a template for the kind of generative policy we so desperately need.

3. While largely absent from the commonly held metanarrative of the American West, the tenet of relational wealth is well documented by

anthropologists and particularly evident in the cultures of Native nations indigenous to the area. For an example from another region entirely, the !Kung people of southern Africa measured wealth according to their breadth of social relations, and gift exchanges and caring connections were seen as necessary for survival. Irenäus Eibl-Eibesfeldt, *Human Ethology* (New Brunswick NJ: Aldine Transaction, 2007).

4. In general, mortality rates have declined over time for all mothers, but deaths among certain segments of the population—especially for women of color—remain startlingly high. For more details, see Mary Beth Flanders-Stephans, "Alarming Racial Differences in Maternal Mortality," *Journal of Perinatal Education* 9, no. 2 (2000): 50–51. In the northern plains Native American mothers and infants died at consistently higher rates than their Euro-American counterparts. J. Hill, "Midwives in Montana," 188.

5. The parallels between women-valuing practices and care for the planet are clear. Viewing all of life, even ants and toads and young girls, as worthy of value is a mind-set identified by scientist E. O. Wilson in his book *Biophilia* (Cambridge MA: Harvard University Press, 1984).

6. Aldo Leopold, "Conservation: In Whole or in Part?," in *The River of the Mother of God and Other Essays by Aldo Leopold* (Madison: University of Wisconsin Press, 1992), 310–19, quote at 318.

7. Unfortunately, abundant examples abound. For instance, the econometrics study referenced at the beginning of chapter 4 has been cited in a number of other publications, including work examining midwifery policies in Indonesia and Guatemala. See, for example, Md Nazmul Ahsan, Rakesh Banerjee, and Riddhi Maharaj, "Early-Life Access to a Basic Health Care Program and Adult Outcomes in Indonesia," USC Dornsife Institute for New Economic Thinking Working Paper No. 18-16, September 2018; and Anna Summer, Sylvia Guendelman, Edgar Kestler, and Dilys Walker, "Professional Midwifery in Guatemala: A Qualitative Exploration of Perceptions, Attitudes and Expectations among Stakeholders," *Social Science and Medicine* 184 (July 2017): 99–107.

8. A multitude of writers and thinkers have eloquently made this point. One of my favorites is Arlie Hochschild in *The Second Shift: Working Families and the Revolution at Home* (1989; New York: Penguin Books, 2012). Hochschild states that "at the very root of a successful gender

revolution is, I believe, a deep value on care—making loving meals, doing projects with kids, emotionally engaging family and friends." She explains that care has "become a hand-me-down job," passed from men to women, and from upper- to lower-class workers, and she posits the critical challenge of "valu[ing] and shar[ing] the duties of caring" (269).

SELECTED BIBLIOGRAPHY

Armitage, Susan, and Patricia Hart, eds. *Women's Oral History: The "Frontiers" Reader*. Lincoln: University of Nebraska Press, 2002.

Armitage, Susan, and Elizabeth Jameson, eds. *The Women's West*. Norman: University of Oklahoma Press, 1987.

Arris, E. Augusta. *Historical Sketch of the Montana State Association of Registered Nurses and Related Organizations*. Butte MT: Convention of the Nurses Association, 1936.

Baillargeon, Denyse. *Babies for the Nation: The Medicalization of Motherhood in Quebec, 1910–1970*. Waterloo ON: Wilfrid Laurier University Press, 2004.

Borst, Charlotte G. *Catching Babies: The Professionalization of Childbirth, 1870–1920*. Cambridge MA: Harvard University Press, 1995.

Bradbury, Dorothy E., and Martha M. Eliot. *Four Decades of Action for Children: A Short History of the Children's Bureau*. Washington DC: U.S. Department of Health, Education, and Welfare, 1956.

Carter, Sarah. *Montana Women Homesteaders: A Field of One's Own*. Helena MT: Far Country Press, 2009.

Cohen, Felix S. *Handbook of Federal Indian Law*. Washington DC: U.S. Government Printing Office, 1945.

Deer, Sarah. *The Beginning and End of Rape: Confronting Sexual Violence in Native America*. Minneapolis: University of Minnesota Press, 2015.

Del Duca, James, "Apsaalooke Maternity: Traditional Practices Compared to the U.S. Techno-Medical Mode." Unpublished paper, Native American Studies Department, Montana State University, 2012.

Dye, Nancy Schrom. "History of Childbirth in America." *Signs* 6, no. 1 (1980): 97–108.

Flannery, Regina. *Ellen Smallboy: Glimpses of a Cree Woman's Life*. Montreal: McGill-Queen's University Press, 1995.

Forssen, John. *Petticoat and Stethoscope: A Montana Legend*. Missoula MT: Bitterroot Litho, 1978.

Garceau, Dee. *The Important Things of Life: Women, Work, and Family in Sweetwater County, Wyoming, 1880–1929*. Lincoln: University of Nebraska Press, 1997.

Gluck, Sherna Berger, and Daphne Patai, eds. *Women's Words: The Feminist Practice of Oral History*. New York: Routledge, 1991.

Hargreaves, Mary Wilma M. *Dry Farming in the Northern Great Plains, 1900–1925*. Cambridge MA: Harvard University Press, 1957.

Henderson, Jennifer. *Settler Feminism and Race Making in Canada*. Toronto: University of Toronto Press, 2003.

Hill, Jennifer J. "Going Public: Childbirth, the Board of Health, and Montana Women, 1860–1920." *Montana: The Magazine of Western History* 65, no. 2 (2015): 3–21.

———. "Midwives in Montana: Historically Informed Political Activism." PhD diss., Montana State University, 2013.

Hoffert, Sylvia D. "Childbearing on the Trans-Mississippi Frontier, 1830–1900." *Western Historical Quarterly* 22, no. 3 (1991): 272–88.

James, Caroline. *Nez Perce Women in Transition, 1877–1900*. Moscow: University of Idaho Press, 1996.

Jameson, Elizabeth, and Susan Armitage, eds. *Writing the Range: Women and Gender in the American West*. Norman: University of Oklahoma Press, 1997.

Kohl, Edith Eudora. *Land of the Burnt Thigh*. St. Paul: Minnesota Historical Society Press, 1986.

Lahlum, Lori Ann, and Molly P. Rozum, eds. *Equality at the Ballot Box: Votes for Women on the Northern Plains*. Pierre: University of South Dakota Press, 2019.

Langford, Nanci. "Childbirth on the Canadian Prairies: 1880–1930." *Journal of Historical Sociology* 8, no. 3 (1995): 278–302.

Lawrence, Jane. "The Indian Health Service and the Sterilization of Native American Women." *American Indian Quarterly* 24, no. 3 (2000): 400–419.

Leahy, Ellen, "'Montana Fever': Smallpox and the Montana State Board of Health." *Montana: The Magazine of Western History* 53, no. 2 (2003): 32–45.

Leavitt, Judith Walzer. *Brought to Bed: Childbearing in America, 1750 to 1950.* New York: Oxford University Press, 1986.

Lemons, J. Stanley. "The Sheppard-Towner Act: Progressivism in the 1920s." *Journal of American History* 55, no. 4 (1969): 776–86.

Libecap, Gary D. "Learning about the Weather: Dryfarming Doctrine and Homestead Failure in Eastern Montana, 1900–1925." *Montana: The Magazine of Western History* 52, no.1 (2002): 24–33.

Linderman, Frank B. *Pretty-Shield: Medicine Woman of the Crows.* Lincoln: University of Nebraska Press, 1932.

Lindgren, Elaine. *Land in Her Own Name: Women as Homesteaders in North Dakota.* Norman: University of Oklahoma Press, 1991.

Litoff, Judy Barrett. *American Midwives: 1860 to the Present.* Westport CT: Greenwood Press, 1978.

Loudon, Irvine. *Death in Childbirth: An International Study of Maternal Care and Maternal Mortality, 1800–1950.* Oxford: Clarendon Press, 1992.

McManus, Sheila. *The Line Which Separates: Race, Gender, and the Making of the Alberta-Montana Borderlands.* Lincoln: University of Nebraska Press, 2005.

McNeely, Alma Gretchen, "From Untrained Nurses toward Professional Preparation in Montana, 1912–1989." DNSC diss., University of San Diego, 1993.

Mead, Rebecca J. *How the Vote Was Won: Woman Suffrage in the Western United States, 1868–1914.* New York: New York University Press, 1998.

Melcher, Mary. *Pregnancy, Motherhood, and Choice in Twentieth-Century Arizona.* Tucson: University of Arizona Press, 2012.

———. "'Women's Matters': Birth Control, Prenatal Care, and Childbirth in Rural Montana, 1910–1940." *Montana: The Magazine of Western History* 41, no. 2 (1991): 47–56.

Montana Nurses' Association. *Nursing in Montana.* Great Falls MT: Tribune Printing, 1961.

———. *Nursing in Montana: The Recent Past; A History of Nursing in Montana, 1962–1992.* Helena: Montana Nurses' Association, 1992.

Nickel, Dawn. "Dying in the West, Part 1: Hospitals and Health Care in Montana and Alberta, 1880–1950." *Montana: The Magazine of Western History* 59, no. 3 (2009): 25–45.

———. "Dying in the West, Part 2: Caregiving in the Home and the Death of Daniel Slayton." *Montana: The Magazine of Western History* 59, no. 4 (2009): 3–23.

Paradise, Viola Isabel. *Maternity Care and the Welfare of Young Children in a Homesteading County in Montana*. Washington DC: U.S. Government Printing Office, 1919.

Parker, Jacqueline K., and Edward M. Carpenter. "Julia Lathrop and the Children's Bureau: The Emergence of an Institution." *Social Service Review* 55, no. 1 (1981): 60–77.

Patterson, Ida S. *The Life of Emma Magee in the Rocky Mountain West, 1866–1950*. Pablo MT: Salish Kootenai Community College, 1981.

Peavy, Linda, and Ursula Smith. *The Gold Rush Widows of Little Falls: A Story Drawn from the Letters of Pamelia and James Fergus*. St. Paul: Minnesota Historical Society Press, 1990.

———. "Women in Waiting in the Westward Movement." *Montana: The Magazine of Western History* 35, no. 2 (1985): 2–17.

Petrik, Paula. *No Step Backward: Women and Family on the Rocky Mountain Mining Frontier, Helena, Montana, 1865–1900*. Helena: Montana Historical Society Press, 1987.

Phillips, Paul. *Medicine in the Making of Montana*. Missoula: Montana State University Press, 1962.

Sands, Diane. "Using Oral History to Chart the Course of Illegal Abortions in Montana." *Frontiers: A Journal of Women Studies* 7, no. 1 (1983): 32–37.

Savitt, Todd. "Abortion in the Old West: The Trials of Dr. Edwin S. Kellogg of Helena, Montana." *Montana: The Magazine of Western History* 57, no. 3 (2007): 3–20.

Savitt, Todd, and Janice Willms. "Sisters' Hospital: The Sisters of Providence and St. Patrick Hospital, Missoula, Montana, 1873–1890." *Montana: The Magazine of Western History* 53, no.1 (2003): 28–43.

Schoen, Johanna. *Choice and Coercion: Birth Control, Sterilization, and Abortion in Public Health and Welfare*. Chapel Hill: University of North Carolina Press, 2005.

Snell, Alma Hogan. *Grandmother's Grandchild: My Crow Indian Life*. Edited by Becky Matthews. Lincoln: University of Nebraska Press, 2001.

———. *A Taste of Heritage: Crow Indian Recipes and Herbal Medicines*. Lincoln: University of Nebraska Press, 2006.

Steele, Volney. *Bleed, Blister, and Purge: A History of Medicine on the American Frontier*. Missoula MT: Mountain Press, 2005.

Taylor, Quintard, and Shirley Ann Wilson Moore, eds. *African American Women Confront the West, 1600–2000*. Norman: University of Oklahoma Press, 2008.

Theobald, Brianna. "Nurse, Mother, Wife—Susie Walking Bear Yellowtail and the Struggle for Crow Women's Reproductive Autonomy." *Montana: The Magazine of Western History* 66, no. 3 (2018): 17–35.

———. *Reproduction on the Reservation: Pregnancy, Childbirth, and Colonialism in the Long Twentieth Century*. Chapel Hill: University of North Carolina Press, 2019.

Wall, Barbra Mann. "Unlikely Entrepreneurs: Nuns, Nursing, and Hospital Development in the West and Midwest, 1865–1915." PhD diss., University of Notre Dame, 2000.

Wertz, Richard W., and Dorothy C. Wertz. *Lying-In: A History of Childbirth in America*. New York: Free Press, 1977.

Wilson, Shawn. *Research Is Ceremony: Indigenous Research Methods*. Winnipeg MB: Fernwood, 2008.

INDEX

Italicized page numbers indicate figures.

abortion, 39, 130, 141

access to medical care, 9, 14, 17,
40–41, 42–43, 60, 78, 101, 116,
133, 171; during Great Depression, 180–82

Adams, Katie, 41

agricultural economy, 16–17, 70,
130–31, 135, 180, 217–19nn39–40

Alderson, Nannie, 44

Allotment Act (1887), 79

anesthesia, 8, 77, 104, 105, 117

Ariss, Augusta, 92

Bauer, Stella Jane, 76

birth and death registration, 24, 42,
43, 82, 85, 88, 88–89, 136–38;
authorized signatures on, 84, 87,
88, 157, 169, 172–73; filing time
frame, 167; incentives for, 142–
43, 155; and national compliance,
138–39, 141, 154

birth control. *See* contraception

birthing locations, 8–9, 31; hospitals, 108, 112, 115–16, 117, 159,
167, 169, 188, 190, 259n44;
maternity homes, 178, 181–87,
256n5; out-of-state, 44–45, 148–
50, 249n8; residences, 7, 77, 161,
184, 185, 187–88, 253n53

birthing positions, 104–5, 107,
233n30

birthing tools, 90, 102, 104–5, 115,
148, 183, 233n32, 237n75

birthweight, 24, 63, 64, 204n23,
225n25

Bourgeois, Louise, 73–75

breastfeeding, 8, 39, 48, 49,
210n11, 236n53

Brodhead Maternity Home, 181,
182, 183–84

childbed fever. *See* puerperal fever

U.S. Children's Bureau, 24, 39,
44–45, 55, 56–57, 67, 86, 149–50,
154–55, 216n15, 246n61

Valleen, Anna, 76
Vanvig, Lena, 23, 92, 108–9
venereal disease, 50, 96, 154,
214n59
vital statistics. *See* birth and death
registration

Walker, Catherine (Mrs. Russell
Brodhead), 42, 177–78, 181–84,
190, 191
Walking Bear Yellowtail, Susie,
204n21
Warkins, Jessie, *88*

weather extremes, 9, 14–15, 18, 57,
70, 132, 133, 180, 242n23
women's labor: nature of, 14,
27–28, 31, 35, 44, 48–49, 58,
62–63, 131–32, 164; statistical
documentation of, 55, 56–59;
value of, 65, 67–68, 70–72,
175, 182–83, 191–92, 217n38,
217n80
women's legal status, 13, 158
women's sociability, 64, 71. *See also*
female companionship
women's welfare, 56–58, 78–79,
104, 114, 131, 133, 135, 149–50,
197–98

Zanto, Mary, 61

CPSIA information can be obtained
at www.ICGtesting.com
Printed in the USA
LVHW040312221222
735707LV00003B/343